THE UP
SIDE OF
DOWN

Megan McArdle has been a correspondent for *The Economist*, *The Atlantic*, and *Newsweek / The Daily Beast*. She is a columnist at *Bloomberg View* and the author of a popular blog, Asymmetrical Information. She also appears regularly on MSNBC, Fox News, and NPR. A graduate of the University of Chicago's Booth School of Business, she lives with her husband, Peter, and their bull mastiff, FitzGerald, in Washington, D.C. Visit her website at: www.meganmcardle.com

More praise for *The Up Side of Down*

'*The Up Side of Down* will teach you to embrace failure and use it to reinvent yourself and your organization.'

Tyler Cowen, author of *Discover Your Inner Economist*

'This is both a surprising and an immensely comforting book. Drawing on academic research, reporting, and not least the failures in her own life, Megan McArdle convincingly demonstrates that avoiding failure isn't what matters, but how we cope with failure. Sparkling with wit and insight in every chapter, *The Up Side of Down* has something for anyone who has ever failed, or lived in fear of failure – in other words, for all of us.'

Greg Ip, author of *The Little Book of Economics*

'Trial and error is the engine of human progress, but we increasingly live in a culture where we teach kids they got it right on the first try. Beautifully written, elegantly argued, and powerfully persuasive, *The Up Side of Down* is that rare book that is just as important for parents as it is for CEOs. Never has an author succeeded so grandly by celebrating failure.'

Jonah Goldberg, author of *Liberal Fascism*

THE UP SIDE OF DOWN

Bouncing Back
in Business and in Life

MEGAN McARDLE

HEAD
of ZEUS

First published in the United States in 2014 by Viking Penguin, a member of Penguin Group (USA) LLC
First published in the United Kingdom in 2014 by Head of Zeus Ltd.

A CIP catalogue record for this book is available from the British Library

Set in ITC Stone Serif Std with Medium
Designed by Carla Bolte

Printed in Germany
1 3 5 7 9 10 8 6 4 2

ISBN (HB) 9781781859506
ISBN (XTPB) 9781781859513
ISBN (E) 9781781859490

Head of Zeus Ltd
Clerkenwell House
45–47, Clerkenwell Green
London EC1R OHT

www.headofzeus.com

To my husband, who has never failed me

PREFACE

When you tell people you're writing a book, everyone tends to ask the same question: What's it about? And when you tell them you're writing a book about failure, most of them want to know why. For two years, I've been giving them the same answer: "Write what you know."

Mostly, they think I'm joking. Or at least they're courteous enough to pretend they do. I've got a great husband, a great job, a hundred-year-old row house near the U.S. Capitol, and an adorable bullmastiff puppy to chew up its woodwork. I've written for many of the top publications in the English-speaking world. And I got Viking to give me a contract to write this book. My life is, I must admit, pretty great.

All these things are true. But this is also true: I am a spectacular failure. I am the Mozart of misfortune, the Paganini of poor luck. I have been laid off from more jobs than most people my age have had—laid off, not fired, though I've been fired too. At one point, my talent for finding employment at apparently healthy companies that went out of business four months later was so amazing that an acquaintance in equity research asked me to let him know if I got an offer from any of the companies he covered, so he could short the stock.

As you'll see in the chapters to come, the amazing husband and the fabulous job are the gifts of my previous failures. By extension, so are the house and the dog. And by "previous failures" I don't just mean a spot of bad luck with the wrong start-up. I mean deep, soul-crushing periods of misery following stupid mistakes that kept me awake until the small hours of the morning in a fog of anxiety and regret. It was only later—much later—that I saw the wreckage of my previous hopes become the foundation for something bigger and better.

There is a famous story of a rich old man being interviewed by a young striver, who asks him for the secret of his success. "Good judgment," says the magnate.

His eager young follower dutifully scribbles this down, then looks at him expectantly. "And how do you get good judgment?"

"Experience!" says our terse tycoon.

"And how do you get experience?"

"Bad judgment!"

Peek into the basement of any successful life and you'll see that they, too, are founded on failure. It would be nice if we could serenely parade from triumph to triumph, but that is not how human beings work.

This is not, alas, a welcome message. Woody Allen once remarked that he didn't want to achieve immortality through his work; he wanted to achieve it through not dying. We feel much the same way about success: it should be achieved by not failing. Most of us hate failure, and spend quite a bit of our lives trying to arrange things so that it can't happen. Too often, when others fail we're tempted to blame them and avoid them, lest some of their failure rub off on us.

Most of us fear failure more than almost anything else. The number-one fear cited by most Americans, above even death and spiders, is public speaking. Which is, of course, just the fear of failing in public. Failure feels bad to us, and worse when we think others can see it. Think about the last time you made a big mistake that a lot of people saw. You can already feel the hairs standing up on the back of your neck and the blush crawling up toward your ears, can't you?

These are deep instincts, wired into our very nature. But we make them worse by the way we think about failure. We tend to assume that failure happens because someone, somewhere, did something wrong. In fact, often failure is the result of doing something very right: trying something that you've never done before, maybe something that no one's ever done before.

But because failure doesn't feel good, we spend an enormous amount of time trying to engineer failure out of our lives, and out of our society. We are devoting ever more of our lives to seeking out what P. J. O'Rourke dubbed the Whiffle Life: the life in which nothing can ever go seriously awry. The upper middle class obsesses about sterling educational credentials. Children are practically encased in Bubble Wrap before they are allowed to step outside—never without copious adult supervision. And if something does, god forbid, go wrong, we start looking for someone to sue. Someone—a regulator, a company, an expert—is supposed to be able to guarantee our perfect safety. The metaphor for our age is the disappearance of high monkey bars from playgrounds across the country. We have made it impossible for children to fall very far—and in so doing, we have robbed them of the joys of climbing high.

This is a terrible mistake. It is the mistake made by the victims of Bernie Madoff's notorious Ponzi scheme, the largest financial fraud in U.S. history. The most amazing thing about Madoff's scheme is that it was a selective club; people had to wheedle their way in. Why were they cajoling their way into a Ponzi scheme? Not because the returns were unusually high. In fact, they were not spectacular by hedge-fund standards. What attracted people to Madoff was the fact that the returns were unusually safe. He delivered 12 percent year after year—bull market or bear, boom or recession. People went to Madoff because they thought they'd found a guaranteed, no-lose proposition.

In hindsight, they should have known that this was impossible. The economy is changing faster than ever, so how could Madoff get the same return regardless of what happened? His victims were seduced by what you might call the technocratic fallacy: the idea that someone who is sufficiently smart and dedicated can engineer the risk out of the system. This gives us a nice, warm cozy feeling. And that nice, warm cozy feeling is the most dangerous sensation we can have. There is no such thing as a risk-free investment strategy—in finance, or in life. As Madoff's victims found out, the riskiest strategy is to try to work yourself into a position where you can't fail. The failure, when it comes, tends to be catastrophic, in part because you haven't prepared for it.

Our declining ability to take risks, and to bounce back when things don't work out, is already beginning to play out. New firms, which have long been the engine of economic innovation and growth, aren't being created as fast as they once were. Laid-off workers aren't being reabsorbed by the job market. We are frozen, unable to tell whether the light we're staring into is the end of the tunnel or an oncoming train.

There's a better way to do this. Since we cannot succeed simply by not failing, we should stop spending so much energy trying to avoid failure or engineer it away. Instead, we should embrace it—smartly. We should encourage people to fail early and often—by making sure that their failures are learning opportunities, not catastrophes. Unfortunately, schools don't teach failure. But maybe they should.

What would such a school teach? It would bring back high monkey bars and let kids learn that the price of reaching lofty heights is the occasional broken arm. It would not try to pretend that there are no wrong answers. Instead of protecting kids from failure, teachers would encourage them to face it, early and often, on sports teams, in the classroom, and in the lab. They'd help kids overcome their natural fear of failure, because failure is often the best—and sometimes the only—way to learn.

But that is just a start. As we'll see, it's not enough to encourage people to fail; it matters as much, maybe more, what we do next. How easy do we make it to recover? Mama bird can't just push the babies out of the nest; she needs to pick them up and bring them back so they can try again.

That means learning to identify mistakes early, so they can be corrected. And it means recognizing when you are on the wrong path. It sounds simple, but the architecture of our brains makes it much harder than you think. We invest in our commitments, mentally and emotionally, and have a very hard time letting go. That is in part what made it so hard for GM to turn around, and why so many of us stay in bad relationships when we know we should move on.

Learning to fail well means learning to understand your mistakes, because unless you know what went wrong, you may do the wrong things to correct it. Some kinds of mistakes require punishment or censure; others are just the natural errors that we'd expect to occur as the result of doing something we're not very good at yet. Mistaking one for the other can be disastrous.

Most of all, learning to fail well means overcoming our natural instincts to blame someone—maybe ourselves—whenever something goes wrong. Societies and people fail best when they err on the side of forgiveness. Not forgetting: the information gained by failing is far too valuable to be lost by pretending that nothing happened. Rather, they recognize the past failure, and then they try to let it go, to always be looking toward a better future. As much as possible, past failures should be "water under the bridge," as my grandmother would say—you don't do much good by diving over the rails in an effort to recapture it.

This sounds really hard. And in a way, it is hard: we have powerful instincts urging us to hide from failure, to wish it away, and if it cannot be avoided, to find and punish the shirkers who made it happen . . . even though the complexity of modern society often makes it harder than we think to identify who they are.

But here's the thing: failing well can't be *that* hard, because America spent several centuries being really good at it. We're the descendants of failures who fled to these shores from their creditors, their failed farms, their disastrous love affairs. If things didn't work out in New York, we picked up and moved to North Dakota. Somewhere along the way, we built the biggest, richest country in the world. And, I'm going to argue, we did it mostly because we were willing to risk more, and forgive more easily, than most other countries. We lend more freely, and let debtors off the hook; we regulate more lightly, and rely on a hit-and-miss liability system instead. These things are often painted as weaknesses, but in fact they are great strengths. They are the sign of a country more invested in the future than the past.

Handle it right, and failure can be the best thing that ever happened to you (though it may sometimes feel like the worst). Handle it wrong and it won't just feel like the worst thing that ever happened to you. I know; I've been there. And the good news is there are concrete things you can do to train yourself to be more resilient, and to turn a very unpleasant setback into an opportunity to do something you might never have had the courage to do otherwise.

CONTENTS

THE UP
SIDE OF
DOWN

1 FAILURE IS FUNDAMENTAL

*How a Brain Scientist and a Psychologist
Helped Me Stop Procrastinating*

Around the turn of the millennium, Peter Skillman embarked on an interesting exercise in design philosophy. Skillman, who is now an executive at Nokia, was the head of "user experience" for Palm, the company that essentially invented the handheld computer. For five years, he ran various groups of people through a design exercise he created, which would come to be called the Spaghetti Problem. He assembled a variety of different groups, from American students to 150 Taiwanese telecom engineers, and split them into smaller units of three or four, at which point they were given twenty pieces of spaghetti, a meter of tape, a marshmallow, and a piece of string. They had eighteen minutes to create the tallest freestanding structure that would support a marshmallow.

This sort of team-building exercise is not new; I did a version of it involving straws and an egg with eight fellow students during my business school orientation weekend. What was new was Skillman's perspective: instead of looking at it like a management guru, Skillman thought about it like a designer. In 2007, he shared what he had learned with the Gel conference, a sort of smaller version of TED.[1]

Unsurprisingly, the engineers did very well. The business school students finished dead last, which is probably also unsurprising to anyone who has spent a weekend doing team-building exercises with future MBAs. According to Skillman, they spent too much time arguing about who was going to be the CEO of Spaghetti, Inc. Lawyers did almost as badly.

1

And who did the very best? Skillman unveiled their pictures, and a wave of laughter swept through the audience. Up on the screen was a series of snapshots of kindergarten students, mugging for the camera in front of . . . well, about what you'd expect if your kindergartner made you something out of spaghetti and tape.

How did the kindergartners beat the engineers? By the simple process of experimentation and iteration. They didn't let themselves get hemmed in by assumptions about what the rules were—they were the only group of people who asked for more spaghetti. And because they had more spaghetti, they didn't have to waste time sitting around talking about how the tower should look, or who should get to write the vision statement. They just dove in and started creating, discarding anything that didn't work. Since, as Skillman points out, "very few people understand the structural properties of spaghetti," this was the fastest route to success.

The structures built by the engineers rose above the workspace with the elegant logic of a suspension bridge. The wild, asymmetrical kindergarten creations lurched drunkenly like modern art installations on a debauched spree. Yet they all supported a marshmallow, at a height that was on average a full inch taller than what the engineers had achieved. The engineers had years of schooling and work experience to teach them how to build sound structures. But the kindergartners had something even more powerful: they were not afraid of failure. By trying and failing, they learned what didn't work—which, it turned out, was all the knowledge they needed to figure out what did.

"Multiple iterations," Skillman told the audience, "almost always beats single-minded focus around a single idea." The people who were planning weren't learning. The people who were trying and failing were.

"If you have a short amount of time, it's more important that you fail," he said minutes later. "You fail early to succeed soon."

I was sitting in the audience the day he gave that talk. Five years later, interviewing people for this book, I have heard this thesis echoed over and over again by entrepreneurs. For most of the rest of us, Skillman's story goes against every instinct we have about how the world is supposed to work. It should not be possible to blunder your way to the top. Success is supposed to be the product of hard-won skill and prudent planning, not breaking spaghetti with abandon. The problem is, most of our instincts about failure are wrong.

Jim Manzi, the founder of Applied Predictive Technologies, tells a typical story.[2] His company, which you'll hear about in a later chapter, was struggling with its business model. They were designing custom software products that they then installed at the client's location using thousands of dollars worth of equipment, and struggling to get enough sales. Then one day, their biggest client happened to notice the on-site team using a Web interface to do some testing. "Can't we just do it this way, on the Web?" the client asked.

Manzi said no. Then he said it again. And again. The client kept asking. Eventually, with money getting very tight, Manzi gave in. He had discovered the software-as-service model of delivering applications to a client, where you own the servers, and they pay you monthly rent to access your product. Then novel, it now dominates most application development.

"It was a combination of luck, having our backs to the wall, running out of money, and listening to what the market was telling us," says Manzi. "In my experience, most entrepreneurs, they'll have a similar story. 'The company almost died, and then we figured out in crisis what we really did for a living.'"

"When we're sitting in our offices perfecting a product," says Jeff Stibel, the CEO of Dun & Bradstreet Credibility Corp, "we're making the product better for us. The problem is, we're not the customer."[3]

Failure, says Stibel, is "the only way a business grows," because it's "the only way you really learn." When he says that, he's not just staking out a philosophical position. Before he was a serial entrepreneur, Stibel was a graduate student in cognitive science at Brown University, where he talked his way into the program by passionately arguing to his adviser that "the Internet is a brain."

Stibel is the distilled essence of a successful entrepreneur: lean and compact, with an intense dark gaze, and the hypomanic charm you find in so many business founders. He fires off ideas like "the Internet is a brain" at a steady rate of about one per minute, usually some mixture of philosophy, management theory, technofuturism, and his beloved cognitive science. Like Skillman, he is voluble on the role that failure plays in learning. Only, he thinks that failure isn't just a way to learn faster: it's the only way to learn at all.

"The brain is a failure machine," he told me. "When you're born, you have about all the neurons you'll ever have. When you're four, you have pretty much all the connections *between* those neurons you'll ever have. Then the brain starts pruning. The brain starts *shrinking.*

"When the brain is shrinking," Stibel says, "you're actually learning by failure."

Think about the last time you tried to learn a new skill—using a spreadsheet, hitting a badminton shuttlecock, baking a cake. When you watched someone else do it, or read the instructions, it probably seemed pretty straightforward. Then you tried it, and nothing came out right. You lost a column and couldn't get it back. The shuttlecock flew off in entirely unexpected directions, or landed, unmolested, on the ground near your feet. The cake was half an inch of soggy crumbs.

Maybe you gave up right then. But if you tried again, you probably had a few more frustrating efforts. And then, after a little while, something clicked. Possibly by accident, this time when you hit the shuttlecock, it went in the direction you'd intended. And you had that little flash of joy that comes from getting something right for the first time.

That flash is your brain's reward system. Dopamine serves a lot of functions in the brain—it's implicated in everything from Parkinson's disease to heroin addiction. One thing it does consistently is regulate your reward systems. It's like a teacher handing out gold stars when your work is done correctly, and an extra sticker or two when your performance is superlative. When you're expecting something to happen, dopamine levels rise in anticipation. And if what you expected doesn't happen, they plummet.[4]

We perceive this rise and fall as elation and frustration. What we don't notice, says Stibel, is the role of dopamine in pruning the synaptic connections we've made. If our anticipation is correct, dopamine levels stay high, and strengthen the association between action and reward. ("When I beat the eggs and sugar together for a full five minutes, the cake is lighter and fluffier.") If something we anticipated fails to occur, the connection weakens. ("I thought moving my hand like that would make the shuttlecock go to the right, but it didn't happen.")

That's why everyone mostly gains skills by practicing, not by watching someone else or developing an elaborate theory of shuttlecock physics. The naturally gifted get a head start, of course. I could practice for ten hours a day, and I still wouldn't be a candidate for the Bolshoi Ballet, or MIT's physics department. But even the most extraordinary prodigy will not qualify for those august institutions unless they spend years practicing their art over and over and over, letting their frequent mistakes and occasional moments of triumph strengthen the neural connections that tell their body how to pirouette across the stage or solve a mathematical equation.

What Skillman and Stibel and Manzi and about a zillion management theorists are telling us is that effective groups work with the brain's natural learning style, instead of trying to supplant it. They fail early and often—"fail heroically," as Stibel puts it. "When most people look back on their successes," he told me, "they realize they were a series of failures that allowed them to navigate to success."

Stibel is very serious about failure. When he took over at Dun & Bradstreet Credibility Corp, a spin-off of Dun & Bradstreet that provides credit counseling to businesses, the company was stagnant— not losing tons of money, but not really succeeding either. He decided he needed to put failure back at the heart of the firm— literally. He, his wife, and his assistant spent an evening with a few gallons of paint and a bottle of wine, stenciling quotations about failure on an office wall. It took almost all night, but when workers came in the next day, there was Jeff, writing on the wall about his own worst failure. Slowly, other workers followed suit.

He knew he'd succeeded, Stibel says, when he overheard one employee yelling at another, "Why haven't you written on the wall? Why don't I get to learn from your failures?" Even his performance reviews include a section on failure—"It's a positive section," he says. "We want to know, has the employee failed? Have they failed enough? Have they shared that with other people?"

That doesn't mean wildly betting the farm, of course; it means calculated risks. "You don't want to fail *too* much," Manzi acknowledges. Rather, it's about "being able to kind of fall down, dust yourself off, get up and move on." Stibel agrees that it's about taking smart chances, not failing for the sake of failure. He is careful never to bet the farm on anything and puts a great deal of effort into ensuring that the failures aren't too costly. The object is to take lots of small, manageable risks, because that, he says, is the only way to figure out what really works.

Of course, as Manzi drily notes, failure is, well . . . "it's very difficult, for obvious reasons." Those plummeting dopamine levels may be doing important work in our brain, but they don't feel good. That's unfortunately inherent: failure feels bad precisely because it's the way your brain says, "Hey, don't do that anymore." That's why Stibel had to work so hard to convince his colleagues that failure was a positive thing. If we want an educated population, a skilled workforce, an innovative society, then we will have to work just as hard as he did to persuade people that the pain of failure is like a blister in tennis—a sign that you are trying hard enough to improve.

THE OPPOSITE OF FAILURE IS NOT SAFETY: IT'S NOTHING

Like most writers, I am an inveterate procrastinator. In the course of writing this one chapter, I have checked my e-mail approximately 3,000 times, made and discarded multiple grocery lists, conducted a lengthy Twitter battle over whether the gold standard is actually the worst economic policy ever proposed, written Facebook messages to schoolmates I haven't seen in at least a decade, invented a delicious new recipe for chocolate berry protein smoothies, and googled my own name several times to make sure that I have at least once written something that someone would actually want to read.

Lots of people procrastinate, of course, but for writers it is a peculiarly common occupational hazard. One book editor I talked to fondly reminisced about the first book she was assigned to work on, back in the late 1990s. It had gone under contract in 1972.

I once asked a talented and fairly famous colleague how he managed to regularly produce such highly regarded 8,000 word features. "Well," he said, "first, I put it off for two or three weeks. Then I sit down to write. That's when I get up and go clean the garage. After that, I go upstairs, and then I come back downstairs and complain to my wife for a couple of hours. Finally, but only after a couple more days have passed and I'm really freaking out about missing my deadline, I ultimately sit down and write."

Over the years, I developed a theory about why writers are such procrastinators: we were too good in English class. This sounds crazy, but hear me out.

Most writers were the kids who easily, almost automatically, got As in English class. (There are exceptions, but they often also seem to be exceptions to the general writerly habit of putting off writing as long as possible.) At an early age, when grammar school teachers were struggling to inculcate the lesson that effort was the main key to success in school, these future scribblers gave the obvious lie to this assertion. Where others read haltingly, they were plowing two grades ahead in the reading workbooks. These are the kids who turned in a completed YA novel for their fifth-grade project. It isn't that they never failed, but at a very early age, they didn't have to fail much; their natural talent kept them at the head of the class.

This teaches a very bad, very false lesson: that success in work mostly depends on natural talent. Unfortunately, when you are a professional writer, you are competing with all the other kids who were at the top of their English class. Your stuff may not—indeed, probably won't—be the best anymore.

If you've spent most of your life cruising ahead on natural ability, doing what came easily and quickly, every word you write becomes a test of just how much ability you have, every article a referendum on how good a writer you are. As long as you have not written that article, that speech, that novel, it could still be good. Before you take to the keys, you are Proust and Oscar Wilde and George Orwell all rolled up into one delicious package. By the time you're finished, you're more like one of those 1940's pulp hacks who strung hundred-page paragraphs together with semicolons because it was too much effort to figure out where the sentence should end.

Most writers manage to get by because, as the deadline creeps closer, their fear of turning in nothing eventually surpasses their fear of turning in something terrible. But I've watched a surprising number of young journalists wreck, or nearly wreck, their careers by simply failing to hand in articles. These are all college graduates who can write in complete sentences, so it is not that they are lazy incompetents. Rather, they seem to be paralyzed by the prospect of writing something that isn't very good.

"Exactly!" said Stanford psychologist Carol Dweck, when I

floated this theory by her. One of the best-known experts in the psychology of motivation, Dweck has spent her career studying failure, and how people react to it. As you might expect, failure isn't all that popular an activity. And yet, as she discovered through her research, not everyone reacts to it by breaking out in hives. While many of the people she studied hated tasks that they didn't do well, some people thrived under the challenge. They positively relished things they weren't very good at—for precisely the reason that they should have: when they were failing, they were learning.[5]

Dweck puzzled over what it was that made these people so different from their peers. It hit her one day as she was sitting in her office (then at Columbia), chewing over the results of the latest experiment with one of her graduate students: the people who dislike challenges think that talent is a fixed thing that you're either born with or not. The people who relish them think that it's something you can nourish by doing stuff you're not good at.

"There was this eureka moment," says Dweck. She now identifies the former group as people with a "fixed mind-set," while the latter group has a "growth mind-set." Whether you are more fixed or more of a grower helps determine how you react to anything that tests your intellectual abilities. For growth people, challenges are an opportunity to deepen their talents, but for "fixed" people, they are just a dipstick that measures how high your ability level is. Finding out that you're not as good as you thought is not an opportunity to improve; it's a signal that you should maybe look into a less demanding career, like mopping floors.[6]

This fear of being unmasked as the incompetent you "really" are is so common that it actually has a clinical name: impostor syndrome. A shocking number of successful people (particularly women), believe that they haven't really earned their spots, and are at risk of being unmasked as frauds at any moment. Many people deliberately seek out easy tests where they can shine, rather than tackling harder material that isn't as comfortable.

If they're forced into a challenge they don't feel prepared for, they may even engage in what psychologists call "self-handicapping": deliberately doing things that will hamper their performance in order to give themselves an excuse for not doing well.

Self-handicapping can be fairly spectacular: in one study, men deliberately chose performance-*inhibiting* drugs when facing a task they didn't expect to do well on.[7] "Instead of studying," writes the psychologist Edward Hirt, "a student goes to a movie the night before an exam. If he performs poorly, he can attribute his failure to a lack of studying rather than to a lack of ability or intelligence. On the other hand, if he does well on the exam, he may conclude that he has exceptional ability, because he was able to perform well without studying."[8]

Writers who don't produce copy—or leave it so long that they couldn't possibly produce something good—are giving themselves the perfect excuse for not succeeding.

"Work finally begins," says Alain de Botton, "when the fear of doing nothing exceeds the fear of doing it badly." For people with an extremely fixed mind-set, that tipping point quite often never happens. They fear nothing so much as finding out that they never had what it takes.

PRAISE AS POISON

Those of us suffering from a mixed mind-set are not just victims of our own neuroses. Everything from the way parents praise their kids to the way the school system rewards achievement creates and reinforces the belief that talent—particularly being smart—is something that happens to you, not something that you make happen. How we treat success, it turns out, has a lot to do with how people will act when they face the possibility of failure.

In one of Dweck's best-known experiments, children were given a simple cognitive task to do and, after they completed it, were praised for their performance. Half of them were told something like, "Wow! You did really well—*you must be very smart!*" The other half were told, "Wow! You did really well—*you must have worked really hard!*"[9]

Even Dweck was surprised by the magnitude of the effects she saw. When they were offered a follow-up test to take, and told that one was easy and the other one was hard, the students who had been praised for their effort eagerly embraced the more challenging test. Those who had been praised for their intelligence were far more likely to choose the easy path.

As you might expect, this eventually translated into performance: during the third round, when everyone was given another easy test, the kids who had eagerly attacked the difficult problems showed improvement, while the kids who had stuck to a task they could do well on actually performed worse.

Think about how grown-ups talk to children. "You're such a good boy!" they'll say. "Look at you—you're so smart!" Or "You're so pretty." The subtle message we are sending is that good qualities are something you *are*, not something you learn or develop. That message is really driven home in school, especially for the kids who have more natural ability. While Dweck believes—and has demonstrated—that people can get better by challenging themselves, she acknowledges that there are natural variances in innate ability. What she's arguing is that focusing on those variances, rather than on the potential for improvement, harms kids. Especially the gifted ones.

"The kids who race ahead in the readers without much supervision get praised for being smart," says Dweck. "What are they learning? They're learning that being smart is not about overcoming tough challenges. It's about *finding work easy.* When they get to college or graduate school and it starts being hard, they don't necessarily know how to deal with that.

"Think about the whole language of school," she adds. "They're put in 'gifted and talented' programs. I'm not saying we shouldn't have those programs; the kids should be challenged. But that wording is very problematic."

The original work on self-handicapping, by Steven Berglas and Edward Jones, studied people who were given a set of impossible-to-answer questions, and then told that they'd aced the test. Since they didn't know how they'd produced this result (remember, the questions were actually impossible to answer correctly), they had no idea how to repeat it. "These are the people who are told they are brilliant, without knowing how that inference is derived," Berglas told the *New York Times*.[10] What he and his colleague saw next was a lot of self-sabotage, designed to protect the illusion of competence.

Our educational system is almost designed to foster a fixed mind-set. Think about how a typical English class works: You read a "great work" by a famous author, discussing what the messages are, and how the author uses language, structure, and imagery to convey them. You memorize particularly pithy quotes to be regurgitated on the exam, and perhaps later on second dates. Students are rarely encouraged to peek at early drafts of those works. All they see is the final product, lovingly polished by both writer and editor to a very high shine. When the teacher asks "What is the author saying here?" no one ever suggests that the answer might be "He didn't quite know" or "That sentence was part of a key scene in an earlier draft, and he forgot to take it out in revision."

I have only ever taken one English class—a college class on Mark Twain taught by Professor Gregg Camfield at Penn—in which we focused on the half-finished, the experimental, and the frankly-not-very-good. Even Sam Clemens, it turns out, had his off days. Lots of them. After a rather speculative and ill-considered publishing venture went bust, Twain spent much of the 1890s sprinting around the lecture circuit and churning out lackluster prose on an almost industrial scale, just to get enough money to maintain his household and pay his debts.[11] But almost no English class ever reads the eminently forgettable stuff he produced during this period. Most English majors have read *Huckleberry Finn* several times. Almost none of them have read poorly structured throwaways like *Tom Sawyer, Detective* or *Pudd'nhead Wilson*. Don't get me wrong: on his worst days, Mark Twain was still a vastly better writer than I am on my best. But the gap was much smaller.

Or consider a science survey class. It consists almost entirely of the theories that turned out to be right—not the folks who believed in the mythical "N-rays," declared that human beings had forty-eight chromosomes, or saw imaginary canals on Mars. When we do read about falsified scientific theories of the past—Lamarckian evolution, phrenology, reproduction by "spontaneous generation"—the people who believed in them frequently come across as ludicrous yokels, even though many of them were distinguished scientists who made real contributions to their fields. And when we lionize people for getting things right, we rarely discuss the false theories they also embraced (Isaac Newton was an avid amateur alchemist; Linus Pauling, who won the Nobel Prize for chemistry, later dabbled in vitamin quackery—he is the reason why you probably erroneously believe taking high doses of vitamin C will cure your cold).

"You never see the mistakes, or the struggle," says Dweck. No wonder students get the idea that being a good writer is defined by not writing bad stuff.

Unfortunately, in your own work, you are confronted with every clunky paragraph, every labored metaphor and unending story that refuses to come to a point. "The reason we struggle with insecurity," says Pastor Steven Furtick, "is because we compare our behind-the-scenes with everyone else's highlight reel."

Somewhat shamefacedly, I confessed to Dweck that I am beset by a fixed mind-set; it is sort of a minor miracle that I got myself to write this book. To my surprise, she admits to being a fixed kind of person herself. It took a lot of hard and painful work for her to adopt a growth mentality. "I knew I had really changed when I heard myself saying, 'Wow, I'm so bad at this! This is really fun!'" she told me. "But it took a long time."

The good news is that there is a way to move people from fixity to growth.

Dweck encourages parents and teachers to praise children for their effort, rather than their intelligence, talent, or looks. She encourages schools to use language that emphasizes that success is a process and ability is malleable—and to teach the struggle rather than just the success. Dweck's research shows that troubled students who are taught that "when they stretch themselves to learn new things, their neurons form new connections and they can, over time, enhance their intellectual skills" often turn their performance around. Adults, of course, can tell themselves the same thing. However, like Dweck (and me) they will probably have to repeat it over and over again for the message to sink in.

And so now when I give talks to aspiring journalists, as I am sometimes called upon to do, I start by telling them that they probably aren't very good writers, and they certainly aren't as good as George Orwell, Tom Wolfe, or Hunter S. Thompson. This is actually a surprisingly welcome message. Of course, I do not stop at crushing the delicate flowers of their egos. What I am telling them is that being a bad writer is normal for someone who is just starting out. They may be no Hunter S. Thompson, but that's okay, because neither was Hunter S. Thompson when he was grinding out minor-league sports coverage for the local newspaper in Fort Walton Beach. There are more talented writers and less talented writers, of course. What there are not, are writers who are unfailingly brilliant from the first moment they set pen to paper to the last manuscript they send off to the printer. Even the very best writers have, over the course of their career, produced some pretty appalling slop.

So instead of fretting that their copy won't be any good, I tell them what it took me years to learn myself: they should give themselves permission to suck. It is easy to begin once you have accepted that what you produce may not be very good, and that *this is normal*. They will get better only by writing—and this can only happen if they sit down and face the page. Or as another writer put it: "You can rewrite garbage. You can't rewrite nothing."

Instead of focusing on chiseling their immortal words into history, something that usually leads to the worst garbage ever written, young journalists succeed by focusing on the things they can control—making lots of phone calls, getting the facts right, and making their deadlines. If they do these things, they will still spend the rest of their career having occasional flashes of easy brilliance, and putting a lot of sweatshop labor into things they wish were better. Just like every other writer who ever lived.

At eighteen or twenty-four or thirty-five they are having to learn what they should have been taught in kindergarten: how to embrace failure rather than avoid it. Not because it's fun, but because it's necessary. So why aren't they learning this in school? Somehow, our educational system has been set up to reinforce the message that failure is somewhere between dangerous and intolerable. That's the bad news. The really bad news is that it seems to be getting worse.

WHIFFLE PARENTING AND THE COLLEGE TRAP

About six years ago, commentators started noticing a strange pattern of behavior among the young millennials who were pouring out of college. Eventually, the writer Ron Alsop would dub them the Trophy Kids.[12] Despite the sound of it, this has nothing to do with "trophy wives." Rather, it has to do with the way these kids were raised. This new generation was brought up to believe that there should be no winners and no losers, no scrubs or MVPs. Everyone, no matter how ineptly they perform, gets a trophy.

Grade inflation has become a rampant problem even in high school; one survey found that more than 45 percent of college freshmen had graduated high school with an A average.[13] A dean of admissions at a selective liberal arts school speaks of seeing thirty to forty valedictorians *at a single school* because no one wants to make a distinction among the kids.[14] Meanwhile, in poor schools, kids who can't read are passed through to the next grade because it's too much trouble—and embarrassment for the teacher—to hold them back. Grades are being compressed into a narrower and narrower range. We have neither exemplary nor poor performance; school is essentially a pass-fail test of whether you can please adults. Actually, given that Fs are increasingly rare, it's pass-pass.

As these kids have moved into the workforce, managers complain that new graduates expect the workplace to replicate the cosy, well-structured environment of school. They demand concrete, well-described tasks and constant feedback, as if they were still trying to figure out what was going to be on the exam. "It's very hard to give them negative feedback without crushing their egos," one employer told Bruce Tulgan, the author of *Not Everyone Gets a Trophy*. "They walk in thinking they know more than they know."[15]

When I started asking around about this phenomenon, I was a bit skeptical. After all, us old geezers have been grousing about those young whippersnappers for centuries. But whenever I brought the subject up, I got a torrent of complaints, including from people who have been managing new hires for decades. They were able to compare them with previous classes, not just with some mental image of how great we all were at their age. And they insisted that something really *has* changed—something that's not limited to the super-coddled children of the elite.

"I'll hire someone who's twenty-seven, and he's fine," says Todd, who manages a car rental operation in the Midwest. "But if I hire someone who's twenty-three or twenty-four, they need everything spelled out for them, they want me to hover over their shoulder. It's like somewhere in those three or four years, someone flipped a switch." Today's new graduates may be better credentialed than previous generations, and are often very hardworking, but only when given very explicit direction. And they seem to demand constant praise.

Is it any wonder, with so many adults hovering so closely over every aspect of their lives? Frantic parents of a certain socioeconomic level now give their kids the kind of intensive early grooming that used to be reserved for princelings or little Dalai Lamas. When I was a child in New York City, middle-class parents worried a bit about their kids getting into a good high school, mostly so that they could get into a good college. Now they worry about getting their kids into a good nursery school, so they can get into a good kindergarten. A good kindergarten, you see, gives you the head start you will need toward the kind of primary school that ensures admission to a decent high school program.

A stock trader of my acquaintance took his daughter, a charming, dimpled dumpling of two and a half, to interview at one of New York's premier nursery schools, where an early childhood specialist asked him, in all seriousness, "What are her aspirations?"

"She's two!" he told me incredulously. "Right now we're working on not eating used gum off the street."

But if she has no aspirations at her advanced age, how can she hope to accumulate the necessary outstanding grades, glowing recommendations, distinguished record of public service, and artistic or athletic prowess (the latter preferably in something obscure and slightly dangerous, like jai alai or the luge)?

New York is extreme, of course, but all over the country parents are engaging in frantic bidding wars on houses in good school districts and micromanaging their offsprings' childhoods in order to produce an end product that will gain admission to a good college. A modern infant needs to be breast-fed until he's old enough to get into PG-13 movies by himself, weaned on organic baby food, preferably homemade, "enhanced" with Baby Einstein tapes (there's no evidence that they work, but . . . *just in case*). By kindergarten, the scheduled activities will have begun: soccer, a musical instrument, maybe something like pottery to make sure that they are, in one memorable slogan I recently heard, "Grounded and well-rounded." By the time they're in high school, a kid on track for an Ivy League school will be spending almost every waking hour practicing, doing homework, or engaging in various résumé-enhancing activities like "founding" charities with the "help" of their parents. It's Whiffle Parenting: everything is arranged so as to preclude the smallest possibility that anything could go wrong.

I went to private school in New York in the 1980s, and it wasn't like that. Don't get me wrong: it was still an elite experience, with two guidance counselors for a class of ninety-four. We had smaller classes than a public school and excellent teachers, and almost everyone was on an athletic team, but we had little of what the *New York Times* recently described as the "nonnegotiable" ancillary costs of private school in New York City: "private tutors, spring training in Florida for sports, unpaid internships at top research institutes to bolster college résumés."[16] We certainly didn't have a problem so widespread that even school administrators admit (privately, quietly) they're trying to crack down: students whose tutors just do their work for them. I am perhaps naïve about these things, but I'm pretty sure that nothing of the sort was happening while I was in school. Our parents were in league with the teachers, not with us. What on earth has changed in twenty years to turn parents into their childrens' willing accomplices as they cheat their way through school? The irony is incredible: parents are willing to sacrifice learning, in order to increase the odds that their children will be able to get a prestige diploma. And yet, if you look at the numbers, you can almost see why.

When my parents went to college, most people chose a school that was close to home. In the 1960s, most cities, and even small towns, offered plenty of opportunity for an ambitious college graduate, so people tended to go to a local college, or maybe the State U.

Plenty of students still follow this path, of course, but they are more likely than they used to be to vie for a spot at a faraway elite college. They know that elite schools are becoming the only path to a lot of lucrative and rewarding careers, like consulting and finance. Even my own profession, which used to be a fairly blue-collar operation, now gets most of its entry-level employees from a handful of highly selective colleges and universities.

Around the time of my birth, the writer Erik Larson was matriculating at Penn. The admissions rate was over 50 percent, a figure, he says, that "Penn officials recall with about as much nostalgia as a Vietnam vet recalls the siege of Khe Sanh."[17] By the time I arrived, in 1990, they were taking about a third of the people who applied. In 2012, just 12.3 percent of applicants, fewer than one in eight, gained admission.[18] And that, reported *Ivy Gate*, was the second *highest* admission rate in the Ivy League, trailing only Cornell.[19] Harvard accepted less than 6 percent of all applicants.[20]

Thanks to decades of expansion, there are still enough spaces for basically every student who wants to go to college. But there's a catch: most of those new spaces were created at less selective schools. The majority of Americans now attend a college that, for all intents and purposes, admits anyone who applies.[21] Spots at the elite schools—the top 10 percent—have barely kept up with population growth. Meanwhile demand for those slots has grown much faster, because as the economy has gotten more competitive, parents are looking for a guarantee that their children will be successful. A degree from an elite school is the closest thing they can think of.

So, crazy as it seems, maybe Whiffle Parenting is not some inexplicable national madness; it's an entirely rational reaction to an educational system in which the stakes are always rising, and any small misstep can knock you out of the race. But is this really good parenting? A golden credential is no guarantee of success (as we'll see later), and in the process of trying to secure one for their kids, parents are depriving them of what they really need: the ability to

learn from their mistakes, to be knocked down and to pick themselves up—the ability, in other words, to fail gracefully. That is probably the most important lesson our kids will learn at school, and
instead they are being taught the opposite.

While I was writing this book, the largest cheating scandal in
decades hit the news: 125 Harvard students were accused of cheating on a take-home exam.[22] This sort of thing happened when I was
in school, of course, but when caught, the cheaters acknowledged
that they'd done something wrong, pleaded temporary insanity,
and threw themselves on the mercy of the court. Not so the Harvard students; they complained to the *New York Times* that the
course was supposed to be an easy A, the exam had contained unfamiliar terms, and anyway, it was an open-book exam and they were
allowed to use the Internet. How were they supposed to know that
when the instructions said "Do not discuss with anyone else," that
meant they weren't supposed to e-mail one another and share
notes?

Judging by my Twitter feed, most recent college grads thought
they had a pretty decent case. If we've reached the point where elite
kids are no longer capable of parsing simple instructions without
someone to hold their hand and explain to them what the words
"do not discuss" might imply, then our educational system is truly
in crisis.

Of course, the crisis that this tournament system has created
among elites is nothing compared with the crisis among poor kids.
Unlike wealthy kids, poor kids are given lots of chances to fail. What
they're not given are chances to recover. As the writer John Scalzi
once noted, "Being poor is having to live with choices you didn't
know you made when you were fourteen years old."[23]

In some ways, the plight of poor kids in failing schools is the
mirror image—and the by-product—of the frantic effort by the upper middle class to ensure their children's economic future. They

seek school districts with low percentages of low-income kids, and press zoning boards to exclude housing that might attract poorer residents and their needier kids. Liberal parents console themselves that their first duty is to their children. And so economic segregation has risen, pushing the majority of the neediest kids into school systems that are overwhelmed by their problems.

It is not impossible to go to a top college if you are poor, but the odds are not great. If you look at the kids coming out of the households in the bottom 20 percent of annual earnings, only 11 percent of them will manage to earn a bachelor's degree.[24] In part this is because they tend to have more trouble in school, but an equal problem is the ease with which kids with ambition are derailed. They don't take the right classes to graduate on time, they mess up their financial aid forms, or they drop out to care for a relative or a boyfriend. While an affluent kid will be protected from his or her mistakes, a poor kid cannot afford to make even one. They are like Olympic gymnasts who can only win if they score a perfect 10. A few do. But the odds are desperately stacked against them.

"WOULD YOU LIKE TO TRY AGAIN?"

There is one place where kids can go to learn to fail the right way: a place where they are rewarded for effort and persistence, for tackling new challenges, failing at them over and over, and then finally prevailing. That place is their video game console. There they have a fail-safe space where they will be continually provided with tasks just a little bit harder than they can handle with their current knowledge. Most of their first attempts to build a city, fly a plane, or conquer a monster will end in disaster. But they'll persist, and most of them will eventually conquer, because in a clever innovation, video game makers have made it easier and easier for them to keep trying.

The early video games that my friends and I played in the 1980s—first in arcades, and then on home consoles like the Atari—were something like running a race where no one actually crosses the finish line. These games had dozens of levels, which almost no one ever actually completed. You started out with a certain number of lives, you got killed when you made a mistake, and even though many games featured opportunities to win bonus lives, eventually the tasks were just too hard. Then the game ended, occasionally with a taunting, "Would you like to try again?" flashing up on the screen.

"Trying again" meant starting again at level one and slogging all the way through a dozen or so levels you'd already mastered before getting to the challenging ones. Getting really good at a game meant playing those same early levels through exactly the same way hundreds or even thousands of times. It's no surprise that almost no one ever completed a game—or that the people who *did* complete them were serious nerds capable of monomaniacal dedication to exhaustive pattern repetition. Most people simply gave up after the twentieth time they'd beaten their way through the same tedious levels only to die, once more, in the exact same place.

When they started putting video games on computers that used disks instead of read-only cartridges, all that started to change. It was possible to save a game (and also necessary—computers were more likely to crash in the middle of game play than their console counterparts). Among other things, this meant that you didn't need an unbroken stretch of hours to play a game through.

The first console game to include a save feature was The Legend of Zelda. Suddenly you could take your game cartridge over to a friend's house and show him how far you'd gotten. More importantly, you could save a game before you died, and then go back and replay just the level you were struggling with until you finally got it. For the first time, games were handing people tasks in chunks small enough to let them focus on a single problem—and rewarding any-one who put in enough effort. You didn't have to be a genius—or obsessive—in order to win a game. You just had to be willing to try, and try again.

As a result, video games have gotten longer, more complex, more fun, and more democratic. They are still primarily male, but not as much as they once were.[25] They get played by adults who may only be able to put in a couple of minutes before setting the controller back down and starting dinner. When I went to college in the fall of 1990, any freshman who brought his game system with him would have been essentially announcing that he did not plan to have sex for the next four years. Now the consoles proudly sit in the living rooms of thirtysomething homeowners.

Educators are trying to figure out how to harness the power of video games to help kids learn math and science. Educational soft-ware can help kids master new skills by pinpointing where they're going wrong, and letting them practice just that task over and over until they get it.[26] And yet, we don't seem to be carrying that lesson outside the computer lab. Perhaps this is because even as our elec-tronics have become a better and better environment for learning from failure, our educational system has become much worse.

The American educational system pays lip service to the ideals of well-rounded kids with plenty of time to explore their passions. But underneath is the remorseless math of the college admissions tour-nament. It's a system that treats success like a fixed quantity, and failure as a disaster. These things didn't use to be true. America has long been famed for the flexibility of its educational system. Didn't do well in high school? Go to community college for a few years and transfer to a four-year university. Turns out you didn't want to be a psychologist? Go back and try something else. If at first you don't succeed, we told students, try, try again. We still say those things, but we no longer act as if they're true.

The good news is that we have what it takes to make them true again. But it will take hard work to get there. In the coming chapters, we'll explore how to build a society that gives people the right incentives to keep failing and learning—one in which our MBAs fail as effectively, and constructively, as our kindergartners.

2 THE VIRTUOUS SOCIETY

*What Two Economists and an Anthropologist
Can Teach Us about Free Markets*

On June 14, 2000, the lights began to flicker out across California. It was a dry, clear day in San Francisco, and abominably hot. California was in the claws of an arid, baking summer. Over to the east, in Solano County, the main interstate that runs from Stockton to San Francisco actually buckled under the heat, and a stray cigarette tossed out of a car triggered a wildfire that consumed 1,200 acres. By noon, the temperature was well above 90, and by 2 p.m., it had spiked to 105 degrees. All over the Bay Area, sweating homeowners cranked up the air-conditioning. Industrial cooling systems clanked into overdrive. Turbines whirred to life as all those hungry motors pulled more and more power out of the electric grid.

Throughout the Pacific Northwest and up into Canada, rivers were running low. Those rivers flowed through hydroelectric dams whose power wound its way down south into Californian homes and businesses. The State of California hadn't built a new power plant in over a decade, and with water levels low, California's Independent System Operator (ISO), the nonprofit that ran the state's newly de-regulated wholesale electricity market, had almost no power to spare.[1] On hot days like this, the difference between the demand for electricity and the total power that the market could supply, was less than 5 percent. The ISO was running with less spare capacity than most American airports on the day before Thanksgiving.[2] On June 14, they ran out. The ISO ordered Pacific Gas and Electric, the utility serving San Francisco, to start rolling blackouts. Ninety-seven thousand customers lost power.[3]

It was the beginning of months of hell. Customers in San Diego, where the retail electricity market had been deregulated, saw their electric bills triple as the utility company desperately sought power on the wholesale market. Los Angeles and San Francisco still had retail price controls, so consumers weren't stuck with outrageous bills. They also had no reason to reduce their power consumption, so they got blackouts instead.

The last blackout occurred in May of 2001. By then, Governor Gray Davis had been forced to switch off the lights on the official Christmas tree to save power, thousands of power workers had been laid off, and two of the state's utilities were teetering on the edge of bankruptcy. Voters were angry. They didn't quite march on Sacramento with pitchforks, but they started signing petitions to recall Davis. During the blackouts, he had famously said, "Believe me, if I had wanted to raise rates, I could have solved the crisis in 20 minutes." His failure to solve it in fourteen months became one of the central issues that led to his recall and replacement by Arnold Schwarzenegger.[4]

Fingers pointed everywhere. The most benign explanation centered on the "perfect storm" of weather conditions (hot, dry weather in the west, and a cold winter in the east that raised demand for electricity and fuel). Others assumed that with so much money flowing out of consumer pockets, there had to be a greedy bastard around somewhere. The new op-ed columnist at the *New York Times*, the economist Paul Krugman, blamed "artificially inflated prices" caused by market manipulation, noting that the "perfect storm" was occurring at an odd time: "State officials have understandably become suspicious about California's current power emergency—an emergency precipitated by the odd fact that about a quarter of the state's generating capacity is off line as the result of either scheduled repairs or breakdowns."[5]

Eventually, we found our villain: Enron. It turned out that when they weren't busy committing accounting fraud, the folks at Enron had engaged in a variety of shady maneuvers to artificially inflate the price of electricity. They jammed up transmission lines in order to create artificial shortages, disguised power generated instate as (more expensive) out-of-state power, and generally worked hard to create scarcity where none should have existed. The utilities had a mandate to provide as much power as customers wanted to consume—and since consumer prices were controlled, there was no way of encouraging them to want less. Enron was selling the last glass of water in a desert they themselves had created.

The peculiar structure of California's energy market encouraged this sort of manipulation. During the recent deregulation, someone had decided it would be a good idea to make the utilities buy their power on the "spot" market, where power is bought and sold for immediate consumption.[6] The idea seems to have been that this would make the market more efficient, but it was a bit like passing a law saying that people would have to do all their grocery shopping at convenience stores. The result was a market that was much easier to game. Utilities never had the luxury of shopping around: when they were buying power, they needed to have it this instant, no matter what the price.

Of course all this analysis came later. At the time, few people understood what was happening, and even fewer had predicted it. Deregulation was supposed to be, in the words of the *New York Times*, "a way to lower energy prices and introduce competition to one of the last bastions of monopoly in the nation."[7] People worried about higher prices, of course, but not *ten times higher*. The biggest concern was lack of interest from consumers, who couldn't seem to be bothered to provide the market with some competition by shopping around among utilities. Even Paul Krugman, whose analysis proved remarkably accurate, was only reacting to events as they happened; it's not as if he had seen it coming.

But a handful of students in Tucson did. In a laboratory at the University of Arizona, a team of economists led by Nobel Prize winner Vernon Smith had set up a working model of California's electricity market. They used undergraduates as the traders, and a small network of computers as the trading system. It was obviously nowhere near as complex as the massive infrastructure that California had set up during deregulation, but it was sophisticated enough to uncover the hidden fault lines in the state's energy market. Even undergraduates were sophisticated enough traders to game the system.[8]

Bart Wilson, a former student of Smith's who had just returned to his team after a stint at the Federal Trade Commission, recalls that he had to keep feeding power into the model market. Just like in the real world, the users were buying at a strictly controlled price, but the sellers could charge anything they wanted. Since consumers paid the same price regardless of how much they consumed, there was no reason for them to be careful about how much electricity they used at peak times—"no priority," says Wilson, "as to whether you are in the elevator or using a clothes dryer." Demand went up, up, up in basically a straight line. His team kept virtual "blackouts" from happening only by feeding the market as much power as it needed.

And just like in the real world, all that extra power at peak times was more expensive.

"There was no way to interrupt demand," says Wilson. "So why not, as a supplier, raise your offer a little? The price will only go up." And up, and up, and up—following demand into the stratosphere as the voracious end users, completely insulated from the rising prices, demanded to be fed. Over and over again in the lab, the undergraduate traders produced massive price spikes. In the lab, of course, they were trading for virtual pennies. But in the real world, this would have been a catastrophic surge, the kind that might push a supplier into bankruptcy—or force them to stop supplying power to all those clothes dryers.

This was May of 2000. In June, the lights went out.

NOT ALL FAILURES ARE GOOD

Most products fail. So do most marketing campaigns. Most firms fail too. Markets take all that failure and turn it into information: This works. That doesn't. And in the process, we all get richer. Apple makes the Newton handheld computer, which bombs—but lays the groundwork for the iPhone. Colonel Sanders loses his truck stop and discovers a late vocation as the nation's foremost purveyor of fried chicken. Yesterday's empty factory buildings become today's high-priced lofts.

California's deregulation was *supposed* to trigger some systemic fallout. Failure is, after all, the point of a free market: things that don't work go away. Joseph Schumpeter famously dubbed this process of incessant renewal from within "creative destruction" and called it "the essential fact about capitalism."[9] But the deregulated market wasn't supposed to fail *like that*. Creative destruction adds value; the debacle in California destroyed it. What markets normally do is fail well. But in California, the process of creative destruction itself failed very badly, in a phenomenon that economists call, appropriately enough, a "market failure."

Why do some things fail badly and others fail well? Why do some kinds of failures create wealth, and others destroy it? How come airline deregulation worked, and electricity deregulation didn't? Why is it easy to get rich in America, and hard to get rich in Zimbabwe?

These are the questions at the heart of economics, the ones that a lot of very smart people are still puzzling over hundreds of years after Adam Smith first published *The Wealth of Nations*. Vernon Smith and Bart Wilson have spent decades studying questions like these. They have tasked themselves with harnessing the power of creative destruction to steady creative destruction. And what they're finding is that how we handle failure is even more important than economists have realized. The way that people, and societies, think about failure and risk is central to the way that they cooperate with others.

It is the difference between a debacle like California's energy crisis, and a pre-success failure like Apple's Newton. It may even be the secret to survival itself.

WHY CAPITALISM WORKS IN NEW YORK BUT NOT IN MOSCOW

In 1955, Vernon Smith was struggling to illustrate to his introductory class at Purdue a fundamental concept known as the equilibrium price, the hallmark of an efficient market. The equilibrium price is the core of many economic models; we test how well a market is doing by how close it gets to this ideal. Economists have outlined a number of conditions under which markets fail to find equilibrium—if there aren't enough participants, or it's too hard for buyers to ascertain the quality of the product—but these concepts weren't necessarily easy to explain to first-time economics students.[10]

Eventually, he hit on an idea: he would build a miniature market in the classroom. Some students would be buyers, and others sellers. They would have no information except their own "reservation price": the maximum price at which it was profitable for buyers to buy, and the minimum price at which it was profitable for sellers to sell. Then he would let them proceed through several rounds of trading. The experiment was supposed to demonstrate how hard it is to trade efficiently. Smith had seen a similar exercise done with graduate students, and the market had failed to reach equilibrium. He expected the same thing to happen here; after all, these were undergraduates with very imperfect information.

Instead, to his surprise, the minimarket converged on the competitive equilibrium almost instantaneously. Smith ran the experiment again. And again. Over the next four years, he created these minimarkets over and over, varying the prices and quantities, but always with the same result: the markets found their competitive equilibrium. Eventually, Smith wrote up the results of his classroom exercises and sent them to the *Journal of Political Economy*, where they were published in 1962—after, in Smith's telling, "two revisions, four negative referee reports and an initial rejection." Smith had just helped to found the field of experimental economics, an achievement for which he eventually received the Nobel Prize, in 2002.

Thirty years after he published his first experiment, Bart Wilson, then a Wisconsin mathematics major, stumbled upon some of Vernon Smith's papers on experimental economics, and was, he says, "blown away."[11]

In the economics textbooks that Wilson was studying, markets worked best under "perfect competition"—markets like oil or corn futures, which have lots of buyers and sellers, undifferentiated products, and very good information about quality and price. But in Vernon Smith's markets, people were quickly finding the equilibrium price under much less than perfect conditions, using only simple trial and error. As Wilson puts it, the notion that supply and demand could work perfectly even without perfect competition "turned things upside down."

Before experimental economists came along, most economics was "blackboard economics": you developed a theory, or a model, or a data set, and then you sat down at the blackboard to do some math. Experimental economists actually built markets, and looked at how, and why, they failed. And so they were constantly discovering things they hadn't expected. "The idea that you could generate your own data was very appealing," says Wilson.

When Wilson discovered Smith's work, he had taken only a few classes in economics. He parked himself in the library and worked his way through every one of Smith's papers. Then he applied to the graduate program at the University of Arizona, where Smith was teaching. A few months later, he was packing his bags for Tucson.

Wilson entered economics at a heady time for all economists, but especially for those, like Smith, who found markets working even when you could think up all sorts of reasons why they shouldn't. The Berlin Wall was coming down and suddenly one of the central arguments of the twentieth century was over. There was no alternative to markets; the only real question was how quickly the socialists and communists and third-world dictators could get with the program. Suddenly, free market economists were powerful figures, charged with rebuilding all these fledgling economies from the ground up.[12]

Mostly, what they tried to do was unleash the market forces that the commissars had carefully suppressed. The Eastern bloc was filled with inefficient firms producing stuff no one wanted, kept on life support by the central planners. They would be privatized and the markets deregulated. Shortly thereafter, creative destruction was supposed to rejuvenate all these wildly inefficient economies.

And why not? Once the heavy hand of the government was removed, it seemed obvious that markets should reestablish themselves fairly quickly, provided you got basic things like a legal system and a functioning currency in place.

A very similar logic animated the California deregulation plan that Smith's team worked on. Reformers thought of markets as the natural state, and government control as an unnatural interference. Take away the obstruction, let the bad products and bad firms fail, and the invisible hand of the market should almost effortlessly guide resources where they were needed.

By the time Wilson joined Smith at Arizona in the spring of 2000, that optimistic theory was slowly being pulverized to rubble by Technicolor failures like California, and the complete refusal of markets in the former Soviet Union to conform to expectations. Markets there were supposed to be just like markets in the West—indeed, the rules had frequently been written by Western consultants. But they didn't work like markets in the West.

There's a legendary story about an economist who showed up a week before the conference he was running on Russian privatization, only to find that the hotel had given away the rooms he'd booked to a higher bidder. "So sue me," the hotel manager said. "This is capitalism." Of course, in most capitalist societies, a hotel wouldn't do something like this. The manager would probably feel ashamed to pull such a dirty trick. Even if he didn't, he'd know the guest would be outraged, and that outrage would quickly turn into scathing complaints that might cost him business . . . and then a lawsuit that might cost him money.

But this was Russia, where endemic corruption meant that markets were something like those cheap knockoff iPods you sometimes find in discount stores. The packaging is almost the same, and even close up they look pretty similar, but they break when you try to use them.

Instead of delivering bourgeois prosperity, in many places the collapse of the Soviet Union delivered kleptocracy. The old apparatchiks bought state assets for a song and became the new oligarchs. Meanwhile, for average people, life savings were wiped out by runaway inflation, alcoholism rose, life expectancy plunged.

Markets, it turns out, are not something that naturally pop into place as soon as you remove an obstructive government, like Athena springing full-grown from the head of Zeus. Nor are they some sort of machine that can be tweaked into perfection by expert planners. They're more like a complex organism. It's a hardy beast—it goes about its work with surprisingly little tending. But you can't just build one like a car. The Eastern bloc countries that did the best after the Soviet Union fell were, by and large, the westernmost periphery—Poland, the Czech Republic: countries that had been taken over after World War II. They were, in other words, the countries where the older citizens still retained a living memory of a market economy.

By 2005, Wilson had done a lot of experiments showing that when you get the rules right, people are surprisingly efficient at making deals together. And he'd done a lot of experiments like the virtual California market, showing what happens when you get the rules wrong. But fiascos like Russia—and persistent poverty in most of the world—were making it clear that it wasn't enough to have the rules; you also needed a society capable of making those rules stick. He started wondering where the rules came from in the first place.

We spend a lot of time asking ourselves why poor countries are poor, but as the development economist William Easterly has pointed out, what we actually want to know is, "Why are rich countries rich?" There's a reason why social scientists now frequently call countries like the United States WEIRD: Western, educated, industrialized, rich, and democratic. In the course of human history, we are the anomaly that needs explaining.

In the spring of 2012, I visited Wilson and Smith's lab, located on the palm-fringed campus of California's Chapman University, where a team of researchers run dozens of experiments a month. The traders are paid, just like real-world traders (though not as much), to ensure that the conditions are as close as possible to a real market. They come up with a question, set up a market to test that question, and then put people in their virtual market, to see what happens.

Almost everyone I met told me the same two things: markets are stronger than you think, and the people in them will constantly surprise you. One of the most profound insights to come out of their experiments is that a person doesn't have to be the coldly calculating, value-maximizing machine that critics of markets refer to as *Homo economicus* in order to trade successfully. If the market is working, it will conjure rational results out of irrational behavior, prosperity out of failure.

"Every experiment I have run has surprised me somehow," Wilson says. But the most surprising thing in the lab is not the lunatic traders who keep demanding irrationally high prices, or those who manage, through trial and error, to find their way to competitive equilibrium despite the most elaborate handicaps the experimenters can devise. It's the stuff they've found poking around at the very foundations of free markets—the way people behave when there aren't any market rules to guide them.

Free markets get called a lot of bad names. Noam Chomsky has called capitalism "anti-human and intolerable in the deepest sense,"[13] and even the conservative commentator Pat Buchanan has accused it of operating by "the law of the jungle."[14] Economists have spent a lot of time asking *how* markets work, but Wilson and Smith are now asking an even more fundamental question: Why and under what conditions are markets created? The first *Homo sapiens* did not spring to life in a trading pit; the Uniform Commercial Code was not inscribed on the tablets at Sinai.

A modern market economy is made up of millions of strangers all doing millions of different things, from teaching yoga to building iPods. Einstein's theory of relativity, *Swan Lake*, and the Chrysler Building all had their roots in two primordial humans deciding they'd both be better off if they exchanged *this* for *that*. Wilson and Smith want to know how we decided—*how we learned*—to do this. Knowing that would tell us a lot about why markets work, and why they sometimes don't.

Some of their answers may surprise you. Markets turn out to rely as much on morality as monetary policy; sociability can be as important as structure. And while our rules for sharing and trading can feel like moral absolutes, they're actually determined as much by our environment as our character. Often when we talk about rights, we should really be talking about risk.

WHO MAKES THE RULES?

Around 2005, when they were teaching an honors course together at Virginia's George Mason University, Wilson came into his office one day to find that Smith had left a sketch on his whiteboard, "to the effect," says Wilson, "that we have no experiment on the bene-fits of specialization." That was, he realized, a big gap in the litera-ture. Specialization is the foundation of all the productivity improvements between us and hunter-gatherers; it is the reason why you have spent the last hour or so reading this book instead of collecting bugs for dinner.

Wilson began to mull over how such an experiment might be designed. But as he thought about it, he realized there was an even bigger gap in the literature: How, exactly, had people figured out how to do this amazing thing that has brought us so much wealth? After all, as far as we can tell, for most of human history, we didn't.

Wilson went to Smith with an idea: What about creating a world where the participants didn't know what the rules were? After all, the first hunter-gatherers didn't have a nice set of market rules handed to them by a professor on an instruction sheet; they had to create them. Why not make students do the same? They could build a world whose inhabitants had to discover that they could trade, and even specialize, in order to make themselves more productive.

"He said something along the lines of 'That's a new kind of ex-periment,'" Wilson recalls. In a field as competitive as economics, that's a ringing endorsement. It was the beginning of what Wilson calls "opening up the action space to see what the subjects would build for themselves."[15]

The answer, quite often, was "nothing." Most of the time, they couldn't build even an elementary trading network. Sometimes they created a prosperous, thriving little society based on Adam Smith's "propensity to truck, barter, and exchange," but more often their dynamic degenerated into what the philosopher Thomas Hobbes called "the war of all against all." Unless they were given clear rules, most people couldn't do something as elementary as trade, something that you do without thinking every time you make a trip to the grocery store.

And yet some could. That was the real head-scratcher: some

groups could do it, and others couldn't. The world had two possible outcomes: one cooperative and prosperous, the other isolated and poor. And the prosperous equilibrium, the one that looks most like the world those of us in wealthy stable democracies actually live in, was harder to reach.

Every experiment may have its surprises, but this result profoundly altered Wilson's thinking. "The more open the experiment," says Wilson, "the more my own thinking is put on the line." Most of his work showed people achieving surprisingly rational outcomes when they were placed into markets. This experiment showed cooperation, and even rationality, falling apart as soon as the rules were removed.

Wilson has now done dozens of these open experiments, and spent endless hours poring through the data, trying to figure out why some groups go bad, and others "go good." All his efforts have come up empty; he sees no way to predict which group will succeed and which group will fail. What he knows is that they seem to settle on one path or the other pretty early—and once they choose, their decision is self-sustaining. Which may explain why so much of the world is still poor and governed by kleptocracy. Failing badly is normal. Failing well, he discovered, is much more unusual, and it turns out to be the key to a thriving economy.

Wilson does know that some of the things the textbooks say make for better markets actually make for worse ones. Larger groups are supposed to make markets more efficient, for example, because there's more competition and scope for cooperation. But in the open world, with no prespecified trading rules, Wilson and Smith have found the opposite to be true: expanding the group to eight people from four made it much more likely to fall apart. "Finding a trading partner got more difficult," Wilson explains. "And people weren't using one person as a bargaining chip to get a better deal from another. They were developing personal social relationships and *from there* discovering the benefits of exchange and specialization." The roots of the market are not in our predatory instincts but in our social ones.

While he can't tell you which groups will be successful before they start, he does know one thing that differentiates the successful groups: talking. He set up the experiment to allow groups to chat with each other through a sort of instant-messaging program. When they started talking to one another, the success rate went up remarkably.

For decades, we thought of these sorts of trading decisions as a simple matter of logic or game theory: people would do what maximized their self-interest, and the brutal evolutionary logic of the market would sort things out. But that is a grossly simplified version of Adam Smith's much-maligned "invisible hand." What Wilson's work suggests is that no amount of rational self-interest will, by itself, enable a group to discover the rules that create that prosperous equilibrium. Wilson began to believe that finding the right rules was only possible if you could build the right culture. But how on earth could you study that?

THE ANCIENT ROOTS OF MODERN MARKETS

How could two economists working at a lab in California study the impact of culture in a meaningful way? The simple answer was to team up with an anthropologist. In 2012, a longtime friend of Smith's named Hilly Kaplan came to Chapman to see if he couldn't replicate, in a lab, the beginnings of cooperative exchange. Kaplan, who teaches at the University of New Mexico, has wide-ranging interests, but one of his main areas of study is how (and why) hunter-gatherers share with one another.

It turns out that what Pat Buchanan once decried as the "law of the jungle" is nothing of the sort. Chimpanzees, our nearest relatives, don't build markets, and neither do hunter-gatherers, exactly. Kaplan and Wilson are trying to figure out why.

Chimpanzees subsist mostly on fruit, leaves, and bugs.[4] They're social, but they're also status-obsessed, territorial, and violent. The dominance hierarchy determines who gets what: higher-ranking males get substantially better opportunities to eat and mate. The hierarchy is defended by regular physical contests—as are other prerogatives. In July of 2012, a Texan working at the Jane Goodall chimp sanctuary near Johannesburg lost an ear, some fingers and toes, and a testicle when two chimps pulled him under a fence and dragged him a hundred feet.[16] It's believed they were reacting to a perceived imposition on their territory.

"Sounds like Hollywood," you may be tempted to remark, and fair enough. And yet somehow we manage to control those urges long enough to build the Eiffel Tower and record stunning performances of Beethoven's Fifth. Chimpanzees can't.

And I really mean "can't." Yes, chimpanzees have smaller brains than we do; they're never going to make the Quiz Bowl squad. But even if they were veritable Einsteins, they probably wouldn't be able to put forth a massive, cooperative effort like that, because chimps just aren't that good at collaboration.[17] They *can* cooperate— researchers have trained them to cooperate on various tasks, often quite sophisticated. But they're not that good at it; chimp cooperation is fragile and tends to fall apart when the chimps see half a chance to monopolize more resources.[18] Put a pile of food in front of a group of chimps and they'll quickly be biting and scratching each other.[19]

A hunter-gatherer band is in lifestyle the closest thing that humans have to a chimp community. And yet in some ways, it's also the farthest thing that humans have from a chimpanzee troop. In the Western imagination, hunter-gatherers were humanity's poor cousins, trapped in an endless search for subsistence. Thomas Hobbes summed up this view when he characterized life in the "state of nature" as "solitary, poor, nasty, brutish and short."

Since the 1960s, new research has revised that view. Hunter-gatherers are actually better fed than subsistence farmers; paleoanthropologists can tell when a group started transitioning to agriculture because the bones show people getting shorter, sicker, and more prone to tooth decay. Furthermore, hunter-gatherers seem to be temperamentally the opposite of chimpanzees. They are egalitarian, male dominance is minimal, and they cooperate—they not only band together to hunt but share the fruits of what they kill on their own. Sometime in our evolutionary history, a radical change occurred: a group of violent, grabby primates settled down and learned to share—consistently, and according to well-understood rules.[20]

And then we unlearned it; sometime around the dawn of agriculture, we started looking a lot more like chimps again. As we settled down on the land, we became more status-obsessed, more tribal, and more possessive. Open-ended reciprocal exchange became less common, and property emerged. Male dominance became much more noticeable, even pathological, and not because men are just so darn valuable in harvesting wheat; in many agrarian societies, women do much of the hard work of food provision, while men provide protection, presumably from other men.[21]

It's easy to see this as a sort of primordial Fall of Man, in which hunter-gatherers somehow banded together to overthrow their alpha-male overlords, only to lose hold of their communist Eden— along with their teeth and their leisure time—when they settled down to farming. The usual story is that when farming comes into existence, the resulting surplus allowed some people to buy the services of others, thereby once again setting themselves up as the alpha.[22]

Kaplan spent years studying the Aché, one of the most communally oriented groups we know about.[23, 24] Aché hunters believed in sharing so strongly that eating from your own kill was taboo; they held that a man who ate from his own kill would lose his ability to hunt. In the 1970s, encroaching farming and logging operations reduced their territory until it was too small to support foraging, forcing them to leave the Paraguayan rain forest and settle down in farming villages. Kaplan observed them during the transition, and he developed an alternative theory about why foragers tend to share more than farmers. This was the theory that he wanted Smith and Wilson to help him test: that how and when we share has as much to do with risk as it does with morals.

RISK, SHARING, AND THE ESKIMO'S DILEMMA

On a frosty morning near the Arctic Circle, an Eskimo hunter sits down next to a hole in the ice and hopes that a seal will show up to catch a breath of air. He may be the most skilled hunter in his group, but that's not going to be the biggest factor in whether he kills something today. No matter how skilled he is, the main question standing between him and dinner is: "Will a seal show up at this hole?"

No amount of effort is going to make the seal come to his hole rather than another a mile away. A crackerjack hunter, the Daniel Boone of the North, could easily sit there for hours and see nothing. Meanwhile a lucky hunter at some other hole will end up with hundreds of thousands of calories, more than he can possibly eat or store. Subsisting on hunting is like playing a meat lottery. Hunters can often improve their odds through cooperation. But even then, the risk remains—and the return to individual skill falls even further. If it takes four people to bring down a moose, it's hard to claim that your contribution was more necessary than anyone else's.

If you're an Eskimo hunting from winter camp, you can at least freeze your extra seal meat. But in sunnier climes, it will quickly begin to rot. Even if it didn't, foraging requires roaming across a large area, with a population density of perhaps one human per square mile. Most hunter-gatherers can't store more than they can carry, so there's no way to set up a savings account. Nor can they really borrow, since they don't know when they'll have meat to repay the debt.

The hunter-gatherer "bank account" is favors, sharing. Anthropologists call it the "gift economy," or "reciprocal altruism." Groups like the Aché make it work on a larger scale, across dozens of people who aren't all parent and child. If it isn't quite the arrival of true communism, it's closer than anyone else has come.

The need for favors, Kaplan argues, explains why status hierarchies are so flat among hunter-gatherers: not because they retain the mystical innocence of the Garden of Eden, but because their inability to store up food for a rainy day makes their lives unusually risky. If you get hurt and can't feed yourself for a month, someone else has to feed you. Hunter-gatherers have quite a lot of leeway about who they take care of, precisely because forager bands are more mobile and fluid than tribal farmers rooted to the land. Unlike tribal societies, where you belong to either your mother's family, or your father's, hunter-gatherer family ties are bilateral. If someone in the group you're living with is making himself unbearable, throwing his weight around, it's pretty easy to decide you'll try living with your brother-in-law's band for a while.

Or if everyone agrees you're really awful, said Kaplan with a mordant smile, maybe someone puts an arrow in your back while you're out hunting.

The result is the sort of society we say we all want, minus the stray arrows: lots of reciprocity, community, and very little jockeying for economic gain or social position. It's the dream that fell apart on thousands of kibbutzes and communes, but for the Aché, for hundreds or maybe thousands of years, it worked. That is, until it didn't.

Kaplan studied the Aché in the 1980s, during their abrupt transition to agriculture. As Paraguayan farmers pushed deeper and deeper into the rain forest, they came into increasingly violent conflict with the Aché. With their territory no longer large enough to support foraging, and their lives under threat from the farmers, the Aché reluctantly agreed to settle in two Christian missions. There they became farmers, tending livestock and small fields of manioc, beans, peanuts, corn, sweet potato, and sugarcane.[25]

This sounds considerably better to me than their traditional diet of palm fiber, insect larvae, fruit, and monkey meat, but the Aché did not quickly resign themselves to agriculture. Bands of ten to fourteen families took frequent foraging trips into the forest, and on several trips, Kaplan followed them, struggling to climb muddy hillsides in his sneakers behind the agile Aché hunters, whose bare feet easily dug into the mud.

In the forest, the Aché were still communal sharers. Data gathered by Kaplan and other anthropologists shows that nuclear families gave away 80 percent of what they acquired to other families—and almost 90 percent of the meat they hunted. Fifteen years later, however, the moral imperative to share had eroded considerably. Hunters had started violating the taboo about eating from their own kill. And back at the settlement, they had begun to restrict their sharing to a tight circle. While a typical food item on a foraging trip was shared with about 40 percent of the group, manioc or sugarcane might be shared with 10 percent. Moreover, that 10 percent was heavily biased toward near relatives. The Aché, in short, looked less like communists than like my mother and me buying each other a few things at the grocery store.

Fifteen years is a pretty short time for such a major cultural shift. It may have been hastened, in one settlement, by fervently anticommunist missionaries who insisted that communal sharing was wrong. But that was not the main reason the Aché started farming individually, says Kaplan. The problem was cultural: the rules that had served them so well in the forest simply didn't work in the farmlands.

"They used to ring a bell in the morning to go into the fields," he explains, just as they had formerly gathered to the hunt. With one key difference.

"People didn't show up."

Kaplan thinks there's a reason for that: exchange is a way of dealing with risk. Societies where there's a lot of variance in the food supply engage in a lot of open-ended reciprocal exchange, and those where it's pretty steady don't. Open-ended sharing is an insurance policy in a world where there's no way to store up physical assets. This instinct for exchange enabled us to survive in a risky world—and if you believe Wilson, it may also have eventually enabled us to build a modern market economy.

That's the theory, anyway. So along with Wilson and Vernon Smith and Eric Schniter of Chapman, he set up an experiment to test it. People were put into a world with two sources of "food"—tokens they could exchange for money when the experiment was over. One source was low risk and provided a steady trickle of resources, while the other was high risk: sometimes you got a huge amount, but often you got nothing.

"The results," says the paper they wrote about the experiment, "provide strong support for the hypothesis that people are predisposed to evaluate gains from exchange and respond to unsynchronized variance in resource availability through endogenous reciprocal trading relationships."[26] In other words, when the connection between work and output is fairly linear, people keep what they earn themselves, or share it with a select circle. When there's a lot of risk, they learn to minimize their downsides by sharing.

Kaplan already knew that foragers and farmers saw morality differently. In some sense, this experiment tells us that they *should* see it differently. Unless they have access to an unusually steady and bountiful supply of food, hunter-gatherers who practice farmer morality will tend to starve to death. And so will farmers who try to do everything communally, as we've proved in endless experiments, from the Plymouth Colony to Mao's Great Leap Forward.

But what does all this have to do with those of us who neither farm nor forage? It turns out, a lot. If you think about it for a moment, you'll realize that many, if not most, of today's angriest political and economic debates come down to forager morality versus farmer morality.

THE FAIRNESS OF FARMERS

As the election ramped up in 2008, the social psychologist Jonathan Haidt published an essay at Edge.org entitled "What Makes People Vote Republican?"[27] Haidt argued that all morality is built on five sets of moral foundations: care versus harm, fairness and reciprocity, authority and respect, purity and sanctity, and in-group loyalty. Conservatives, said Haidt, tended to weight all five equally, while liberals tended to emphasize care and fairness.

Haidt wasn't particularly surprised to receive a flood of e-mails from liberals tut-tutting him for suggesting that Republicans might have different priorities, rather than twisted and cruel personalities. One reader wrote to say that he had overlooked Republican narcissism, which, sadly, would prevent them from understanding Haidt's valuable perspective on their "illness."

But Haidt was surprised at the e-mails he got from conservatives. Some had liked the essay. But many were angry that he had misunderstood them. They cared about fairness a lot, they said, and they didn't think it was fair for the government to take their hard-earned money and give it to people who didn't work for a living. They viewed liberals as indifferent to the morality of spending tax dollars on people who didn't work, or worse, actively encouraging poor people to live off the taxpayer. The e-mails were larded with colorful and contemptuous language, like the one whose subject line read "Head up ass."

Haidt realized that he'd made a mistake when he thought that conservatives cared less about fairness than liberals; rather, they cared about different fairness. Liberals worried about the fairness of equality. Conservatives were animated by the fairness of proportion: Are people being rewarded according to the effort they put in? Haidt realized he needed a sixth moral foundation, one that would capture what these conservatives were talking about. "It was the fairness," writes Haidt, "of the Protestant work ethic and the Hindu law of karma: People should reap what they sow."

Haidt might also have said it was the fairness of farmers.

Foragers live in a fluid, mobile world where they excercise very little control over their environment. Their power lies in movement. If the pickings are thin in one area, move to another. If your brother-in-law isn't pulling his weight on the hunt, go live with someone else. That's easy to do because it's easy to see. If there's no game—or no hunter hunting it—you can react right now.

Farmers can't exit. They are tied to the land. The punishment for laziness—no food later—is hard to enforce right now, when you need people to show up and go into the fields. And so instead of exit, their morality focuses on control. Someone who puts in the work of tending their fields will almost always reap a harvest, and anyone who stores up a harvest will have enough to tide them over an illness or injury. Forager values are focused on providing immediate social insurance: reciprocity and equality. Farmer values are focused on providing the incentive to produce for the future: proportionality and justice.

This is a simplification, of course; farmers share, and hunter-gatherers reward individual effort. But which value is emphasized differs greatly. Kaplan thinks that this is a rational—and necessary—response to the structure of their food supply.

When you see a liberal and a conservative hotly debating welfare policy, isn't this what they are arguing about? The liberal says "It's not their fault that they were born poor" and the conservative says "They could stop being poor if they waited to have kids until they got married, worked full-time, and finished high school." Both statements are true. And so how you feel about poverty and social policy depends on whether you think that living in the American economy is mostly like being a big-game hunter, where rewards are largely dependent on luck, or whether it's like being a farmer, where rewards are mostly a function of effort.

And of course, so does how you feel about progressive taxation. If you think that people get rich mostly because they work hard, then you'll favor low taxes and a less generous safety net. If you think that wealth is mostly luck, then you'll believe in a lot of redistribution—and get mad at lucky people who refuse to contribute their "fair share." Our forager instincts are constantly at war with the bourgeois culture we inherited from thousands of years of farming.

What we need is a synthesis, and over the years, America has mostly found one. The American Bourgeois Synthesis can be summed up like this: If you pursue the bourgeois goals of ownership and prosperity by the bourgeois means of saving and work, we will share generously. If you pursue other goals, or use other means, you're pretty much on your own.

Some version of this synthesis prevails in every country, but in America, it is particularly extreme. We are the most generous nation on earth to the failed entrepreneur, who will find it fairly easy to get a new job from a boss who admires his hustle, and be offered extremely generous bankruptcy protection from any debts he has left over. We are one of the harshest to the criminal, the shirker who is trying to live off the work of others. That's why we have federal help for the middle-class Staten Island homeowner who just wanted, as so many of us do, to have a nice home near the ocean, and why we don't offer similar help to someone who forgets to pay the insurance premiums before their house burns down. It's why we're the richest big country in the world, and the biggest rich country in the world, and why our underclass is among the world's most pronounced.

While the synthesis is good, it is far from perfect. We treat some things as bad luck that aren't—if you built a house on the Mississippi flood plain, it is not "bad luck" when your house gets inundated, but the federal government will still give you money to rebuild. And in other areas, we are far too ready to view the unlucky as the undeserving. If you're farming or hunting, it's easy to distinguish bad luck from laziness or incompetence. But in a modern industrial economy the line is blurrier.

The main engine of our growth, entrepreneurship, is particularly hard to classify. The problem is that becoming an entrepreneur is really an incredibly stupid thing to do. Most entrepreneurs fail. It's tempting to think that this statement actually means "most entrepreneurs have bad ideas" or "most entrepreneurs don't know how to run a business," but that's wishful thinking. There's no evidence that "bad entrepreneurs" fail while "good entrepreneurs" succeed. Take a successful entrepreneur, one who has already founded at least one thriving company. Pair him with an experienced venture capital firm that's able to offer him good support and advice. Research shows that in this, the best-case scenario for a would-be start-up, he still only has one chance in three of succeeding the second time.[28]

Perhaps that's why a lot of them don't try. One entrepreneur I spoke to, who founded a very successful firm and sold it shortly before the financial crisis, says he would never do it again. "When you start it, there's a 90 percent chance that it's going to fail. You'll be worse off financially for having done it. It's hard to communicate how energy-sapping that is."

How do we encourage people to take these sorts of crazy risks? One way is to offer lavish rewards to those who succeed, which America does; our tech billionaires litter the lists of the richest people on earth. But that's not enough. German tech successes could also make billions, and yet relatively few of them even seem to try.

Americans aspire to start businesses noticeably more than their European counterparts; they are more likely to try to start a business, and as a result, they are more likely than the citizens of most European nations to end up owning a new business.[29] This has big implications for economic growth. During political campaigns, you frequently hear politicians begin a song of praise for small business by noting that most new jobs are created by small businesses. This statistic is true, but it's also misleading. In fact, small businesses do create a lot of jobs, but they also destroy a lot of jobs. Net new jobs—what you get after subtracting all that churn—are disproportionately created by a handful of fast-growing small businesses, the ones that are on their way to becoming the next Google or Walmart.[30] It isn't the number of small businesses that makes our economy so strong; it's the rate at which daring and a trifle foolhardy entrepreneurs found *new* businesses.

So what explains the difference? It's not genetics—there are plenty of entrepreneurs in America whose ancestors hail from countries with low rates of entrepreneurship. The difference is the culture and rules surrounding risk and failure. When you talk to Europeans who have done business in America, and Americans who have done business in Europe, they tell you the same thing: a European executive who works for a company that has failed is an executive who no longer has a career. In America, by contrast, having tried (and failed) to start your own company is often a résumé booster—particularly in the fertile fields of Silicon Valley. It marks you as a risk taker, a self-starter, someone who is not afraid to shoulder a whole lot of responsibility. And the (correct) assumption is that in your failure, you've learned a lot of valuable lessons that your new employer will benefit from.

On the two continents, the exact same set of circumstances signal wildly different things: in Europe, that you are irresponsible, and perhaps too lazy and incompetent to run a business, in America, that you are a risk taker and a visionary.

Europe, in short, treats entrepreneurial risk-taking like farming: success is a result of hard work and good planning, so if you fail, it's because you did something wrong. America, by contrast, treats it like foraging: results are highly uncertain and always driven by luck, so if you fail, it's a healthy sign that you were trying hard. And to an extent, these expectations are self-fulfilling: in a culture where people are discouraged from taking these kinds of risks, the people who *do* are probably, on average, pretty far out there.

When it comes to poor people, the positions are reversed. Europeans treat poverty, unemployment, and so forth as mostly a matter of luck. They respond by generously sharing community resources, taxing those who are working to give lavishly to those who are not. Americans are more likely to treat those people as the authors of their own fate. The primary focus is on making sure that people contribute their fair share.

Americans often fail well, but this book will argue that we can fail even better, if we change the way we think about risk. We need a little more forager, a little less farmer—a little more forgiveness, a little less judgment.

Now let's get back to California for a minute. For most people, the villain of that story is Enron, traders who profited while costing taxpayers millions. That's one way to tell the story. Here's another: the people who deregulated California's energy market set up a system with bad rules, one that was bound to create an expensive mismatch between demand and supply. Because of the faulty environment, the incentives to manipulate the market were high. That meant the only thing standing between California and disaster was the moral restraint of traders in the energy market. And as we've seen, when there's a mismatch between morality and the environment, there is a good chance morality will begin to slip.

Markets work best when formal rules are supported by a strong set of informal moral rules—by that cultural operating system we talked about earlier. And those informal moral rules work best when they're in tune with the risk environment. When the most moral actions are also the most likely to be rewarding, it's relatively easy to keep the system working. When they're not, the whole system tends to fall apart. It's as true for us as it is for the Aché.

In some ways, it's even more true for us. Life for the Aché may not be a simple, bucolic paradise, but it is more comprehensible. It is easy to observe what the other members of your band are doing, and because there's very limited specialization, easy to see whether or not they are doing it right.

By contrast, a modern person lives surrounded by strangers who are doing things they may not understand. We cannot rely on our instincts and our relationships to keep society working. So it's more important than ever to make sure that we get the rules right. If we want our economy to grow, it means looking for ways to support experimental risk-taking by trading a little more than we may instinctively be comfortable with. It means offering big payoffs to those who are willing to take big risks but also making sure that the unlucky don't starve. In short, it means accepting that a high degree of unpredictability goes with the hunting ground.

3 THE EXPERIMENTERS

*Why There Are No Guarantees in
Hollywood or Silicon Valley*

You've probably heard the story of what's arguably the biggest movie disaster of all time. The script required a massive set built in the middle of an even more massive body of water, even though water is both difficult and dangerous to work with—if you've ever had a bathroom flood, you can imagine what thousands of gallons can do to the kind of temporary construction that normally suffices for sets on land. The director became obsessed with perfecting his vision of a script he'd been developing for years and the studio let him run with it because, by that time, they were already in way too deep—and hadn't he shown he knew how to make a big hit?

The budget marched rapidly north toward $200 million, which in the mid-1990s made it the most expensive picture ever made. The sheer scale of the project attracted guffaws and predictions of doom from a gleeful press. To top it all, the picture was plagued by production delays (did I mention that water is difficult to work with?). The producers pushed back its release date, originally scheduled for one of the biggest weekends in summer.[1] Moving a big budget film off a release date like that is usually a sign that things have gone so wrong that no amount of extra spending or corner-cutting can make the film work in time. As the media swarmed, cast and crew leaked tales of a director who continually "lost it" on the set while the unwieldy production became totally unmanageable.

"Yeah, the horror stories are true," an assistant director told the *L.A. Times*. "If anything, the fault of the movie is just its sheer size.

It was just so huge, there was no way to control it."[2] By the time of the release, the studio heads had privately started saying things like, "If we can just break even . . ."[3] The director himself admitted—well after the release—that he "labored on" for the last six months "in the absolute knowledge that the studio would lose $100 million. It was a certainty."

The film finally debuted four months late, in Tokyo, to a reception that the *New York Times* described as "tepid," "muted," and "subdued." Journalists and movie buffs across America had by then already spent months wallowing in schadenfreude. How could the studio have let this happen? How could *the director* have let this happen? How could anyone have thought this was a good idea?

Which just goes to show why so few journalists end up making millions in Hollywood. *Titanic* went on to become the top-grossing picture of all time—at least until its director, James Cameron, went on to make the even more successful *Avatar*. The movie stayed in theaters for nearly a year, grossing $600 million in domestic box office sales in its initial run, and double that worldwide. Fifteen years later, it is still earning money for its creators.

Perhaps you were expecting me to name *Waterworld*, the Kevin Costner extravaganza that cost almost as much as *Titanic*, and grossed just $85 million in domestic box office sales before an ignominious close. That's certainly what many people were expecting when *Titanic* hit movie screens in 1997. The 1995 *Waterworld* debacle was still a fresh memory when *Titanic* debuted, and the parallels must have chilled even James Cameron.

Consider: two producers with previous blockbusters under their belts who nearly doubled their initial budgets in order to pursue their vision. Both had a string of problems with the water environment and their complicated sets—Costner saw an expensive set washed away by a hurricane, while Cameron had to contend with extended construction time and further delays—as cast and crew members, including Kate Winslet, became ill after spending so many hours immersed. Both had a gloating press awaiting their demise long before they made it into theaters.

In fact, before the film debut, many of the comparisons seemed to be running in *Waterworld*'s favor. *Waterworld* came in at just over two hours, while *Titantic* ran over three. The extra length created two potential problems: people are reluctant to see very long movies, and theaters can't pack as many screenings into a night, both of which cut down on box office returns. Unlike *Titanic*, *Waterworld* actually made its July release date, giving it a built-in audience of bored teenagers whiling away the summer. And *Waterworld* had Kevin Costner, a certified Big Star who could open movies. *Titantic* had Kate Winslet, veteran of a couple of roles in small-budget films, and Leonardo DiCaprio, who had had one star turn in *Romeo+Juliet*, but was otherwise mostly famous for his portrayals of the drug addicted and mentally challenged.[4]

All of which illustrates William Goldman's famous observation about Hollywood: no one knows anything.[5] Until you put a movie into a theater, there's no way to tell for sure what's going to happen.

But there's something else our exercise illustrates even more compellingly. It's easy to believe, especially in hindsight, that you can reason your way to a good prediction. I fooled you a bit by telling you that it was arguably the greatest movie disaster of all time, rather than the greatest disaster movie. But the reason I was able to get away with this is that the line between the two is much thinner than we like to think.

It wasn't crazy to think that *Titanic* would be a bomb; it would hardly have been the first time an epic movie had failed spectacularly. It wouldn't even have been the first time this happened to James Cameron: his first water picture, *The Abyss*, went through a similar saga of set problems and cost overruns. Conditions were so bad that decades later, the lead, Ed Harris, basically refuses to talk about it.[6]

When he was making *The Abyss*, James Cameron didn't say to himself "You know, I've already made *Terminator* and *Aliens*, and in a couple of years I'm going to have smash hits with *Terminator II* and *Titanic*. So I think I'll go make this awesome picture that no one will want to see." Nor, as I believe William Goldman originally pointed out, did Steven Spielberg decide he wanted to take some time off between *Close Encounters of the Third Kind* and *Raiders of the Lost Ark* to make *1941*, a forgettable and now-forgotten period comedy. Two of the most successful directors in history *didn't have a clue.*

People desperately want to believe that prediction is possible, if only you are sufficiently smart and well informed. We cling to this belief even in the face of massive contradictory evidence. But if that's so, why do movies fail? Studio heads are not stupid people. They have every incentive to work hard to figure out what movies will do well—and they do work hard at it, commissioning survey after survey, paying professional consultants to do computer analyses of scripts, putting films in front of test audiences. Certainly, they know more about the business than any of us, and given Hollywood's famously opaque accounting, they have access to much better information about how much movies cost, and what they earn. Nonetheless, the public knows something that they don't: whether they prefer *Titanic* to *Waterworld*. In *The Big Picture*, his book of essays on Hollywood, Goldman describes the opening night of *Beloved Infidel*, a big-budget 1959 picture starring Gregory Peck as F. Scott Fitzgerald. Members of the studio's publicity department were pacing the lobby, waiting to see if the public would, voluntarily and with its own money, want to see the film. Seven hundred fifty people would be a blockbuster; something less than that would at least let the studio make its money back. The actual size of the audience they got was . . . four.

"Reeling and ashen," says Goldman, one flack turned to another and asked the eternal question that still plagues Hollywood: *"How do they know?"*[7]

Most business books, indeed most public commentary, are written with the underlying assumption that there is an answer to that question—that there is some way to figure it out short of making a movie and seeing if people like it. And why shouldn't there be? Engineers can build big suspension bridges that we drive across twice a day because they can figure out what will happen when you put all that steel and cement and cabling together in a certain way. "We got better at predicting the future" is a not-so-bad way of describing the entire march of human civilization.

But there is a catch: people cannot be treated like engineering problems. We have a very good idea how a piece of steel will behave if we heat it up to 1,000 degrees, but no scientist can predict exactly what you will do if you burn your tongue on a hot cup of coffee. You might spit it out, or painfully swallow; you might say "Ow!" or "Ouch!" or start swearing. Or you might fling the cup across the room. Still less can scientists predict the reaction of the people around you, which depends on what you do, where you are, the culture you live in, and the individual temperaments of all those other people. When it comes to popular entertainment, there is also the knock-on effect of one person influencing another, which has been dramatically enhanced by social media.

Of course, human behavior is not totally random. We can predict that you won't smile after that coffee burn. Still, it's surprisingly hard to predict what will succeed, and what will fail. Just look at the entertainment industry's history of surprise hits and equally unexpected bombs. The majority of start-ups, even those with venture capital funding and previously successful entrepreneurs at their helm, are failures. Once you account for fees, most professional money managers underperform broad market indexes like the S&P 500. For that matter, they more than occasionally underperformed a portfolio selected by *Wall Street Journal* staffers throwing darts at their stock pages, as a ten-year series run by the newspaper showed.[8]

PAST PERFORMANCE IS NO GUARANTEE
OF FUTURE RESULTS

A few years before the financial crisis, a psychology professor named Philip Tetlock published the results of a landmark study of experts in various fields who had spent years making predictions about world events from the Cold War to Argentina's GDP.[9] The results were shockingly, embarrassingly bad. The experts didn't do all that much better than you could have done by randomly selecting possibilities from a hat.

Drawing on concepts originally articulated by Isaiah Berlin, Tetlock notes that some experts are better than others: "foxes," who have a lot of little theories about the world, do better than "hedgehogs," who have a single grand theory that explains everything. In part, they did better because they were less willing to make the strongest predictions that would most easily be proved wrong. Hedgehogs were more likely to be "very right" (think of Winston Churchill declaring Hitler's Germany an existential threat to Britain while Neville Chamberlain was declaring that he'd secured "Peace in Our Time"). But they were also more likely to be "very wrong" (think of Winston Churchill's disastrous decision as Chancellor of the Exchequer to return Britain to the gold standard after World War I at a grossly overvalued exchange rate with the dollar. Churchill believed he was restoring Britain to her former glory, but in fact he pushed the country into a decade of underperformance).

We think that experts do better than they actually do because we tend to remember their successes, but not their mistakes. That's particularly true if their predictions are spectacular and bold. An economist who goes on television and says that it's hard to know what the stock market will do is undoubtedly correct, but he will not be famous. One who predicts that it will soar to new heights and sees this prediction borne out will win renown as a prognosticator, particularly if everyone else is predicting a bear market. And if the prediction proves wrong, he can always defend himself by arguing that some surprising piece of information confounded his prediction.

By gathering data systematically, Tetlock exploded this conceit. The best experts did a little bit better than people who didn't know much about world politics; the worst experts did a little worse. But this is a little like being the best student in remedial math: you're still not where you should be.

Tetlock's work is frequently played for comedy value—ha, ha, they think they're so smart! But it doesn't tell us that experts are rubbish. It tells us that human systems are too complex to predict in the mechanical way that we analyze the potential stresses on a bridge. We should not be laughing and pointing the finger (though we should certainly be cautious about banking too much on any specific prediction). Rather, we should be marveling at the incredible variety of possible futures when we throw hundreds of millions of people together.

We are good at engineering problems because they're easy. We think that they're hard because most of us couldn't do the math, but here's the evidence that they're easy: we've solved them. By contrast, we still don't know how to get people to take the blood pressure medication that can save their life—more than 50 percent of people with hypertension don't take their medicine regularly.[10] And that's a comparatively easy problem in social science. The pills are cheap, have virtually no side effects, are distributed to millions of convenient locations, and require users to do nothing more than pop a small, easy-to-swallow pill in their mouth. But people won't do it.

Don't despair: I'm not saying that we can't get better at human engineering. We just have to do it the way we got better at regular engineering: we need to experiment, and see what works.

CHAOS IN THE LAB

In the late 1990s, a sociologist named Duncan Watts became interested in Malcolm Gladwell's famous debut book, *The Tipping Point*.[11] The book is, as Watts notes, "catnip to marketers" because it theorizes that a few influential people can, "through social connections and energy and enthusiasm and personality" spread trends, such as the revival of Hush Puppies by Brooklyn hipsters. It's a very compelling story, which is why the book sells so well. But what bothers Watts is that *it is a story*. It is piecing together bits of information after the fact in a way that is extremely intuitively plausible.

"Storytelling is so ingrained in us," Watts told me, "and it's so natural to us—rationally it shouldn't matter how good-looking you are when you're telling the story, or how funny your jokes are, or how you make them feel emotionally when you're telling it but in fact, it matters a lot." The fact that my science teacher is able to illustrate the principle of gravity with a neat parable about two young teenagers who are in love doesn't make the theory of gravity any more true. But it makes it *feel* more true.[12]

When people try to explain why the *Mona Lisa* is the most famous painting in the world, they talk about her mysterious smile, the gauzy technique, the background. And yet Watts points out that they are not really explaining the painting's appeal; they're just describing the painting.[13] What they are really saying is that the *Mona Lisa* is a great painting, because . . . um . . . it is more like the *Mona Lisa* than any other painting in the world. Interestingly, he says, this tends to leave out an inconvenient fact: the *Mona Lisa* was a fairly minor work until 1911, when a disgruntled employee of the Louvre stole it.[9] It was only after the painting was recovered two years later that we started thinking of it as, well, the *Mona Lisa*.[14]

Our brains, says Watts, are "causality machines": you see something happen and your brain creates a causal story that accounts for it. This is useful in many contexts, but it's also extraordinarily dangerous. "Your brain didn't see all the things that could have happened but didn't. So your explanation is only explaining the one thing. And then other things, that you don't resonate with emotionally, they cease to have any grasp on your attention." Watts wanted more than a story about these sorts of phenomena: he wanted a test.

As it happens, Duncan Watts was in a position to do that test. With Matthew Salganik of Princeton, he designed a novel experiment.[15] They set up a Web-based music download site that simulated a market for music. Fourteen thousand teenagers were recruited to listen to forty-eight songs and rate them on the website. If they wanted to, they could then download the songs they liked.

Teenagers are the most avid consumers of new music, and they are the ones who drive the pop charts. Songs sweep through the teen population almost like epidemics, spreading from friend to friend like the measles. Yet we tend to explain this success in terms of the characteristics of the songs, or the singers: Madonna's outrageous personality, the exquisite angst of "Smells Like Teen Spirit," Bob Dylan's counterculture message. But of course, this is the *Mona Lisa* argument all over again: we love Bob Dylan because he's just so . . . Dylanesque.

At some level this is true. Most markets have what economists call threshold effects: below a certain level of quality, you can't compete. Jim Manzi, whom you met in chapter 1, and who happens to be an expert in retail experiments, puts it rather pungently: "You can't sell people a cow patty on a plate."[16] Hollywood may not be able to tell which scripts will be blockbusters, but it does know roughly what sort of structure makes a good story. (Boy on a quest to fight the evil galactic empire: possibly. Boy stares sullenly at a wall for two hours while complaining bitterly about his parents: probably not.) We know that certain plot lines have a tendency to appeal, but we have a very hard time explaining why one romantic comedy or disaster movie is so much more popular than the next.

At any given time, there are lots of very talented people trying to make it in the music business, most of whom can sing or play an instrument. Most of them will fail; only a few will go double platinum. Did Madonna become a top star because she was the absolute best, most awesome performer out there? Or did she get lucky? Was it predestination or chance?

We don't get a do-over to see if Madonna's success was predetermined, or essentially random. But Watts and his coauthors figured out a way to simulate a do-over with his online experiment, by using a randomized controlled design. The researchers created their little music site, and advertised it on a social network aimed at teens. A computer randomly assigned some of the teenagers to a system where they could only see the names of the songs. Others got the names of the songs, plus another piece of information: how many times the songs had been downloaded by other teenagers.

Randomization was important because it ensured that the teenagers couldn't self-select into groups: moody loners on one side, extroverted crowd-pleasers on the other. All an experiment like that tells you is that different groups of people are different. That's also why the control group—the people who could only see the names of songs—is just as important. Randomization and control let Salganik and Watts observe the effect that social networks have on song popularity. Would the different groups of teenagers all end up rank-ordering the songs in the same way? Or would their social network influence their choices?

Salganik and Watts divided the people who could see the preferences of their peers into *eight different* social groups, which they called "worlds." People in a given world could only see the song rankings of people in their own world. And while the list of songs was the same in each world, the order in which people saw them was different. There was no cheating: each world started off with zero downloads. But after that, the choices of the people before them would influence what the new arrivals saw.

The differences were striking. For one thing, popularity was much more uneven in the social worlds: the hits had more down-loads, and the unpopular songs had fewer downloads, than in the world where people couldn't tell what others were listening to. Even more striking, in each social world, the hits were entirely different. Quality obviously mattered somewhat: songs that were number-one hits in one world never ended up on the bottom of the list in another world. But they might be number 40. The social influence, wrote Watts in his book, *Everything Is Obvious Once You Know the Answer*, increased both inequality and unpredictability.

"People think that social science should be like engineering science," says Watts. "It's not, not just because you're dealing with people, but because you're dealing with complex systems. The properties of the system are separate from the properties of the components that make it up." He pauses, as if searching for the right words. "Your sense of self," he says finally, "is not just a bunch of cells." Which is why, if you had never seen a brain, you could not look at one and say, "That's where our sense of self lives" much less, "That's Fred. He enjoys Italian food, French New Wave film, and long walks on the beach."

Let's go back to *Titanic* for a moment. One of the notable things about the film's success was its longevity. Most movies have a big opening weekend, and then a sharp drop-off, while *Titanic* opened at $52 million, shot to $71 million the following week, and kept packing theaters for months.[17] The film was in U.S. theaters for ten months—not that unusual in 1950, but a standout these days, when ten months is about how long it takes a moderately successful movie to reach the Walmart bargain bin.

Even more surprising was the audience: teenage girls. Most box office, like most pop music, is driven by the tastes of teenagers; it's somewhere they can go with friends and hang out when they're too young to get into bars. But for most movies, the teenagers who matter most are teenage boys.[18] That's why budgets have soared over the last few decades as directors and marketers seek ever more spectacular car chases and explosions.

Titanic was different. Teenage girls went, and went again.[19] They dragged their girlfriends to giggle over Leonardo DiCaprio. They dragged their boyfriends. *Lord of the Rings*, which had a spectacular $90 million opening week over Christmas 2001, was down to $3 million a week at the beginning of March. *Titanic*, on the other hand, was still pulling in over $20 million.[20]

Was this because of some intrinsic property of *Titanic*? Did it capture a unique moment? Or was *Titanic*'s success an emergent property of thousands of social networks combining into a gigantic *Titanic*-loving machine?

What Watt's work suggests is that there may be no way to know in advance—or even after the fact. The modern world has an enormous amount of complexity, endless potential interactions between the millions and billions of people your product might reach. One of the important things that experiments can reveal, as unsatisfying as it sounds, is the limit of experimentation.

WELFARE REFORM: EXPERIMENTS COME TO GOVERNMENT

One of the reasons that we are better at building bridges than getting people to take their blood pressure medication is that we've run a lot of experiments on the structural properties of steel and bridges. Say you want to find out the effects of health insurance on health and mortality. Ideally what you'd do is take a pair of identical twins and give one health insurance for life, while forcing the other one to stay uninsured as long as he lived, then see how the two differ. Actually, you'd like to do that thousands and thousands of times. But fortunately, the constitutional amendments forbidding slavery prevent us from carrying out such experiments.

As a result, most public policy has been designed with a very shaky experimental foundation. Experts can draw on their experience, of course. But the more innovative the policy, the less useful that experience tends to be. New policy programs are essentially based on thought experiments: mental models of the world. No matter how well-informed or carefully constructed those models are, there is always the risk that they are missing something, or that there will be unintended consequences.

Consider welfare benefits. Aid to Families with Dependent Children (AFDC) was conceived as a small program for widows and other "deserving" mothers who had been left alone with small children through no fault of their own. The New Dealers who framed the program expected it to wither away as Social Security's widows and orphans benefits replaced it with a more generous system.[20]

The widows and orphans did indeed switch into Social Security, but welfare rolls grew. The women on the rolls were now those who society had never seen as pure victims of fate: the divorced mothers, the abandoned mothers, and, increasingly, the never-married mothers. The legislators who passed the initial program had never imagined that the eligibility requirements would be loosened to include all single mothers, or that single motherhood and welfare would explode in the second half of the twentieth century—arguably, in part because it was now easier to support a child without a father. The people who had argued for expanding eligibility certainly never imagined that changing the criteria could have such an effect; life on welfare is no picnic, and it seemed absurd to think that a woman would have a baby just to get a welfare check. Of course, that is absurd . . . but it is less absurd to think that if you make it easier to have a child without a father or a job, people might do it more often. That slight omission in their mental model meant that those who crafted the bill radically underpredicted what happened.

In the late 1960s, the sociologist Carol Stack spent years among a poor black community in a midwestern city she calls "Jackson

Flats."[21] Her account is already dominated by the group that would come to be known as "the underclass," characterized by intermittent or nonexistent work histories, intermittent or nonexistent relationships between women and the fathers of their children, and increasing dependence on the government. Stack focused on the rich social networks and endlessly inventive survival strategies of the people she studied, and these are indeed amazing. But what also comes through is that both she and her subjects regarded the American taxpayer as some sort of delightful natural resource, like wild raspberries: it may be occasionally troublesome to harvest the fruit, but there's no reason why you shouldn't take as much as you can get. As the welfare rolls grew, taxpayers sensed this. And they resented it.

Ronald Reagan's 1976 campaign against a probably fictional "welfare queen" tapped into middle-class America's growing belief that welfare was rewarding idleness and irresponsible child rearing—no, not just rewarding it, but subsidizing it, and thus inadvertently expanding it. In vain did liberal academics, social workers, and poverty activists point out that the rolls had grown even as the real cash value of benefits had declined; in vain did they ask, incredulously, whether Mr. and Mrs. Middle Class would quit their job and start having babies for the princely sum of $500 a month. Alternative theories, such as William Julius Wilson's work on the decline of urban manufacturing jobs and the flight of the black middle class, found a wide audience among the media and the academy, but Republicans, and increasingly the vast majority of the American public, found a simpler theory much more attractive: women were choosing welfare over work, welfare over marriage, welfare over the bourgeois values that provided the tax dollars that paid for welfare in the first place.[22]

Reagan's first budget, in 1981, cut welfare rolls by making it harder to collect benefits if you got a job. But it also authorized what came to be a radical new experiment in policy design. A bipartisan coalition was forming between governors and the Reagan administration to support the broad outlines of what would eventually be called the "new consensus": stiff work requirements, combined with more programs to support welfare recipients in finding and keeping jobs. In 1983, thanks to the new rules, states began to experiment with work requirements under the aegis of the Manpower Demonstration Research Corporation, a nonprofit consortium of foundations and government agencies founded in 1974 to analyze the effects of government policy design. These studies were randomized and had a control group, allowing the researchers to see how the test subjects differed from those left in traditional welfare. Eventually, they covered eleven states, 65,000 subjects, and a variety of different approaches to getting workers into jobs, used singly and in combination: intensive job search, temporary public jobs, and a plethora of different training programs.

These programs demonstrated conclusively that it was possible to get recipients, lots of recipients, into work. Earnings increased—though because of lost government benefits, incomes didn't. The cost savings, however, were dramatic. And the children didn't seem to be any worse off. Almost as important, noted Gordon Berlin, president of the social policy research organization MDRC in a 2007 speech, was that "while the results of experimentation told the nation what worked, it also showed what did *not* work, and what we still did not know."[23] In the face of these gaps, America did the right thing: it did more experiments. The 1988 Family Support Act included funding for a further round of testing for things like wage supports and additional investments in education and training.[24]

Eventually, the insights from Manpower's research led to substantial expansions of the Earned Income Tax Credit, a system of refundable tax credit that now helps support an estimated 26 million poor households in work rather than welfare.[25] They also helped support the landmark 1996 welfare reform, which set lifetime limits on the number of years that women could collect benefits, instituted broad work requirements, and gave broader latitude to the states to get recipients off the rolls.

The result, as Jason DeParle chronicles in the book *American Dream*, was a dramatic shift in America's poverty support system. After bottoming out in the 1970s, the poverty rate had been on a slow, unsteady, but quite noticeable upward trend: 11.7 percent in 1979, 12.8 percent in 1989, 13.7 percent in 1996, the year that welfare reform passed. That was also the year that the welfare rolls peaked at over 5 million families, which contained just about 5 percent of the U.S. population. At any given time, the majority of those families were long-term welfare recipients, the average woman on the rolls would stay on welfare for ten years.[27]

When welfare reform was being debated, poverty activists and policy analysts warned of dire consequences for those long-termers. Wendell Primus, a deputy assistant secretary at the Department of Health and Human Services, commissioned a study, which showed the proposed reforms would push an additional 2.6 million people, including 1.1 million children, into poverty.[28] Edward Kennedy thundered from the floor of the Senate that the bill was "legislated child abuse." After it finally passed, Marian Wright Edelman, the head of the Children's Defense Fund, declared that "President Clinton's signature on this pernicious bill makes a mockery of his pledge not to hurt children," while her husband, Peter, resigned from Health and Human Services in protest.[29] A year later, he would write an article for *The Atlantic Monthly*, calling welfare reform "The Worst Thing Bill Clinton Has Done," and painting a dystopian future of misery for America's most vulnerable families.[30]

Virtually none of these frightening visions came to pass, except one: enrollment in America's welfare programs dropped as if it had been flung from the top of the Capitol dome. In 1995, 12.3 million people were being supported at least partially by a welfare check. By 2000, the number was less than half that. Some of this had to do with the economic boom, of course; welfare rolls were already dropping by 1996 as the country shook off the lingering effects of the 1992 recession. But the boom could not explain why the number of people on welfare stayed low even after George Bush took office. As of 2010, only 4.6 million people were being supported by a welfare check.[31]

The size of the drop surprised even welfare reform's proponents; Robert Rector, the Heritage Foundation analyst who had pushed hardest for strict work requirements, told Jason DeParle that his estimates of the caseload reductions were off "by a factor of three or four." And for the bill's opponents, there was another surprise: the poverty rate did not rise dramatically. Actually, it dropped, from 13.8 percent in 1995, to 11.7 percent in 2001. Instead of 1.1 million more poor children, we had almost 3 million fewer. Those numbers got somewhat less rosy when the dot-com boom ended, but only somewhat. By 2007, despite substantial population growth, 1.3 million fewer children were living below the poverty line than had been doing so in 1995. Only after the worst recession in 70 years did poverty rates begin to approach the levels that had been common in the 1980s and early 1990s.[32]

Of course, one can argue that there should be more people on the rolls right now—that in desperate times, we have left needy Americans without a safety net. But one also has to acknowledge that for more than a decade, welfare dependency dropped while incomes rose. Unless you think that fewer people should work on principle, this is an unequivocally good development. The mental models of poverty alleviation had failed—and in their wake, a great experiment in social policy produced greater-than-expected social change.

KNOW YOUR EXPERIMENTAL LIMITS

After more than a decade of trial and error, welfare experts thought they knew what would happen when work requirements were instituted without the kind of extensive (and expensive) supportive services that earlier "new consensus" experiments had called for: small caseload declines, skyrocketing poverty. They were wildly wrong. Rector, the person who came closest to forecasting the result, was a conservative outsider who worked at the Heritage Foundation. "To the poverty establishment," writes DeParle, "Rector was a joke." Yet the joke was on them.

In 2012, Jim Manzi, whose company specializes in helping companies run experiments on everything from compensation to retail product placement, published *Uncontrolled*, a book on how to harness the power of experimentation to make better corporate and government policy. But though he is perhaps the world's biggest booster of the randomized controlled trial, he notes that a big part of the power of experimentations is understanding their limits. They need to be replicated, over and over, before one can be at all confident about their results. And often results don't hold up. One recent survey of major cancer studies indicated that the overwhelming majority of the results—47 out of 53—could not be replicated.[33]

And even when things do seem to work more than once, the universe can always surprise you. Sales tactics that used to work stop working. Trading strategies that used to make money now produce losses. Manzi reminds us of the banks that issued mortgages on the basis of little more than a credit score and a borrower who attested that he made enough money to repay the loan. Widely reviled now, this was a profitable strategy early in the bubble, when rising prices allowed creditors who were in trouble to get out with a quick sale before they missed a mortgage payment. Bankers had reams of data, and long experience, showing that people with high FICO scores virtually never defaulted.

"Correlations like that work until they don't work anymore," says Manzi. "And it's unpredictable when it's going to stop working."

This problem is most acute with what you might call "pseudo-experiments": things that look like a rigorous test, but which serve only to give people false confidence in what they are doing.

THE PERIL OF THE PROMISING PILOT

Like many of us, the L.A. Unified School District has been trying to eat more healthfully in recent years. In 2011, they overhauled their menu, getting rid of their pizza and chicken nuggets in favor of nutritious options like black bean burgers and quinoa salads. The initiative won awards from the USDA and the Physician's Committee for Responsible Medicine. The students were less enthusiastic; they dropped out of the lunch program by the thousands, and many of those who stayed started throwing away their entrees and unflavored milk unconsumed, which has disturbing implications in a district where 80 percent of the students qualify for free or reduced-price lunches. A black market rapidly developed in forbidden foods, and the *L.A. Times* found high schoolers lunching on the Flamin' Hot Cheetos and soda they brought to school in their backpacks.[34]

Believe it or not, the LAUSD put a lot of thought into the program that flopped. They ran extensive community taste tests and solicited feedback, 75 percent of which was positive. But when the food was put into schools, students—even those who had liked it in the taste tests—started refusing to eat it.

Government—so stupid! (said the conservative blogs). And hey, government is often stupid. But they're hardly the only ones who get taken in by promising pilot projects. When I was in business school, I took a class in new-venture strategy with James Schrager, who along with being an outstanding teacher has worked on virtually all stages of a start-up: founder, investor, turnaround. Faced with sixty MBA students filled with dreams of fabulous Internet wealth (it was, after all, 2000) he set about rapidly puncturing our confidence.

"How will you know," he asked, "if your idea will work?"

"We will do market research!" said sixty MBA students, all of whom had gained admission to the Booth School mostly on the strength of their ability to do research, or at least type it up into pretty PowerPoint presentations.

Whereupon Professor Schrager told us this story:

> Once upon a time, there was an old company with a very old problem: their formerly very successful product wasn't selling as well as it used to. An upstart competitor was cutting into their sales. So they started a top-secret project to develop a replacement product. These men weren't stupid: they knew that this was risky. And so they commissioned market research. They commissioned more market research than maybe anyone else in the history of the planet. Even before they had finished developing the new product, market research teams were criss-crossing the country, asking people how they might feel about the change. They did surveys and focus groups, and then they did them again. They test-marketed free samples. And while a minority of customers were resistant, the overwhelming majority said "Yes! Yes, we love the new product! Please give it to us!" So they did. They got rid of their old product and replaced it with this astonishingly popular new creation.

New Coke lasted less than three months and nearly took the company down with it.[35]

The problem with the executives at Coke, and with the people at the L.A. Unified School District, was not that they didn't test. It was that they didn't understand the limits of their experiments. They assumed that a successful limited pilot program necessarily translated into a successful organization-wide rollout. They were so convinced of the splendors of their pilot programs that even after it was obvious that things weren't working out—as the press mocked them and an elderly consumer told a reporter that "in the vernacular of

teenagers, it sucks,"[36] Coke executives were celebrating the free publicity. In similarly blind fashion, the chef who designed L.A. schools'
new menu simply denied that meals were being thrown away.

The L.A. Unified School District and the Coca-Cola company
were afflicted with what I call the Curse of the Successful Pilot Project. It's what happens to organizations that forget the cardinal rule
of experimentation: many results are spurious, and most pilot projects don't scale. Most things that work great in the lab, or the taste
test, or the focus group, nonetheless bomb when you attempt to roll
them out system wide.

This isn't because they did the test wrong. And it isn't (necessarily) because they screwed up the implementation. It's because, to
return to our opening story, there is ultimately no way to know
whether something works until you put it out there and see how
your target audience reacts. A good experiment can tell you a lot,
but Manzi, who runs a lot of tests for retailers, says that even the
most successful test doesn't tell you "this strategy works"; what it
actually shows is something considerably more modest, like "this
strategy seems to be successful on Saturday mornings in midwestern supermarkets located in busy shopping centers." And quite often, experiments are better at telling you what doesn't work than
what does. "Experiments falsify or corroborate," says Jim Manzi.
"They don't *prove.*"

After all, sometimes the "success" of your stellar pilot project was
simply a result of random chance—you taste tested your quince mus-
tard jam on a group full of avid mustard-lovers. Apparent success may
also be due to what researchers call the Hawthorne effect, named after a factory outside Chicago that ran tests in the 1920s to see whether
workers were more productive at higher or lower levels of light. When
researchers raised the lights, productivity went up. When researchers
lowered the lights, productivity also went up. Obviously, it wasn't the
light that boosted productivity, but something else—the change from
the ordinary, or the mere fact of being studied.[37]

Sometimes the success is due to what you might call a "hidden parameter," something that researchers don't realize is affecting their test. People told market researchers that they loved New Coke. And they did, in the taste test. But they were being offered a three-ounce cup of the stuff in a shopping mall lobby or supermarket parking lot, often after they'd spent an hour or so shopping. New Coke was sweeter, so (like Pepsi before it) it won the taste test, because very sweet things are quite appealing in small doses. But that didn't mean that people wanted to drink a whole can of it with a meal—especially if it cost them the option of drinking "Old" Coke.

The market researchers had, in short, stripped the choice of all of its context—all the brand associations, the packaging, and the activities, like eating a meal or cooling off after a hot day in the sun, that we normally associate with drinking a familiar soda. Just as "opening Christmas gifts" is a lot more than just the physical act of untying ribbons and tearing wrapping paper, "having a Coke" is far more than just taking a few sips of a mystery drink. The question they thought they were asking was "If we replace Coca-Cola with this new soda, will you buy more of it?" But the only question their test could actually *answer* was "Which of these small samples would you prefer to drink in a parking lot, if I gave it to you for free?"

There are other problems that make even rigorous pilots into something more like a pseudo-experiment than a valid test. The personnel you hire for the pilot are usually top-flight professionals who are really excited about the project and committed to rigorous standards, while a system-wide rollout will mostly involve people who already work there, who often at best aren't particularly interested in your goals, and at worst actively disagree with them. The pilot projects that eventually led to Head Start had significant, measurable effects on the lives of the participating children. Head Start—implemented with a less-skilled workforce and a lot more bureaucracy, does not.[38]

Small, successful pilots are frequently very difficult to bring up to scale, for some of the same reasons that it's fairly easy to get two or three friends to agree to meet for dinner, and very hard to pull the same trick with two hundred. The mechanism that works with a small group—phoning, texting, sending an e-mail—has to be replaced with something entirely different, like Evite, if you want to scale up. And the features that worked in a small system often won't work at all in a larger one. With a few people, you can let the group decide where to meet. When there are hundreds, that would be absurd. You pick a place and tell them where to go.

So consider the LAUSD test. In the testing phase, when the program was small, they were working with a small group of people who had been specially chosen to participate. They were cooking in relatively small batches, and could choose their ingredients carefully because they did not have a sprawling supply chain to manage. The kids and the workers knew they were being studied. And they were asking the kids which food they liked—a question that, social science researchers will tell you, is highly likely to elicit the answer that they liked *something*. "If you go into someone's home or business, and you ask them to sample a product, there's a lot implied in that," says Bart Wilson. People are reluctant to tell any chef that their food sucks.

Politely sampling something at a tasting is very different from choosing to eat it in a cafeteria when no grown-up is looking and you're surrounded by a bunch of friends, just as drinking three ounces of free mystery soda is very different from choosing to march into the grocery store and buying some with your hard-earned money. And producing the food is also very different. Cooking palatable food in large amounts is hard, particularly when you have a tiny, school-lunch-size budget—and the things that make us fat are, by and large, also the things that are cheap and palatable when mass-produced. Bleached grains and processed fats have a much longer shelf life than fresh produce, and can take a hell of a lot more handling. Salt and sugar are delicious, but they are also preservatives that, among other things, disguise the flavor of stale food.

One anecdote in the *L.A. Times* report was particularly telling. People complained that salads dated October 7 were served on the 17th—and the district responded first by pointing out that October 7 was the "best served by" date, not the date when the food actually went bad; and second by removing the labels because they were "confusing." Now, as anyone who has forgotten to eat a bag of lettuce knows, while it may not actually be rotten after ten days, it probably doesn't look much like something you'd eat voluntarily. This is not something that you can change by stamping a different "sell by" date on the container. If that were my choice, I too would come to school with a backup bag of Cheetos.

The school lunch distribution system was probably not set up to ensure fresh, crisp greens every day—at least at the budget they had to work with. And probably the mind-set of the managers was still locked in "don't poison them" mode, rather than "salad lover's delight." There is, after all, not that much difference between chicken nuggets at their absolute peak of freshness and chicken nuggets that have been sitting in the refrigerator awhile. Those subtle changes in mind-set are very hard to roll out in a large organization.

That's what real-world applications are up against. They're not jazzy pilot projects with everyone pulling together and a lot of political push behind them; they're being rolled out into a system that already has a very well-established mind-set, and a comprehensive body of rules. The new program implemented by the old rules often turns out to be worse than the old program. Instead of moving kids from pizza to salad, you move them from pizza to Cheetos. You move customers, screaming, from Coke to Pepsi.

LEARNING THE RIGHT LESSON

But even though you can't always run definitive experiments in advance of a project or product launch, you can still be experimental. Hollywood is actually very good at postproduction experimentation. I told you at the beginning that no one in Hollywood knows for sure what's going to be a hit and what isn't, and that's true. But it's also true that by the time a movie gets into theaters, they usually have a pretty good idea if it's going to totally bomb. That's because Hollywood makes extensive use of screenings in front of test audiences. Films that get a bad reaction have been recut, and sometimes whole new endings have been reshot, because the test audiences gave the original a thumbs down.

Of course, there are limits on how much postproduction experimentation can do. If you have given a star director like Michael Cimino $30 million to shoot hundreds of hours of footage, and he turns in a five-hour film with nothing recognizable as a normal story line, there's not much you can do to save *Heaven's Gate* other than insist that he cut it down to a shorter film with nothing recognizable as a normal story line. (The shorter version made just $4 million in theaters, making this one of the most legendary film disasters of all time.) On the other hand, *Fatal Attraction*, the hit 1987 psychological thriller that was nominated for six academy awards, was saved by a last-minute reshoot when test audiences panned the original ending.[39]

When things go wildly wrong, people often blame the experiment: "Market research doesn't work." "Pilot programs are useless." But this is the wrong lesson. We have to experiment to find out which good ideas actually have promise—and be prepared to keep experimenting, because the path-dependence uncovered by Duncan Watts, and the changing market conditions that Jim Manzi talks about, means that we'll never be sure whether success or failure are just around the corner. As we do, we always need to keep in mind that subsequent failures don't mean that the initial experiment was a bust; it means that when we structure our experiments, we must be careful to understand what they can tell us and what they can't.

We've learned from experiments what government programs

can work, Manzi told me ruefully, but what we've also learned is that even the programs that work don't work that well. They generate small improvements, not the lightning transformations that proponents expect. Even welfare reform, which succeeded beyond the dreams of its architects, was not as transformational as they might have hoped. Members of a previously permanent underclass left the welfare rolls, got jobs, and improved their incomes somewhat. But they mostly did not join the stable, prosperous middle class.

In other words, experimentation is not enough, by itself. You also need iteration, to find out whether your experimental results are consistent or a fluke and, after you've made one small improvement, to find the next. We need a culture of experimentation as much as we need the experiments themselves.

Experiments give us some of our greatest hope for building better companies, better policies, and better lives. But that doesn't mean that we can make everything great by doing an experiment and then rolling it out on a grand scale. We need to prepare to spend our lives experimenting: lots of tests, incremental rollouts that can be modified, or scrapped entirely, if it turns out that our experiment doesn't scale. We have to be prepared to take *Titanic*-size gambles. But we have to be prepared to recognize if it turns out we've made *Waterworld*.

The business writer Harvey Mackay tells a story about Tom Watson, who was president of IBM during the first half of the twentieth century. A young executive was called in to Watson's office after a string of bad decisions had cost the company a hefty sum. As he entered the office, the executive said, "I suppose after that set of mistakes you will be wanting to fire me." Watson is said to have replied, "Not at all, young man. We have just spent a couple of million dollars educating you."[40]

The story may be apocryphal, but the sentiment is not. It's why in Silicon Valley, having worked on a start-up that failed is viewed as a résumé enhancer. Good judgment, as the aphorism goes, comes from experience—and experience comes from bad judgment.

We can't necessarily tell in advance whether we're making *Titanic* or *Waterworld*. What we can do is make sure that when things do fail—and they will!—we react the right way. Figuring out what that right way is will be the task of the rest of this book.

4 ACCIDENTS, MISTAKES, FAILURES, AND DISASTERS

What the Hospital System Can Teach Us about the Mistakes We Make

"Failure" is sort of a junk drawer of a word. We dump all sorts of meanings into it, and then when something goes wrong, we rummage around and pull one out. The word "fail" covers everything from the unexpected termination of a computer program to the 2008 financial collapse; from forgetting Grandma's birthday to dying halfway up Mount Everest. If we're going to spend hundreds of pages talking about failure and making the case that harnessing its power is vitally important, we'll need to sort out the junk drawer a bit.

The first thing we need to get out of the way is what failure is not: an accident. *Accidents* are coincidences that could not have been plausibly expected, or planned for.

A few years back a friend of mine was driving a rental car around a curve on a highway when suddenly the steering stopped working. She was hit by (she thinks) five other cars and sent hurtling across the median strip, stopping just short of plunging into the oncoming traffic. It was only when the state troopers came that she realized how bad the accident had been; the car was totaled, and she should have been killed, instead of hobbling away with a banged-up knee.

Obviously, she was shaken by it, but this was a true "auto accident": there was nothing she could have done to prevent it. The car was from a reputable company. The steering had failed with very little warning. The only lessons she might have taken from the accident would have been ridiculous ones, like "don't rent cars," or "don't drive on highways." If you're standing on the street and an air conditioner falls out of a window and conks you on the head, you were just in the wrong place at the wrong time. Assuming you survive, you will undoubtedly find yourself wistfully thinking that you really should have stopped three blocks earlier and gotten that Frappuccino you were craving. But that doesn't mean you should spent the rest of your life at Starbucks.

The hallmark of an accident is that while there may be lots of things you *could* have done differently, there's absolutely nothing that you *should* have done differently. Aside from perfect foresight, there is no hard-won knowledge that you wish you could have applied, no error in judgment that can inform your decisions in the future. While someone else should probably learn a much-needed lesson about air-conditioning maintenance (our accidents are often other people's failures), the only thing *you* can do is accept that sometimes, things happen.

In many ways a *mistake* is the opposite of an accident: it's where you could and maybe should have done something differently, but nothing really bad happens as a result. You spell "embarrass" wrong and the spell-checker corrects it before you're even finished typing. You enter the wrong number into the budget spreadsheet, and then have to spend your lunch hour hunting down the discrepancy. You forget the grocery list and come home with wine instead of the milk your spouse wanted.

Most mistakes are trivial. But even big mistakes usually turn out all right. When I was a technology consultant, years ago, I once got called in to a firm because a secretary had accidentally deleted a file, and she needed it restored from their tape backup. That was when I discovered that their tape backup apparently hadn't been running for years. They should have been periodically checking to see that the system was working, but their previous consultant had left under cloudy circumstances, it had taken them a while to find someone new, and the office full of English majors was somewhat afraid of the equipment in the back room.

If it had been the company budget—or worse, a server failure—their mistake might have been catastrophic. As it was, the file turned out to be fairly unimportant, and fortunately modern computer systems have redundant fail-safes in place so that it's very difficult to permanently delete files; I was able to retrieve it without much difficulty. Instead of a disaster, the secretary's minor mistake was actually a bit of serendipity; it led me to fix their backup system before something went seriously wrong.

Failure is what could have happened; it's a mistake performing without a safety net. The fail-safes aren't failing safely any more. Suddenly, something has gone terribly wrong, and worse, if someone had only done things differently—better—it could have been prevented.

When I wrote the proposal for this book, I promised a section on medical failures. Every year, some thousands of Americans die of medical errors. They go into the hospital for something we can cure, and they are released to a funeral home. We don't know exactly how many people die this way—it's what statisticians call a "dark number," one that's inherently virtually impossible to measure. Some people do go into the hospital and die despite the very best efforts of their caregivers. Others could have been saved, but aren't—and it's often very hard to tell one from the other.[1]

But we do know that it's much higher than it could or should be. Hospital-acquired infections, mistaken diagnoses, surgeons who cut out the wrong organs or leave instruments inside the patient: these things all happen far more often than they should. It seemed like a good place to examine how and why things go wrong, especially because right now there are so many people working on ways to reduce the error, using everything from basic checklists to bleeding-edge computer systems.[2]

Then, just as I was starting to write, I found myself sitting in the cavernously empty preoperative ward of a local hospital, trying not to cry while my sister and I waited for the doctors to take my mother in to surgery for a ruptured appendix.

That doesn't sound so bad—these days, it's practically outpatient surgery. But while a ruptured appendix is minor in a twenty-four-year-old, in patients over sixty it is less likely to be correctly diagnosed, and more likely to kill them, because their immune systems are often too weak to overcome the payload of deadly bacteria that escapes into their abdominal cavity. Because I cover the health-care system, I knew how to look up the relevant studies, which means that as I sat there holding my mother's dry, frail hands, I knew that there was a 5 to 10 percent chance that she was going to die.[3] Abruptly, life cured me of the delusion that there is any such thing as an easy checklist for error prevention. Over the next few weeks it became clear that I never understood just how easy it is for things to go wrong in the medical system, or how hard it is to do them right.

I was shocked by the level of error I witnessed—errors easily detectable by me, a journalist, not a trained medical professional. We made bad initial decisions, and then the people taking care of her made many more. Most of the errors in judgment were small, simple things, but each error made the other ones more dangerous, like sticks of kindling igniting a roaring fire.

Unlike many others, my mother's story has a happy ending. She is alive and well, taking her bullmastiff on long walks and grousing about DC traffic. I think it's because there was a happy ending that I can now look back on the experience and see all the bad things that almost happened, all the incidents that could have had very different results. I am a journalist who covers this stuff for a living, and my sister and I took my mother to the best ER in the city. The fact that so many bad things happened, or almost happened, was a powerful reminder that none of us is ever very far from a terrible medical mistake. It was also a real-life illustration of the different ways that we can make mistakes.

My mother was lucky. During the month she was sick, there were a number of mistakes. But there was no failure. The safety net held.

MY FIRST MISTAKE

My mother stopped by our house on Thursday night to drop off her dog; she and my sister were taking a short trip to New York the next day. I was on deadline for a column and slightly frantic; my mother was racing from errand to errand. She looked slightly pale, but otherwise, exactly how she always does, which is to say about eight feet worth of energy packed into a five-four frame. Despite our mutual hurry, I offered her a glass of wine.

"No, I have to pack," she said. "Anyway, I have indigestion."

My sister called me from work the next day. The indigestion had turned into a stomach bug, and they'd canceled the trip to New York. I wrestled with the column for another hour or so, and then, grateful for the break, called my mother to check in. Her voice at the other end of the line sounded very sleepy.

"I'm really sick," she said. "I've never been this sick."

"Do you want me to come take you to the emergency room?" I asked anxiously. The column was due that day. On the other hand, well, *Mom*.

"No," she said weakly. "I just got to sleep. I didn't sleep all night. I have terrible, terrible pains in my stomach."

"Are you sure?" I asked.

"Yes," she said. "I just want to sleep."

"Okay, I love you," I said, and hung up the phone. That was my first mistake.[4]

THE SPELL-CHECK FACTOR

Modern life has a lot of what you might call a "spell-check factor." The complexity of modern society often works against us, but it also conspires to keep most of our mistakes from mattering. We all go through our lives making a constant string of mistakes, but because nothing bad happens, we're barely even aware of them.

Think of how many times you've made a few little mistakes while driving: gotten lost in a strange town, drifted out of your lane, crept up too close on another car, or accidentally run a stop sign that was semi-hidden by some foliage. And those are only the inadvertent mistakes that we *know* about. We didn't include the things you know you shouldn't be doing, or didn't even know you did. Yet despite all these mistakes, you probably think you are an above-average driver.

Half of all drivers in America admit to having driven while drowsy, and one in five say they've actually nodded off behind the wheel.[5] About a quarter of American adults confess they've sent or received text messages while driving and three-quarters of Americans say they've driven while talking on the phone, which can impair your driving performance as badly as driving while drunk (yes, even if you use a headset).[6, 7]

But despite all this, unless you have a serious substance abuse problem it is very, very unlikely that you have been behind the wheel in a fatal car crash. Only about 30,000 people a year are killed in car crashes. That's about 0.02 percent of Americans with licenses, and almost a quarter of those accidents were the fault of a drunk driver. The number of serious incidents (injuries, but not death) is much higher—about 2 million—but it still adds up to well under 1 percent of American drivers. Since some of those drivers will have more than one accident, this means that most people will go their whole lives without more than a little ding.[8]

A society as rich as ours is set up to leave lots and lots of margin for error—a sort of well-padded safety suit in which we live almost all our lives. Our highway lanes are wide, state police cruise the highways looking for drunk drivers, and our cars are designed to swaddle us in multiple overlapping safety systems, from seat belts to antilock brakes to front and rear "crumple zones" carefully calculated to make the car, rather than the passengers, absorb most of the force of a collision. The impact of our mistakes is absorbed by our safety suit. We walk away unscathed.

You can think of that safety suit as being made of layers of Kevlar—all the overlapping safety systems that modern America has built to keep us from hurting one another, and ourselves. It takes either enormous force, or very bad luck, to penetrate all those layers.

James Reason, a psychologist who studies accidents, has dubbed this the Swiss Cheese Model.[9] Imagine each safety layer not as Kevlar, but as a slice of Swiss cheese. Each layer has at least one hole in it—state troopers don't always spot drunk drivers, and antilock brakes can actually make us less safe sometimes. You only get a failure if all the holes line up; otherwise, a mistake that makes it through one hole is stopped by the next layer.

When automatic systems catch most of your errors, the safety itself becomes a bit dangerous. You are so used to thinking that nothing serious can go wrong that when the holes finally do line up, it's hard to believe that your fail-safes have actually failed. In my mother's case the holes didn't quite line up. But it was close.

Why didn't I insist that my mother go to the hospital? I should have known something was wrong, and though memory can be tricky with events like these, I think I did know that something was wrong. My mother is not one of those people who takes herself to bed with a moderate case of the sniffles: she hates being sick, and possibly because of that, she almost never is. And when she describes being ill, even very ill, as when she hemorrhaged after having me, she's always quite stoic about the pain. So when she told me a terrible stomach pain had kept her awake all night, that should have been enough information for me to know she needed to see a doctor.

So why didn't I insist? I probably could have made her, if I'd really pushed. But insisting would have meant a fight with my sick yet determined mother. And, well, I was distracted by my column.

Writing those words now, I flinch. My mother could have died, and I was worried about a column! But of course, I didn't actually know she was in danger of dying. If I had known, I would have broken the land speed record from my house to hers. All I really knew was that she had a bad stomachache.

My sister stayed with her that night, and in retrospect, that too was a mistake. I've done enough health-care reporting to have a rough idea of the sort of symptoms that mean "Get to an emergency room *right now*"; my sister didn't. My mother's house was close to my sister's office, however, and I already had her dog, which needed to be fed and walked. At the time, it seemed like a sensible division of labor.

At 7 a.m. the next morning, my sister called. "Mom needs to go to the hospital," she told me. I was a little worried as I drove the fifteen minutes to her house, but I was still unprepared for what I saw. My mother couldn't sit or stand or lie down without obvious terrible pain, and she couldn't move without screaming. She cried out when I braked, when I accelerated, when I drove as slowly as I could over DC's many, many speed bumps. I think it took us approximately seventeen years to drive the three miles to the hospital, where the triage nurse took one look at her and called for a wheelchair.

The hospital was switching over to a new medical records system that weekend, one that used handheld scanning devices to keep track of every patient interaction. Ordinarily I would have been fascinated, but at the time what I mostly noticed was that the unfamiliar equipment had slowed everything to a crawl. The emergency room was backed up and overflowing, because everything was taking two or three times as long as it should. I spent thirteen hours in an ER cubicle with my mother while she had her stomach pumped, her abdomen prodded, and liters of fluid infused into her veins. The one thing she did not have was a diagnosis. All the doctors knew was that her belly was hard and very, very tender. I spent a helpless day at her side while she trembled on the brink of unconsciousness.

At one point in the early afternoon, a nurse came and told me that my sister wanted to come in and sit with her for a bit. Since only one person was allowed to stay with the patient at a time, that meant I would have to go out into the waiting room. We exchanged places, and I found a seat in the waiting room under one of the many televisions. For a moment, I closed my eyes and leaned my head back against the cool wall. It seemed to me that I heard someone singing gospel music.

I'd just about managed to keep from sobbing like a toddler when I was sitting next to my mother, but now the tears overflowed my closed eyes and flooded down my cheeks. The voices of the choir swelled, as if in stereo. It sounded as if they were right overhead. I opened my eyes. They were right overhead. With the cheerful heartlessness of people who see death every day, the ER nurses had tuned in to Whitney Houston's funeral, which was at that moment occurring in New Jersey. I cried so hard that a complete stranger walked across the room to offer me a packet of tissues.

Eventually my sister came out and I went back in, to where my mother was being tended by a nurse. The problem, they explained, was that we had waited so long. She was dehydrated, and blood tests indicated her kidneys were under stress, which meant they couldn't inject the contrast fluid for a CT scan. Normally, that would just mean she needed to drink the contrast fluid, but there was rather a lot of it, and she was having trouble keeping anything down. They hoped that with hydration, her kidneys would improve, but hours passed, the IV bag was changed two times, and her blood levels still looked too risky. Sometime in the early evening, nine or ten hours after we'd gotten there, they decided that they'd just have to try getting her to drink the fluid. "Drink as much as you can," the nurse said. "When you can't drink any more, we'll take you to the scan."

My mother is tough. Though it tasted terrible and nauseated her, she willed it down in small sips. Eventually, the nurse took the cup away and said, "I guess that's enough." That was the second big mistake.

HOW FAILURES CASCADE

In 1984, in the wake of a partial meltdown at the Three Mile Island nuclear facility, the sociologist Charles Perrow wrote a landmark book called *Normal Accidents*. His thesis was simple and alarming: complex systems like nuclear plants are inherently prone to periodic disasters. Accidents aren't aberrations that can be avoided simply by designing more safety features into the systems; indeed, since safety features themselves add complexity, they may raise, rather than lower, the chance that something will go wrong.[10]

At the beginning of the book, Perrow proposes a thought experiment. You have an important job interview across town, and as you are preparing to leave, you discover that your spouse broke the coffeemaker. A coffee addict, you rummage around and find your old machine, but now you are late and anxious, and you rush out the door without your keys, only to find that the door has locked behind you. Luckily, you keep a spare key under the mat; unluckily, you gave that key to a friend who is coming by to pick up some books later, when you expect to be downtown talking to your potential employer. No problem—your neighbor never uses his car, and is normally happy to let you borrow it. Unfortunately, today he needs it. Okay, you'll take the bus . . . but oops! There's a bus driver's strike going on. A taxi, then. Well, what with the bus strike, the cab companies are all booked. Eventually you have to call and explain that through an extraordinary series of events, you will not be able to make your interview. The employer's secretary says of course, perfectly understandable, but you know that she doesn't understand, and you will not be getting the job.

At the end of this extraordinary story (though not so extraordinary that most of us have not experienced something like it at least once), Perrow poses a little quiz. What caused this disaster?

1. Human error (leaving the heat on under the coffee, or forgetting the keys in the rush)? Yes__ No__ Unsure__
2. Mechanical failure (the generator on the neighbor's car)? Yes__ No__ Unsure__
3. The environment (bus driver's strike and taxi overload)? Yes__ No__ Unsure__
4. Design of the system (in which you can lock yourself out of the apartment automatically)? Yes__ No__ Unsure__
5. Procedures used (warming up coffee in a glass pot; allowing only normal time to get out on this morning)? Yes__ No__ Unsure__

What would you answer? Perrow's point was that the error does not lie in some specific decision, person, or procedure. The failure is inherent in complex systems that are what he called "tightly coupled": elements interact in complex and unpredictable ways, so that one problem tends to show up somewhere else, unexpected. Sure, you made a mistake, but people lock themselves out of the house all the time. It doesn't usually result in losing out on a great employment opportunity, because most of us have multiple layers of Swiss cheese—or, as Perrow puts it, "redundant pathways"—between us and actual failure. But when something does go wrong, those pathways are like a maze—they make it harder to discover, and correct, when you've gone astray.

My mother is covered by Medicare, which is supposed to ensure that she can go to the doctor whenever she feels ill. But it's incredibly hard to find a primary care physician who is accepting new patients in DC, especially new patients with Medicare, which pays doctors less than private insurance. My mother, who moved to

Washington five years before, still hadn't found a doctor. So when she got really sick, she had to go to the ER because she had no one to call. Which meant that she resisted going.

It would be silly to say that my mother would have been better off without Medicare (for one thing, she'd have had a very large hospital bill). Or that we should strip everyone else in the District of their insurance to make more doctors available. The problem is that it's all bound tightly together. It's hard to pull out any one element to fix.

When I asked her, much later, why she had resisted going to the hospital, she looked surprised. "No one wants to go to the emergency room," she said. After a pause she added, "Well, now I'd go."

The surgeon who eventually saw her had a very good bedside manner: firm, calm, and respectful. He listened carefully to what she told him about her symptoms, and then he said he was going to admit her for observation. They couldn't get a good image on the CT scan, he said; all they could tell was that there seemed to be some fluid between her bowel loops, which indicates inflammation. This seemed to confirm his initial suspicion, which was an intestinal obstruction.

Intestinal blockage is usually caused by either adhesions from prior abdominal surgery, which my mother had never had, or by what the surgeon called "a mass" and most of us call cancer. But they can arise "idiopathically," which is what doctors say when they have no idea why the hell you got sick. Cancer has to be cut out, of course, but the hope with the other sort of intestinal blockage is that if you give the patient enough fluids, painkillers, and time, it will resolve on its own. On the basis of the CT scan, he decided to admit her to the surgery service for observation while continuing to pump out her stomach and pump in IV liquids, in the hopes that the symptom would resolve. If she didn't get better in a day or so, they'd do an exploratory laparotomy to see what was going on in there.

Hospitals are very complex systems, and the parts don't always work smoothly together. We'd spent most of the afternoon waiting for the CT machine to be ready (at one point she was bumped at the last minute for a gunshot victim). Now we waited a few more hours for a bed in surgery to open up. My mother couldn't get comfortable on the thin foam mattress of the ER bed, and her inability to get comfortable (or drink coffee) had left her with a ferocious headache. I spent hours meekly pleading for analgesics, a real hospital bed, and information, but none of these things seemed to be obtainable so instead, I rubbed her temples, a gesture more active if no less futile.

Sometime during the thirteen hours we spent together in that cubicle, I made a list of the things I did to keep myself busy on that long day:

Tweeted about the misery
Googled what causes snoring
Looked up intestinal blockage on the Mayo Clinic website
Tried fruitlessly to charge my iPad
Held her frail, frail hand
Rubbed her head
Thought how much she looked like my grandfather when he
    was dying
Rubbed her neck
Tried to craft a neckroll out of a hospital blanket
Ate 150 calories worth of diet cookies
Tried not to let Mom see me cry
Acquiesced to my mother's insistence that she not have an
    open casket funeral service

Eventually, around ten o'clock at night, an orderly showed up to wheel her to the surgical ward. Once she was installed there, she rapidly became much more comfortable. At the time I attributed this to the plusher regular hospital bed and the IV opiates, which gave me hope that the surgeon's diagnosis was correct: a simple, if somewhat surprising, intestinal obstruction that would pass in a few days. Of course, I now realize that this was probably a sign that things had just gotten much, much worse. "When a patient with suspected appendicitis suddenly experiences a sudden relief of their pain," say the authors of *Principles of Clinical Gastroenterology*, "one must worry that the appendix has perforated."[11]

STANDARD ERROR

Medical error is a problem so large that it essentially forms its own category. In some ways, it is the perfect recipe for catastrophic failure. Most of the worst problems occur in hospitals, which are large, complex places filled with large and complex pieces of equipment. There is an elaborate hierarchy of specialties, each one jealously guarding its own little part of the process. And the object of all this attention is an even more complex system: the human body.

We often call the human body a machine, but the machines we are currently capable of making don't even begin to compare to the complexity of the body. Take something like a car, itself an amazingly intricate piece of equipment. And yet compared with your body, it might as well be a yo-yo. We know how your car is put together, and what all the parts do—and if it breaks, your mechanic can take it apart and then put it back together again in perfect working order.

The bacteria and viruses and cancer cells that make us sick aren't as complex as we are, but they are extremely adept at hijacking this incredible system to their own ends. Your body has evolved elaborate defense mechanisms in order to defeat them, which leaves doctors in the position of a ham-handed imperial power trying to intervene in a local war—they frequently don't know who the combatants are, where they are located, or what they might be up to.

And because it's dangerous to just rip your way in and take a look, they're reliant on snatches of information that they can cull from your blood, your urine, and advanced imaging systems that still can't see as well as the human eye, plus subjective reporting from patients who sometimes lie and often don't know what might be important. The body may actively work against the doctor's healing efforts—and the opposite is also sometimes true.

We were all glad that my mother was resting more comfortably in her hospital bed. But what did that tell us? That she was getting better? Or that painkillers dull pain?

In such an environment, errors are inevitable. They can be reduced. But they cannot be eliminated. There are simply too many potential unexpected interactions, and too little information. Despite this, most medical interventions end successfully. The patient gets better from some combination of the body's incredible healing powers, the inventions of modern medicine, and dumb luck. Happily for us, we had luck.

I went home to sleep a bit, and when I returned, two new surgeons were at my mother's bedside. They no longer thought it was intestinal blockage, they told me. The chief radiologist had come in Sunday morning and taken a look at my mother's images, which had earlier been read by a more junior staffer. He didn't think it was an obstruction at all. The chief radiologist thought she had appendicitis.

"It's really rare in people your age," said the doctor, in a tone that seemed carefully calculated to fall exactly halfway between an apology and a defense. "And your symptoms weren't at all typical."

As it turns out, this isn't quite true. Most cases of appendicitis do occur in young people between the ages of ten and thirty, but a substantial fraction fall outside that range. And studies show that in elderly patients, appendicitis is much less likely to present with the "classic" symptoms, like sharp pain localized on the left side. This is one reason why the elderly are much more likely to die from appendicitis: since their symptoms are often less severe, and they are used to feeling not-quite-right, they wait longer to get treatment, and when they do they are often misdiagnosed. All this is exacerbated by the general deterioration in the immune system and other body repair mechanisms that comes with aging. The doctors missed it because they were trained to look for "typical" symptoms that aren't typical at all in older patients.

My mother's ruptured appendix was a cascade of failures. Consider all the holes that had to line up to put her on the gurney they wheeled away from us on Sunday afternoon:

1. Because doctors in DC weren't keen to take new Medicare patients, she had a hard time finding a physician she could call when she got sick.
2. Because she didn't have anyone to call and wanted to avoid an emergency room visit, she stayed home too long.
3. Because we waited, she went to the hospital on a Saturday, when the hospital was short-staffed.
4. That was the week that the hospital was switching over to a new record system, which slowed everything down.
5. Because things were slow, she became dehydrated, so her kidney function suffered.
6. The hospital safety procedure (do not inject contrast fluid into anyone whose kidney function is down) delayed the CT scan and forced them to use an oral contrast solution.
7. Because my mother was now very, very sick, it took her a long time to drink the contrast solution. The overburdened emergency room nurse stopped her halfway through, presumably to keep patient flow moving as fast as possible.
8. Because it was a weekend, her images were seen by a less experienced radiologist, and because the contrast was poor he did not recognize appendicitis.

9. Because her symptoms were not the "classic" presentation of younger patients, the radiologist's report led the surgeons in the wrong direction.

10. Because the surgeons misdiagnosed her and didn't operate in time, her appendix perforated, spraying dangerous bacteria across her abdominal cavity.

The surgery itself went very well, but the errors didn't end there. The bacteria from her appendix formed colonies in her abdominal cavity, and she had to stay in the hospital for over a week while they drained the abscesses and pumped her full of powerful intravenous antibiotics. During that time, I saw mistake after mistake.

I'd written about medical error before, as tidy columns marching across reports from the Institute of Medicine: errors in the thousands and hundreds of thousands, with no names attached. Even the mortality rates seemed less like deaths than statistics. Now I watched them dramatically illustrated on my own mother's body.

The surgical drain they used to evacuate her largest abscess became blocked soon after it was put in and stopped draining. This was probably because no one was following the standard procedure of flushing it once a day with saline. My sister and I pointed out the conspicuous lack of drainage to several people, including both her day and night nurses, but they all insisted it was fine. More than a day went by before the surgeon who had operated on her noticed the problem and flushed the drain out himself.

Then there was the handwashing. Hospitals are fundamentally unsanitary places, not because the staff is filthy, but because hospitals are where we stick sick people who are loaded with dangerous bacteria. Hospitals are also where we pump those people full of antibiotics, which is what has led to the rise of antibiotic-resistant superbugs. Fortunately, the superbugs are still rare, but they're growing a lot faster than our stock of new antibiotics. Our best guess is that nosocomial infections (sickness contracted as a result of medical treatment) kill about 100,000 people every year—about three times as many as are killed in car accidents.[12]

Picture Yankee Stadium during a playoff game, with every seat filled and the standing-room crowds packed stem-to-gills. Then picture everyone in that stadium suddenly dying a gruesome death as virulent bacteria roam from organ to organ, shutting down the kidneys, then the liver, then the heart and lungs. After you have pictured that, picture it happening all over again. That's what our hospital-acquired infection mortality would look like if it all happened at once in one place, instead of spread out across tens of thousands of American hospital rooms over the course of a year. And a huge proportion of those deaths could be prevented if doctors and nurses and other staff just washed their hands the way they're supposed to.

Over the course of ten days, I witnessed multiple people come into my mother's hospital room, touch various surfaces, and then put on gloves to touch her without washing their hands. This is, to be sure, better than if they had touched her bare-handed, but it is not standard procedure, and for good reason. Just putting on the gloves transfers bacteria from your hands to the latex. And for a small number of patients, this is a fatal mistake.

I knew all this before my mother went into the hospital. I have written articles on the poor state of hospital hand hygiene, exhorting doctors to do better and patients to demand that they do. And yet when I was in the hospital room, watching someone approach my mother with gloved but unwashed hands, it suddenly didn't seem so easy. It is hard to accuse someone of something that you both know they shouldn't be doing, particularly if that person is responsible for your mother's life. What good would it do to get them to wash their hands while I was there, if they took out their resentment on her during the many more hours that I was not?

I did speak up a couple of times—couched in an elaborate lie about this terrible series I'd seen on the Discovery Channel—I know that you probably already did it, but I can barely sleep as it is, and would you mind just once more before you touch her? But often I didn't. As I discovered when I myself had to spend ten days administering IV antibiotics at home, the reason that handwashing is so hard to do consistently is that it's not actually that risky to forgo it. The odds that any one slip will cause an infection are extremely low, well under 1 percent. And since it's tedious and often must be done multiple times while touching a single patient, it's very tempting to skip it sometimes. Over thousands of repetitions, this kills people. But most of us don't judge our actions over thousands of repetitions.

Weighing those odds against the risk of pissing off one of her caregivers, I let it go, along with a dozen other little things, like the kinked IV lines. At one point, they tried to insert a permanent IV line so that she could go home on drip antibiotics, but my mother had to stop the procedure because of the excruciating pain. Google informed me that this is an extremely common occurrence with PICC lines. When my mother apologetically told her surgical resident that she couldn't handle the pain, the resident responded with a verbal shrug: "Well, I can't make you get one." So my sister and I took on the job of making sure that the compression leggings that prevent deep vein thrombosis were working, bed linens and hospital gowns were changed, and my mother understood that, no matter how much inserting the permanent line hurt, it was better than an out-of-control infection in her abdominal cavity.

It was easy to forgive the failure to recognize a swollen appendix on a blurry image. It was much harder to forgive these tiny but constant failures of attention to simple, obvious details. And yet, this was not a bad hospital; it was actually a very good one. Her surgeon was excellent. Errors were common, but not constant: most of the time, the nurses washed their hands, the doctors were helpful and informative, and the system worked.

HOW DOCTORS MAKE MISTAKES

In an article for *The New Yorker*, Atul Gawande, a surgeon who writes eloquently about his practice, once described the enormous complexity of a modern cutting-edge procedure:

> What makes her recovery astounding isn't just the idea that someone could come back from two hours in a state that would once have been considered death. It's also the idea that a group of people in an ordinary hospital could do something so enormously complex. To save this one child, scores of people had to carry out thousands of steps correctly: placing the heart-pump tubing into her without letting in air bubbles; maintaining the sterility of her lines, her open chest, the burr hole in her skull; keeping a temperamental battery of machines up and running. The degree of difficulty in any one of these steps is substantial. Then you must add the difficulties of orchestrating them in the right sequence, with nothing dropped, leaving some room for improvisation, but not too much.[13]

Forty years ago, the sociologist Charles Bosk decided to study how surgeons learned to master this environment: how they learned to improvise without ad-libbing their way into fatal mistakes. For over a year, he embedded himself with the surgical teams at a leading teaching hospital, moving equipment, fetching X-rays, and observing how aspiring surgeons were taught to handle errors.[14]

From watching them, Bosk identified four types of errors that surgical residents made. There were technical errors, like nicking a blood vessel during surgery, which resulted from insufficient skill or experience in the delicate manual work of surgery. He separated this from judgment errors such as waiting too long to operate or ordering the wrong treatment for a patient. Both judgment and technical errors were expected, if not exactly welcome, because surgery is fundamentally a hands-on specialty; there is no way to learn to do it except by practice.

We saw technical errors, as when the nurse didn't exactly know how to insert the tube to pump my mother's stomach. And we saw some serious errors in judgment, as when the radiologist missed her swollen appendix. But these were fundamentally forgivable; they were the sorts of mistakes you could imagine yourself making.

Bosk also identified two types of errors that aren't expected, and which ultimately call into question the resident's fitness to be a doctor. The first of these is what he called a normative error. It is somewhat harder to define than the previous two categories, and it may be easier to demonstrate by example: the foremost normative error that Bosk cites is failing to give the supervising attending surgeon all the information about a patient. "No surprises" is one of the foremost rules of surgical residency. It was okay to make a mistake in surgery or treatment, but it was not okay to hide those mistakes from your attending physician. Nor was it acceptable to be unfamiliar with the latest information on your patient's condition.

Every new resident has to learn how to make incisions—and decisions about a difficult case. A technical or judgmental error usually simply indicates that the resident doesn't have enough experience. As with every other skill, medicine must be learned through failure. A normative error, on the other hand, indicates that the resident is not fully committed to the system of learning, and caring, for patients. It calls into question whether they have what it takes to be a doctor.

If the distinction seems confusing to you, think back to your own college education. You might have points docked off a paper for technical errors, like spelling and grammar, or judgment errors, like misreading sources. But if you plagiarized a paper, or cheated on an exam, you risked being expelled. This is true even if you turn in an excellent paper, or score 100 on the exam, because these errors aren't about the outcome; they're about the process. They demonstrate that you haven't internalized the values that make this complicated system work—in the case of a medical resident, either you are not attentive enough to finding out everything about the patient, or you are trying to hide mistakes from your superiors.

The fourth kind of error that Bosk identifies is possibly the most interesting; it's what he calls "quasi-normative" errors. Normative errors violate the shared understanding of what it takes to become a surgeon. Quasi-normative errors, on the other hand, are specific to the attending physician under whom a resident is training. A quasi-normative error involves doing something that your supervisor has told you not to do, even though lots of doctors might recommend you do it.

There's something autocratic and distasteful about quasi-normative error. And yet, in the context of a surgery ward, when keeping people alive is often a matter of doing everything almost exactly right, it makes a sort of sense. The legendary rock band Van Halen used to demand that all concert venues provide them a bowl of M&Ms with all the brown ones picked out. The presence of even a single stray brown M&M was grounds for canceling the contract. For years, this was cited as an example of typical prima-donna rock-star behavior. But in fact, it was a very sophisticated device for detecting normative error. Lead singer David Lee Roth explained the whole thing in his autobiography:

> Van Halen was the first band to take huge productions into tertiary, third-level markets. We'd pull up with nine eighteen-wheeler trucks, full of gear, where the standard was three trucks, max. And there were many, many technical errors—whether it was the girders couldn't support the weight, or the flooring would sink in, or the doors weren't big enough to move the gear through.
>
> The contract rider read like a version of the Chinese Yellow Pages because there was so much equipment, and so many human beings to make it function. So just as a little test, in the

technical aspect of the rider, it would say "Article 148: There will be fifteen amperage voltage sockets at twenty-foot spaces, evenly, providing nineteen amperes . . ." this kind of thing. And article number 126, in the middle of nowhere, was: "There will be no brown M&Ms in the backstage area, upon pain of forfeiture of the show, with full compensation."

So, when I would walk backstage, if I saw a brown M&M in that bowl . . . well, line-check the entire production. Guaranteed you're going to arrive at a technical error. They didn't read the contract. Guaranteed you'd run into a problem. Sometimes it would threaten to just destroy the whole show. Something like, literally, life-threatening.[15]

For someone who works in a hospital to perform a procedure such as inserting an IV line without washing their hands is a normative error. Talk to any doctor, nurse, administrator, or a member of any one of a dozen academic fields that study the health-care industry, and they'll all agree that washing your hands every single time is an absolute imperative. This is true even though most of the time, the outcome is just fine. The outcome doesn't matter. What matters is that by not washing you're demonstrating that you're willing to harm a patient. And yet, for all the agreement that this is a normative error, a lot of health-care workers seem to treat it as a quasi-normative error—as something that can safely be skipped depending on the circumstances.

In the end, none of it mattered. My mother lived even though her nurses forgot to unclog her surgical drain, even though her doctors didn't spot the appendicitis in time, even though we didn't make her go to the doctor when she really should have. What saved my mother was a drug called Tygasil, an antibiotic so powerful and toxic that it can only be administered intravenously.

"It's pretty hard core," said a drug researcher of my acquaintance.

Another was more blunt. "Tygasil? That's a freaking monster. Kills everything."

It doesn't, quite—if your immune system isn't strong enough to do the mop-up work, you can still die, even on Tygasil. But it's very strong, and it's used rarely, so bacteria haven't built up defenses. In my mother's case, it was strong enough.

Antibiotics are unquestionably the single greatest advance of the twentieth century in terms of the number of lives they have saved.[16] They're like the superman of infection prevention. It hardly matters what the doctor does, because in the end, they can always call in antibiotics to save the day. They are the single biggest Spell-Check Factor of modern life; if you doubt it, just go walk through an old graveyard and note how many people used to die at age two, or sixty. Antibiotics have been a boon to everyone, but particularly the elderly, whose immune systems decline, and infants, whose immune systems are still learning to identify invaders. Before the invention of penicillin, pneumonia in patients over sixty was almost always fatal; in fact, pneumonia was known to doctors as "the old man's friend." Now it is almost never fatal unless you are already very sick.

Along with all their good effects, antibiotics have had a bad one: they make it easy for us to be less careful. We have fewer failures—but we make more mistakes.

We can wait longer to call the doctor, and the doctor can maybe be a little sloppy about keeping the work area sterile.

The most dangerous thing about the Spell-Check Factor is that we forget it's there; we don't register all the times that we have come close to making fatal mistakes. That one moment when a doctor decides not to wash her hands almost never kills anyone. But millions of such moments kill tens of thousands of people every year.

Mistakes are most likely to be identified when they lead to a failure. When the patient dies, the heartbroken family wants to know why; if they don't like the answer, they may sue the doctor. When the patient walks out of the hospital on the road back to health, we act as if things must have gone all right. But that is not necessarily the case. One study of the health-care system showed that about one-third of hospital patients can expect to be the victims of a serious mistake—an estimate that, judging by my experience, seems ludicrously low. Most victims of a medical mistake never sue, and many of the people who do sue were not victims of negligence, but of simple bad luck.[17]

None of this is unique to health care. When Ron Johnson was fired as chief executive of JCPenney after barely eighteen months, he exited to catcalls from the press about his "disastrous" results— even though his hiring was a Hail Mary move by a company that was already in steep decline. Meanwhile, numerous CEOs have been feted as solid managers for presiding over steady earnings while slowly but steadily eroding the value of their brand with cheaper products, ill-considered brand extensions, or empire-building mergers that dilute management focus. We remember MCI Worldcom and Enron as abusive fraudsters who violated the trust of their investors—which they were. But we've forgotten the name of other firms who grossly misstated earnings during the 1990s—and got away with it because the boom bailed them out.[18]

Most of the time you can get away with launching a terrible product, or with not washing your hands. But one time in a thousand, you will kill a person, or a company. Unfortunately, the very fact that you've gotten used to taking these little shortcuts will make it hard to identify what went wrong. It will look like you didn't do anything different from what you normally do. And that will be true. When your mistakes rarely lead to a bad outcome, you lose the necessary feedback that helps you improve.

Over the years, companies and professions develop standards to protect themselves (and others) from bad outcomes that only happen some of the time. A rogue trader usually can't destroy the company with a judgment error unless he has also circumvented the internal controls designed to prevent him from taking on too much risk. A technical security glitch in a software program should not mean the end of a big software company, unless they try to hide it from their clients rather than fixing it. If you want to minimize the risk of catastrophe, you focus on the process much more than the outcome.

People who commit normative errors are generally too focused on the result, and not enough on the process. They are willing to cut corners, to bend the rules, and that is a very dangerous thing. The problem is that while normative errors are the most dangerous, they are also the hardest to identify. We'll spend the next two chapters looking at why it is so important to identify mistakes before they turn into disasters—and why it's so damn hard to do.

5 CRISIS

What a Bad Breakup Can Tell Us about the GM Bailout

Take a moment and try to guess what phrase is usually paired with "the best thing that ever happened to me." If you did a Google search (don't cheat), what do you think would come up?

I've got a pretty good idea of what you guessed. Was it, "Meeting my spouse"? "The birth of my child"? "Getting my dream job"? "Winning the lottery"? In June 2012, I administered a Web survey to several hundred people and in almost every survey, at least one of those four answers appeared. Respondents also thought well of "Being born" and—to my surprise—"meeting my favorite celebrity."[1]

But I'm afraid you're wrong. Oh, to be sure, if you do a Google search of the phrase "The best thing that ever happened to me," marriage and childbirth certainly do pop up. But those halcyon moments are actually a distant third. The most common result is (darn you, Google) the lyrics to a Gladys Knight song. And if we can agree to ignore Gladys Knight, the things that come up aren't things we wish for; they're things most people fear more than anything. They're, well, the worst.

Here's a partial list of the unexpected items that make up life's Greatest Hits:

Divorce
My husband's affair
Cancer
Getting fired
Being left at the altar

Prison

Dyslexia

After asking my survey takers what they thought *other* people would most commonly identify as the best thing that had ever happened to them, I asked them the same thing about *themselves*. The answers were revealingly idiosyncratic. Marriage and childbirth were still among the most popular options, but a surprising number reported that their luckiest break was being born—in the United States, to solidly middle-class parents who gave them good values and a head start on education. And while almost no one predicted that negative life events would turn out to be peak life moments for others, when asked about their own "best thing," a lot of them described what could only be considered catastrophic crises.

"Surviving a should-have-been-fatal car accident."
"When my family and I were accepted as refugees to the US
    from Afghanistan."
"Divorce."
"During a period of underemployment, getting a phone call
    asking me to help start a business."
"Not getting a job I wanted but in retrospect would have
    ended up trapped in."
"Got sober."
"Trying and failing at multiple entrepreneurial endeavors."
"Getting a job, getting off drugs."
"Dropping out of school (and going back)."

Surprised? I was. That list reads like a country song, with better grammar. But I really shouldn't have been. Most of us can look back at some moment of crisis and realize that this is when life, after years of sending us more-or-less-polite cease-and-desist notices, finally punched us square in the face as if to say, "I'm not kidding around! Cut it out, you stupid moron!" Moments of crisis can be transformative. They are awful, yes, but they also open up new opportunities that you wouldn't—or couldn't—otherwise have taken. In fact, the great mystery is not why crises so often seem to change our lives for the better. It is why we seem to be unable to change them any other way.

THE BEST THING THAT EVER HAPPENED TO ME

I didn't get married until I was thirty-seven. Demographic data indicate that I was part of a fast-growing trend, which, like most such trends, has spawned its own little publishing boomlet.[2] The past few years have seen a spate of articles by women in their late thirties explaining why they didn't get married. My case is a little different, though, because unlike these other women, I didn't just somehow forget that I wanted to get married. Nor was I a victim of my own excessively high standards, or too attached to the freedom of my own bathtub, the deep satisfactions of Saturday brunch with the girls, and the possibility that I might—suddenly and for no apparent reason—decide to pick up and move to Rome.

I very much wanted to get married. I had even picked out someone to marry. One giddy Wednesday night, after months of those tedious will-we-or-won't-we negotiations that afflict almost all couples at a certain point in the life cycle of their relationship, he indicated to me that yes, he was ready to get married, and for two days I literally skipped down the subway platform on the way home from work. And then on Saturday he quietly told me that he'd made a mistake, and I should move out.

Pick your cliché: slapped in the face, punched in the gut, heart ripped out, stomped on. It felt like all of these things had happened at once, as if I'd gone twelve rounds with a bare-knuckle boxer who really didn't like me. One who'd caught me with a tricky sucker punch.

There was nothing obviously wrong with our relationship, but for a long time there had been something not quite right. We never fought, which at the time seemed like a good sign, but in retrospect was a symptom of a puzzling distance between us. Only much later, when we were both in new relationships, were we able to diagnose it over a friendly round of drinks. He didn't think you were supposed to have to work at relationships, and so when there were difficulties, he gently detached himself. I wanted to get married so badly that I was terrified of making any demands at all. The result was something like those sugar sculptures you see at fancy parties. Superficially, it looks great, and but the slightest pressure might cause it to collapse into a thousand shards.

If he'd just said it a few days earlier, I might have stood it better; at least I'd have been prepared. As it was he caught me completely by surprise. Worse, I felt like a fool for having been so happy. It was spectacularly cruel.

Before that morning, I'd always held the theory that it was harder to break up with someone than to be broken up with. This theory, I can now report, was wildly wrong. He was wistful but I was shattered. I missed him and, more important, I was thirty-three and had wasted the last of my prime dating years on someone who now didn't want me.

That afternoon I moved back into my Manhattan apartment (no wonder he wanted me to keep the lease) a 435-square-foot "one bedroom" half-sunken below street level, trapped in such perpetual gloom that even on the sunniest day, I needed to turn the lights on to read. For months I watched television with a determination that should have earned me some sort of VIP award from Time Warner Cable. I never turned it off, a trickier feat than you might think given the fact that I absolutely couldn't stand to watch any shows about happy people, because they would make me terribly sad. Nor could I watch any shows with sad people, because they would make me even sadder. Mostly, I watched the Science Channel. And by mostly, I mean for eight or ten or twenty hours a day. I believe I may still be one of the world's leading experts on supervolcanoes and the asteroid belt.

This went on for the better part of a year. We tried seeing each other again a couple of times, but one Saturday, on a wretched car ride from the train station, he made it clear that it was really never going to work. Unable to spend another year in that apartment, on Monday, I did the only thing I could think of: I asked *The Economist* for a temporary transfer to DC.

I ended up staying in Washington longer than expected. Once I was at a safe distance, I found myself wondering how on earth I could have let everything drag out for so long. In another city, with an entirely new group of friends and, eventually, a new job writing for *The Atlantic*, my old self seemed like a lunatic fifth cousin—that person looks sort of like you, but what on earth are they doing?

It wasn't until the financial crisis happened, rapidly followed by the disintegration of the American auto industry, that I really started to understand my behavior.

GM'S LONG AND NOT-SO-MYSTERIOUS DECLINE

For those of us who are not yet forty, it's hard to remember that GM was not always the bumbling butt of late-night-television jokes. For most of its existence it was the Apple Computer of its day: technologically advanced, a master of consumer marketing, and probably America's best-known company. In 1953 GM's president, Charlie Wilson, famously testified to Congress that "what was good for the country was good for General Motors and vice versa." This may sound to modern ears like the self-serving justifications of a greedy kleptocrat (and he took some ribbing even then) but if you look at the company's record in 1953, it seems more like a simple statement of fact. For one thing, GM had played a significant role in producing armaments for World War II. And that year, in record peacetime prosperity, it was the country's largest private employer. When America prospered, GM sold more cars. And because GM employed more than half a million people, when it sold more cars, America prospered.[3]

Back then, GM was a radical innovator. Most people know that Henry Ford essentially midwifed the modern auto industry when he started to build his cars on an assembly line, which allowed them to be produced cheaper, faster, and with more consistent quality. Far fewer people are aware of the fact that GM, not Ford, invented the way that consumers experience the auto industry.

Ford wanted his customers to wait obediently at the end of his production line to hop in and drive off in whatever he chose to make. He famously remarked "You can have any color—as long as it's black." His company produced one car, the Model T, from 1908 to 1927, and then, when sales finally started to flag, it rolled out another car, the Model A, as its lone successor. Ford thought his customers shouldn't go into debt and refused to provide financing, until the late 1920s.[4]

By contrast, GM pioneered annual model changes and attractive styling, was an early leader in auto financing, and developed multiple brands to suit different demographics and personalities—"a car for every purse and purpose," as the longtime GM executive Alfred P. Sloan put it. Henry Ford's big idea was to do one thing and get very good at doing that thing. He ran his company like a not-so-benevolent dictator, right down to creating a "Social Services" department that pried into the personal lives of his employees. General Motors was the liberal democracy to Ford's quasi-theocracy. The nice managers at GM didn't want to tell you what car you should drive. They just wanted to help you find the car of your dreams.

Such was the power of the assembly line that by 1918, one in two cars on America's roads was a Model T—a record never since equaled by any single car.[5] But people eventually got tired of the Model T, and Ford refused to innovate. By 1960, GM had matched Ford's 1918 feat in company-wide sales. They held just about 50 percent of the domestic market, employing more than 400,000 hourly workers who averaged more than $100 a week, at a time when the average annual wage was closer to $3,000.[6]

GM workers were making twice as much as most of the American labor force not because their union was too powerful (that came later), but because the company was running its production facilities flat out, trying to keep up with seemingly insatiable demand. Americans loved GM cars the way they have never loved another company's product. "If we were to publish a list of those who own Cadillac cars," said a 1947 ad, "it would be recognized throughout the world as an honor roll of contemporary achievement."[7] This was immodest, but it was true. American cars were the gold standard the world over. GM wasn't just providing cars and jobs to Americans; it was serving as a goodwill ambassador.

"Ford at the time was a classic innovator who changed the world and then refused to change himself," says my old professor James Schrager, a turnaround consultant who also teaches strategy at the University of Chicago's Booth Business School. "GM came in and said 'We'll make many cars, many colors.' They were a brilliant technology company. First electric starter. First automatic transmission. First car with overhead valves. They came out of World War II in a cannon, and that cannon just shot them all the way to 1965."[8]

It took the most successful company in the world more than forty years to finally acknowledge that the magic was gone. As GM entered its death throes, every business journalist in America tried to answer the same question: How do you let your company lose market share for forty years running without, y'know, doing something about it?

I once listened in on an earnings call with the CEO of a biotech firm who had covered some holes in his cash flow by selling off the rights to all his firm's patents. Nothing in their drug pipeline was even remotely close to being approved by the FDA. They had, in other words, absolutely no means of generating any income and they were burning through the company's remaining pile of cash at a pretty brisk clip. Yet the CEO was cheerfully talking about "the firm's future" as if it had one, other than receivership.

"This man is obviously crazy," I thought. "This must be why his firm is doing so badly."

But the other analysts on the call took it in stride. They weren't insane; they were just used to it. They knew what I eventually learned, writing about business for the next decade: this is how companies act when things go badly wrong. Turnaround experts will tell you that they usually get called in when a company is about to miss payroll or a big loan payment. This is not because they didn't realize that something was wrong long before that; accounting knows that the bank balances are dropping, sales knows that customers are unenthusiastic, production knows that the line has slowed down. "Everyone kind of knows when things aren't going well," one turnaround expert I talked to said. He paused for emphasis. "*Everyone.*"[9]

So why do they go on pretending that everything will be fine when that patently isn't the case? Why don't they change course when they have plenty of time—or make only cosmetic changes, rearranging the deck chairs on the *Titanic* while the ship is sinking? Well, why does everyone pretend that Great-Grandma hasn't launched into a racist tirade in the middle of Thanksgiving dinner? Pretending everything is fine even when it's not is so common that cognitive scientists have given it a name: the normalcy bias.

When management seems oblivious, we tend to look for explanations in the specifics of the company: the management is stupid, the unions are greedy, the regulators weren't doing their job. But in fact, this is a general problem, and it's not special to corporations. The long answer to "How could they let this happen?" is that when it comes to responding to change, unfortunately corporations are all too human.

THE NORMALCY BIAS

Picture yourself in a plane crash or a terrible fire. What do you see?

Most likely you imagine people around you screaming hysterically, maybe trampling one another to death. It looks, in short, just like every disaster movie you've ever seen. If you're very lucky, one calm, clearheaded person, probably played by Liam Neeson, will get things under control and help lead the group to safety.

This makes for great movie drama, but it has nothing to do with real life. You shouldn't worry about getting trampled if something really bad happens, because most people don't necessarily freak out when disaster strikes. Many people, in fact, don't do anything.

Hundreds of people died in the World Trade Center because they wandered around talking to one another and wondering if they should leave rather than picking up their bags and getting the hell out of there. Many of the people who failed to evacuate ahead of Hurricane Katrina were stuck because they had nowhere to go, but lots more decided to stay put because they didn't believe the storm would be so bad. According to Amanda Ripley, author of *The Unthinkable*, a book about disasters, an astonishing number of people die in airplane disasters because instead of evacuating the plane, they sit in their seats and worry about their hand luggage. When a plane crashes, there is a high risk of fire, so it's important to get to the exits and away from the airplane as quickly as possible.[10] Most people don't do that. They just don't seem to grasp the danger and, as a result, they die.[11]

That's the normalcy bias: acting as if things are fine even when they quite obviously are not.[12] There are many evolutionary theories for why this might be, none of which are very satisfactory. What is clear is that even in the most extreme circumstances, when it is very, very clear that things are not normal, people have a very strong propensity to act as if they are.

Eventually they figure things out, of course—the passengers who stayed put were presumably not planning to spend the rest of their lives sitting in those seats—and there are ways to speed things up. Flight attendants who scream at passengers to GET OUT NOW are more effective than those who calmly and politely point out the exit.[13] People who take a moment to think through a disaster plan before something terrible happens (a fire, a break-in, a medical emergency) are more likely to execute it. But while there are ways to accelerate the process of adjusting to the new normal, there are also a bunch of mental brakes that slow things down. And the longer you have had to get used to the old normal, the more powerful those brakes tend to be.

After all, they are still in their seats, with their seat belts on. It doesn't feel that different from getting ready for takeoff. If things were really bad, people would be screaming and running around, so that must mean it's safe to stay put. The more things look normal, the more likely you are to act as if they are. When the planes hit the World Trade Center, the building was on fire. But the fire wasn't close to most peoples' offices at first; their work space looked exactly like it did twenty minutes before. This made it easy to think they could take a few minutes and check out what their coworkers thought about the situation, rather than grabbing their stuff and heading for the stairs.

Of course, not everyone freezes when disaster hits. Lots of people do nothing, but there are also plenty of people who do something—but not enough. They take inadequate half measures until they reach a crisis point: the moment when it is no longer possible to pretend they are facing anything except imminent doom. Until then, they sit tight and ask the flight attendants to do something about the air-conditioning.

THE HIDDEN COST OF HALF MEASURES

You often hear analysts say that GM did nothing while its market share vanished, and indeed, I've just suggested as much. But this is not actually true. In fact, the company did try to do something about its woes. Many, many somethings. There were very small cars, and very big ones. There was NUMMI (New United Motor Manufacturing), a joint venture with Toyota that was supposed to teach American workers and managers how to be nimble and quality-focused like the Japanese. There was Saturn, "a different kind of car company," which, it was hoped, would provide a distinctly American model for reform. For all the finger-pointing about its failure to change, the company tried more turnarounds than an all-night Macarena marathon.

What you see when you look into the history of GM—or Kodak— or any number of other once-mighty industrial giants—is not quite the idiot Goliath most people like to picture. In popular legend, these companies (or their unions) are like that smug, grasping villain in caper films, who never suspects that his richly deserved comeuppance is upon him. But in life, they're more like that stupid bureaucrat who pops up in every disaster movie, the one who almost lets the asteroid hit Earth because he doesn't want to worry the president.

This tendency to accentuate the positive probably has its uses. There's a scientific name for people with an especially accurate perception of how talented, attractive, and popular they are—we call them "clinically depressed."[14] Optimism may sometimes be the only thing saving us from despair in our ordinary lives. Unfortunately, when everything changes for the worse, our natural optimism starts to work against us. Often, indeed, it goes so badly awry that we're not merely staying in our seat while smoke fills the plane; we're lashing ourselves to the fuselage and screaming at people to go away when they try to help us.

THROWING GOOD MONEY AFTER BAD

In May of 2011, the White House posted a heartwarming video on its website, showing how the 2009 stimulus was "helping to create long-term manufacturing jobs that will help ensure America's leadership for the twenty-first century."[15] A grateful worker explained how happy he was to have found a good, steady job in a growth industry, right there in the Bay Area where he could stay near his family. Other workers in sterile white lab gear were shown in various stages of an apparently painstaking manufacturing process, while a manager explained that, thanks to the loan they'd gotten with the help of a federal government guarantee, they were in the process of building a second fabrication plant to allow them to ramp up production and hire even more people. The White House's blog told the rest of the story: there would also be construction jobs, jobs with suppliers, and eventually, jobs for the people who sold and installed the product.

Less than four months after that video was posted, Solyndra filed for bankruptcy, laid off all the workers in the video, and announced that the government would not be getting its money back. In less than three years, the company had somehow managed to burn through almost a billion dollars, including $535 million worth of loan guarantees from the U.S. government, building novel solar panels that cost more to make than they could possibly sell for. Much of what they'd spent the money on seemed phenomenally stupid: robots that whistled Disney tunes as they rolled about the plant; stunning conference facilities; that second, larger fabrication plant even though they hadn't even been able to sell all their output from the original, smaller operation.[16]

Conservatives had a jamboree: The president had been frittering away taxpayer money in order to ingratiate himself with his fundraisers (one of whom was a major investor in Solyndra) and environmentalists. Nonsense, the administration's supporters retorted; when they'd made the investment, silicon prices were sky high, and there was every reason to think that Solyndra's novel design, which didn't use all that expensive silicon, would be a solid bet. The only way to foster innovation is to take some calculated risks. Yes, some of those bets would fail, but overall, the payoff from the wins would more than make up for the losses.

Conservatives retorted that the risks didn't seem all that well calculated. Silicon is also known as "sand" before it is melted down and turned into solar panels, and while the manufacturing process for high-grade silicon is a bit fussy, the fact remains that the planet is awash in the basic materials needed to make it. The odds that silicon prices were going to remain high were very slim—and indeed, they began a long and dramatic decline shortly before the administration signed off on its investment.

The supporters had one thing right: Creative destruction is about risk. Risk means that even a good decision can result in a bad outcome. During the financial crisis, even incredibly conservative and prudent stock index funds lost almost half their value. That didn't mean that the people who'd poured money into their 401(k)s were stupid.

But all this partisan bickering missed the point. They were essentially debating the question "Can the administration unerringly predict the future?" which has an obvious answer. What they should have been asking is "Did the administration use a good decision-making process?" And here the evidence suggests they did not.

The administration is, understandably, not eager to discuss what they were thinking. But reporting by various news outlets and internal documents subpoenaed by a congressional committee make a few things fairly clear.

Energy secretary Steven Chu, who was a fan of thin-film solar panels before he took office, was touting the Solyndra loan guarantee even before it was finalized. He'd mentally invested in the company before the due diligence was complete.

The administration was trying to push money out the door as fast as possible, both to provide economic stimulus, and to find environmental projects they could show to the Democratic base. They were eager to give speeches in front of Solyndra's new gee-whiz factory, which included autonomous robots that whistled Disney tunes as they moved around the plant.[17]

That factory was built with Solyndra's loan money, even though the company hadn't been able to sell all the output from their older, smaller factory. The company's manufacturing process was tricky and their costs were higher than those of traditional photovoltaic cell manufacturers. The company seemed to think that if they could just build a big enough factory, with enough lab-coated employees and whistling robots, they'd be able to drive costs down. This is what corporate strategists call "chasing your competitor down the cost curve," and it rarely works, because your competitor can also build a bigger factory—especially if he is profitable, and you are not. (This is basically what happened.) The company's strategy was a real-life example of the sardonic economist's joke: "We're losing money on every unit, but we'll make it up in volume!"

Silicon prices began to fall in June 2009, before the loan guarantee was finalized. Since cheap photovoltaic cells would make it impossible for Solyndra's technology to become cost competitive, this should have caused the administration to pause before they cleared the loan. There's no evidence that this happened.

The administration made Solyndra a poster child for its environmental agenda, ignoring clear warning signs that the investment had been a mistake.[18] Between June of 2009 and August of 2011, traditional silicon-based photovoltaic cell prices dropped more than 50 percent. By March 2010, less than a year after the loan guarantee had been finalized, Solyndra's auditor, PricewaterhouseCoopers, warned that the company's financial problems "raise substantial doubt about its ability to continue as a going concern." Nonetheless, despite the unease of some staff members, the president gave a speech at Solyndra in May. All those workers surrounded by whistling robots, said the president, showed that "the promise of clean energy isn't just an article of faith."

Even when it should have been crystal clear that the investment was not working out, the administration engaged in desperate long-shot attempts to save it—possibly because the president, had, embarrassingly, given a big speech touting his loan guarantee. That guarantee was senior to all the other funds invested, meaning that if Solyndra folded, the taxpayers would be repaid before any other creditors or shareholders saw a dime. But in February 2011, the administration allowed a couple of the VC investors to pour an extra $75 million into the company, in return for an assurance that they would get to cut in line before the taxpayer in a bankruptcy proceeding. If the company went into bankruptcy and had to sell off its inventory of unsellable solar cells and whistling robots, there probably wasn't going to be enough money to pay everyone back. Letting the VC investors jump the line meant that they would probably get their $75 million—and the government would be out-of-pocket.[19, 20]

The initial decision to invest can be forgiven. If we want creative destruction, we need to take risks, and by definition many, maybe most, of those risks won't pan out.

What is troubling is their pattern of escalating commitment. By late 2009 it was clear the company was in trouble; by the end of 2010, it should have been clear that Solyndra could not possibly scale up enough to ever make a competitive product. But everyone kept going for another year, money and labor turning expensive raw materials into garbage.

To understand why this happens, we need to go back to my terrible, horrible, no good, very bad year.

SUNK COSTS, OR THE DANGER OF DOUBLING DOWN

The most embarrassing part of my breakup—the part I almost didn't tell you about—was how desperate I was to get him back. Over the years we'd been together, my life had come to revolve around our relationship, because so many of my friends were absorbed in new babies, and most of the rest had, for various reasons, moved out of New York. When he pushed me out, I looked at all the parts of my life and saw mostly . . . nothing. There were my parents (who were themselves in the middle of divorcing and selling their apartment). There was my job. And there were the shows on supervolcanoes.

Alone in my apartment, faced with the terrifyingly shredded remains of my future, I became obsessed with the past. I could remember all the great moments we had, how perfectly suited we were. What were the odds that I was going to meet another tall, libertarian New Yorker who liked the same movies and books that I did? No, it seemed obvious that my only hope was to somehow convince him to plug back in to all the holes in my life.

Six months later, the day before Valentine's Day, I ran into him at the supermarket. You can guess what happened next. Though we were nominally seeing other people, it didn't stop us. I waited patiently for things to fix themselves. And then a little less than a year after we'd broken up for the first time, he did it again.

How could you be so stupid, you may ask? How indeed. The answer is what economists call "sunk costs," and what I like to call "the three years I had already invested in a failing relationship."

A sunk cost is, well, like a sunken ship: an asset that has already been expended, and cannot be recovered. It's the money you wasted painting the bathroom that dreadful shade of blue that looked so nice in the store, the six years you spent getting that PhD in English that no employer wants. It is very sad that you wasted $140.73 and your Memorial Day weekend painting the bathroom, but there's no way to scrape the paint off the wall and take it back to the store.

As economists know, and most people don't, the right way to deal with sunk costs is to ignore them. When I was in college, I dated the son of an economist, who took me to see *The Road to Wellville*, which was aptly described by Roger Ebert as "an expedition through the digestive tract with gun and camera." The *Austin Chronicle* called it "a muddled mess of boorish scatological jokes and preachy asides that goes nowhere, does nothing, and ultimately dies a grim, humorless death."

"As comic material," said Janet Maslin of the *New York Times*, "it doesn't even approach the cornflake, which also figures in this story."

We watched all 119 painful minutes, at my insistence. My boyfriend wanted to leave after ten minutes, but we had paid good money for our tickets, and I wasn't going to get cheated out of my money.

"Seriously, let's go," he whispered after twenty minutes. "It's not going to get better."

"Those tickets cost ten dollars," I said indignantly.

When the movie was over, and we were finally, thankfully, regurgitated into the outside air, he took my hand and looked into my eyes.

"Megan, I want you to come home and meet my father."

"You want me to meet your parents?" I asked, heart fluttering.

"Yes," he said. "So my father can explain the concept of sunk costs to you."

My boyfriend was quite right. The money for the tickets was gone. There was nothing to be gained by also wasting two hours that we could have spent doing something that was actually fun, or at least something that wasn't actively unpleasant.

But like most people, I couldn't let go of the money we'd wasted. That's why so many people eat awful meals, watch horrible movies, read terrible books, and suffer through dreadful relationships. It's why I am far from the only woman who wasted her early thirties on a relationship that wasn't going anywhere. The psychological cost of conceding that you've made a huge mistake—worse, a mistake you can't fix—is too great. So you waste even more money, or time, or effort trying to somehow salvage what you've lost.

The administration and I had essentially the same problem: we'd invested something very valuable, and irretrievable, and we wanted that investment to pay off. So when things started looking a little shaky, we invested more: more time in my case, more political capital in theirs. Instead of cutting our losses, we doubled down.

LOSS AVERSION, OR WHY WE CAN'T LET GO OF BAD DECISIONS

Gambler's Anonymous notes that one of the prime signs of someone with a compulsive gambling problem is that after you lose, you want to get back to the casino as soon as possible in order to win back your losses.[21] It's a crazy idea—doesn't every frequent gambler know that the odds are stacked in favor of the house? Over a lifetime of gambling, the chance that you will win back your losses is, statistically speaking, zero.

But when it comes to other kinds of losses, most of us turn into gamblers. Almost everyone is what psychologists call "loss averse": we worry more about losses than potential gains.

Think of it this way: Would you take a gamble that offered a 50 percent shot at losing half your income, permanently, and a 50 percent shot at becoming as wealthy as Paris Hilton? If you're like most people, you wouldn't. You're more worried about even a relatively small loss than you are excited by the prospect of millions.

Ah, you may say, but losing half my income would mean a huge reduction in my happiness. Sure, I'd be happier if I had all of Paris

Hilton's money, but my life is already pretty okay. The potential gain in happiness is just not worth what I'd stand to lose.

Fair enough. So consider an experiment conducted by the well-known behavioral psychologists Daniel Kahneman and Amos Tversky. They posed the following scenario to a large group of college students:[22]

> The U.S. is preparing for the outbreak of an unusual Asian disease, which is expected to kill 600 people. Two alternative programs to combat the disease have been proposed. Assume that the exact scientific estimates of the consequences of the programs are as follows: If program A is adopted, 200 people will be saved. If program B is adopted, there is a one-third probability that 600 people will be saved and a two-thirds probability that no people will be saved. Which of the two programs would you favor?

Note that the expected value of the two options is the same. In the first scenario, you will save 200 people 3 out of 3 times; in the second, you save 600 people one time, and 0 people the other two times. Either way, over three trials, you'd expect to save 600 people.

The difference is in the risk. Do you take the sure thing and know that 400 people will definitely die, while 200 people are definitely saved? Or do you risk losing everyone—if it gives you a chance at saving everyone?

Most of the students opted for the low-risk strategy. You probably think that's the sensible course, because most of my readers, like most doctors, are risk averse. But consider the following scenario, which Kahneman and Tversky also posed to college students:

> The U.S. is preparing for the outbreak of an unusual Asian disease, which is expected to kill 600 people. Two alternative programs to combat the disease have been proposed. Assume that the exact scientific estimates of the consequences of the programs

are as follows: If program C is adopted, 400 people will die. If program D is adopted, there is a one-third probability that no-body will die and a two-thirds probability that 600 people will die. Which of the two programs would you favor?

Clever readers will have noticed that this is the same question. It's just phrased differently; instead of focusing on the people being saved, this scenario highlights the ones who will die. Yet changing the words slightly produced radically different answers. In the first scenario, 72 percent of subjects wanted to take the low-risk course, while the remainder chose to gamble on saving everyone. But when the question focused on losses instead of gains, the proportions flipped: 78 percent of subjects wanted to go all in on a possible cure.

In other words, the bigger our losses, the more we are willing to gamble. Even when that gamble is unwise.

WHY ONCE-SUCCESSFUL COMPANIES HAVE A HARD TIME CHANGING COURSE

You've often heard it said that companies or people are "victims of their own success," but in the case of GM, that was literally true. "The great problem with successful companies is that they have been successful," says Schrager. "Most don't call people like me until they are quite obviously unsuccessful. They don't develop their own internal thinking to say, 'Yup, we used to be great, but that was yesterday.'"

But it isn't just nostalgia that makes the turnarounds so hard. That history of success means the potential losses are enormous. Years of wealth building means that everyone has more to lose—and thus, that people will try very hard to avoid the losses.

Through the 1970s, the UAW had negotiated a series of incredibly generous contracts. There were double-digit annual wage increases. Health benefits were gold plated and continued into retirement, along with very substantial pensions.[23]

The work rules also became more elaborate. If a machine broke down, everyone on the line got to take a break while they waited for an electrician or machinist to come make the repair—even if the line workers could have repaired it themselves. And it was so difficult to penalize workers for unexcused absences that the Big Three essentially gave up and closed the plants on the first day of hunting season. By the late 1970s, Leonard Woodcock, the UAW president who had negotiated the most generous of these contracts, seemed nonplussed by the dynamic he'd helped create. In *Crash Course*, author Paul Ingrassia quotes Woodcock's confession to a friend after he'd retired. "Our members have the best contract that people with their skills and education could ever hope to get. But we've convinced them that with every new contract, they're entitled to more."

All this drove costs up. When the Big Three enjoyed a cozy little oligopoly over the market, that didn't matter so much: the costs just got passed on to consumers. But in the 1970s, with gas prices soaring, the American consumer discovered that foreign cars cost less and got much better gas mileage. Eventually, they discovered that they were also better made.

The declining quality of American cars over the last few decades is usually blamed on management, but in fact management had no choice. By the 2000s, higher hourly wages and ballooning retiree benefits meant that they had a cost disadvantage of several thousand dollars per car. That money had to come from somewhere, and where it came from was the quality of the product. Cheaper materials on the seats and dashboard, less insulation so that the cars were noisier . . . despite the advertising slogans and the breathless Sunday supplement articles, quality is not just magicked up by fine German engineering or Japanese teamwork. It costs money. And the American automakers had to put that money elsewhere.[24]

The alternative was a massive showdown with the unions. Many of the workers in the plants, and in management, were second- or third-generation GM employees who had watched the company provide their parents a steadily increasing standard of living and a very comfortable retirement. But it was especially hard for the union workers, many of whom had chosen the line over college or a skilled trade precisely because it offered lifetime job security and guaranteed retirement benefits. Now, decades later, they were not going to quietly admit they'd made a bad bet and see if they could get into nursing school. The kinds of cuts in wages, benefits, and staffing levels that could have made the company competitive with foreign firms, whose cars were mostly assembled in nonunion plants down south, would have triggered a nuclear showdown with the unions. Even if the company won, it would have suffered a massive loss of market share while the factories were shut down.

Their dealer network was also a big problem. Auto dealers are a very powerful political force: there is an auto dealer in almost every congressional district, and its owner is often among the richest men in town. Over the decades, they too had striven to secure for themselves a right to well-padded lifetime employment, in the form of franchise laws that made it difficult and expensive to shut down a dealer franchise. Like the unions, the dealers were not interested in hearing that they had to lean into the strike zone and take one for the team.[25]

When Rick Wagoner became head of GM in 1998, he very sensibly decided to shut down the Oldsmobile brand, which had seen its sales decline 75 percent over the previous fifteen years. Thanks to state franchise laws that forced GM to compensate dealers when they dropped a brand, that decision cost the company north of a billion dollars, and made sure that the company would never again try to close a product line, no matter how badly it was selling.

Wagoner also cut a deal with the union to lower costs somewhat, including off-loading a big chunk of retirement benefits onto the UAW. But this didn't mean that they could make a successful small car. GM had done decades of damage to its brand in order to keep peace with the union. If people were willing to compromise on quality, they would go to a lower-priced Korean import; if they wanted a high-quality gas-sipper, they bought a Honda or a Toyota. In order to compete in the small car business, GM functionally had to sell the cars at a loss.

So instead, GM returned to what had worked in the past: big, gas-guzzling vehicles. Americans were willing to pay extra for the space and comfort of an SUV, which gave Detroit some breathing room. It's hard to lose $2,000 worth of labor costs in a $13,000 compact car. It's a lot easier with a $35,000 truck.

They also pushed harder and harder on their financing. In the late '80s, two prices started falling rapidly, and kept falling for fifteen years: the price of oil, and the price of credit. Detroit exploited both those trends to the fullest, with ever-more-massive SUVs sold on ever-cheaper financing.

Obviously, any increase in the price of gasoline, or auto loans, was going to make this strategy something of a disaster. And yes, management understood this. But the alternative was to have a disaster right now. Maybe it would be a smaller disaster, and maybe it would put the company on a sounder long-term footing. But just like the people in Kahneman's experiment, when they were faced with the choice of a definite small disaster, or a maybe big one, they chose to gamble on maybe.

GROUPIDITY

You would think that big, respectable companies, and big, respectable government agencies, would be less prone to doubling down this way than individuals. After all, they have teams of auditors, accountants, and expert analysts to tell them when things aren't working. They have all sorts of oversight panels that are supposed to keep them from throwing away the money that taxpayers and shareholders have entrusted to them. But in fact, groups are capable of much more stupid behavior than individuals are. They frequently fall prey to what I've taken to calling "groupidity": doing something stupid because other people around you seem to think it's safe.

Fundamentally, people are herd animals. We band together for safety. We look to other people to see what is dangerous, and what is not. This is an important part of asset price bubbles: it feels safe to herd into stocks, or flipping houses, and safest when the most people are doing it . . . even though this is actually when it is the most dangerous.

Ask yourself why children now have to be escorted at all times by their parents until they're old enough to sit for the SAT, even though my generation—the people arranging all this intensive supervision—managed to survive to adulthood just fine without it.

My best friend started riding the crosstown bus to school by herself in first grade. Because I walked to school, I had to wait until fourth grade for independence, when I was allowed to walk, along with two other fourth graders, across two busy avenues and past a number of housing projects. This was in the early 1980s, when crime in New York was a very serious problem. I was nine, and I would have died if my mother had insisted on walking me to school. In 2008, a woman made national news for letting her nine-year-old son ride the subway alone.

I routinely meet parents who feel that they have to escort their junior-high schoolers past Fifth Avenue's multimillion-dollar co-ops. All the parents I know complain about having to spend all this time supervising their kids, and lament the loss of the freedom we had. But none of them dare to put their kid on the subway alone because of the sneaking feeling that if no one else is doing it, it must be more dangerous than they remember. Besides, if anything *did* happen and they were the only ones doing it, they'd be destroyed by guilt and regret.

A crisis can make the group collectively much stupider than the people in it. You wonder if you should undo your seat belt and run, but you look at your neighbor, who seems to be calmly sitting there, so you calm down and sit there too. Meanwhile, your neighbor, who was preparing to run, notes that you don't seem worried, so he can probably take his time about getting out.

The instincts that can make us too cautious can equally make us think that we are safe when we are not. In the aftermath of the Solyndra bubble, one of the most noticeable things was the way that everyone justified the investments on the grounds that all these other smart investors were investing. Solyndra prominently advertised the government's new loan guarantee when it sought another round of VC financing. Then later, when things went south, the administration's defenders pointed out that there was all this private equity money going into Solyndra, so wasn't that proof that they weren't so stupid after all? At GM, too, the herd thinking seems to have made everything worse—in part because of the stakeholder battles, but mostly because the management talked themselves into behavior so bizarre that it bordered on mass psychosis.

By early 2008 GM was burning through about $1 billion a month, which put them less than eighteen months away from bankruptcy even if things didn't get worse. But there was no radical restructuring announced.[26] Rick Wagoner, the CEO, refused to even line up the debtor-in-possession (DIP) financing that might be needed to see the company through a bankruptcy reorganization. Without DIP financing, the company might be forced to liquidate in a fire sale rather than going through an orderly restructuring. But Wagoner was adamant: bankruptcy was out of the question. No one would want to buy a car from a firm that might go bankrupt.

There's some logic to his position: the publicity from seeking DIP financing would have been very bad. But by summer, he was on track to run out of cash in less than six months. Unless something changed incredibly quickly, GM was going to end up in bankruptcy, whether or not they sought DIP financing. The only question was whether the process would be orderly, or catastrophic.

Wagoner seemed to believe that by not admitting GM might

declare bankruptcy, he could somehow keep it from happening. What he thought would take place when the company ran out of cash is not clear. Nor is it clear why his executives and his board of directors nodded and said "Yes, Rick" rather than insisting that he confront reality. Instead, they helped him sustain his delusion by formulating a mad plan to merge with Chrysler, as if strapping together two nearly bankrupt auto firms would somehow make both of them solvent.

But Wagoner's mute refusal to plan ahead isn't even the craziest part of the story. That honor goes to the leadership of the UAW, which seems to have been genuinely surprised to learn, three weeks beforehand, that the company was about to run out of money and be forced into receivership. Mind you, it had been widely reported that the financial crisis was causing both car buyers and car loans to dry up. Surely, the union must have noticed that they weren't putting out so many cars. And both the amount of cash that the company had in its coffers, and the fantastic rate at which that cash was being consumed, were public information, available to the union and everyone else in GM's publicly audited financial statements.

Arithmetic is not some sort of arcane art. And these people weren't all crazy; they had risen to the top of one of the most complicated industrial organizations in the world. Yet somehow, thousands of people decided that the laws of mathematics no longer applied to them. It took actually running out of cash—plus a bankruptcy court, a special task force, and about 300 million angry taxpayers—to get GM to stop pretending and do what had been obvious for decades: drastically trim the workforce, slash the wage and benefit package until it was competitive with Toyota and Volkswagen, and close over a thousand underperforming dealerships.

Somehow, taking risks in groups makes us more, not less, likely to make dumb gambles that give us some remote hope of maintaining the status quo. We look around at all the other people strapped into their seats and say, "Never mind the smell of smoke." While you'd hope that adding more people would make it more likely that someone would state the obvious, in truth, it often just gives our play-acting a larger and more convincing cast.

If I'd been sitting alone in my apartment, it would have been hard to convince myself that I was on the right track. But as long as I had someone else there who was willing to say that we might get married someday, I had just enough reason for optimism to keep on doing what I was doing.

THE THREE PATHS

Ultimately, the inevitable crisis killed Solyndra, and it took with it more taxpayer money than it had to because government officials could not bring themselves to admit it was over. Ultimately, my inevitable crisis saved me. I fled our failed relationship and went to Washington, DC, where I got a job with *The Atlantic*. A month later, I met the man who is now my husband.

With GM, the case is more complicated.

After the government bailout and bankruptcy, GM made a lot of changes. The workforce was cut, the dealer network streamlined, the retiree benefits pared back. Some brands were shuttered. The company emerged from bankruptcy a leaner, tighter operation, and most importantly, it no longer had that thousands-of-dollars-per-car cost disadvantage. That meant it could raise the quality of its cars to be competitive with what Japanese and German manufacturers were doing.

But it is far from clear that this is enough. By the time GM declared bankruptcy, the firm had spent the better part of several decades steadily but implacably grinding down the value of its brand with low-quality products. The bailout was not the first drive for

quality the company had made; there had been a similar push earlier in the decade, which showed results in places like the J.D. Power
survey. But their market share just kept sliding.

A successful car company, notes James Schrager, has one job: "to
build cars people will pay full price for." To do that, the company
can do one of two things: build "really, really, exciting cars," or
build "really, really, mundane reliable cars." GM, he says, has done
neither; instead, they've oscillated.

"That second strategy takes a long time to build—Japan was in
the trenches with that strategy for well over a decade," he says. "By
the time they turned around their quality in mid-2000, it was too
late."

The crisis gave GM a chance to finally do the kind of radical
transformation that many people had been urging. And for all the
carping, they did everything that a think-tank wonk could name.
Conservatives may complain that the government stiffed bond-
holders in favor of union retirees, but the company emerged from
bankruptcy with a leaner cost structure that allowed them to invest
in higher-quality components and better insulation or a quieter
ride.

And yet, the company's global and domestic market shares have
continued to slide; they now stand at the lowest level in decades.[27]
Worse, GM is still struggling to sell those cars at full price. They
have to use a lot of "cash on the hood"—incentives and discounts—
to keep their market share even as high as it is.[28]

There is a point beyond which even radical transformation will
not save you. GM may not have passed that point yet; Schrager says
that big firms like GM are like floating fortresses, hard to turn but
even harder to destroy. But even if they haven't passed the point of
no return, they've certainly flirted with it.

Two thousand nine may still end up being the best thing that
ever happened to the company. But it would have been better if

they'd admitted they had a problem sooner. As we'll see in the next chapter, it is possible to turn around sooner, if you pay attention to outside information. The problem is that we have a bad tendency to invest ourselves emotionally in our mistakes and cling to them until it is too late.

6 ADMITTING YOU HAVE A PROBLEM

*What Gamblers Anonymous
Could Have Taught Dan Rather*

Journalists almost all share two dreams in common. One is covering a story that might actually get you shot. The other is getting a scoop that will cause a sitting president to lose his job. These are the kinds of stories that sell memoirs and nudge other journalists into envious silence as you sit down at their table.

As a foreign correspondent in Vietnam, Dan Rather had already fulfilled that first dream. When he sat down in front of the camera on September 8, 2004, he must have wondered if he wasn't on the brink of achieving the second, joining a superelite group that so far contained only one famous team, made up of Bob Woodward and Carl Bernstein. With the 2004 election season in full swing, President Bush was locked in a neck-and-neck race with the twice-decorated senator John Kerry. Now CBS was preparing to break a tremendous story: documents showing that President Bush had gone AWOL during his Vietnam-era service in the Texas Air National Guard.

This was not a new story. There had been rumors about it for years, and scattered reports of favoritism had already made it into the newspapers. But the stories were hard to pin down. Memories had faded after thirty years, and lots of people had died in the interim. Only now *60 Minutes* had obtained proof that didn't depend on the flighty memories of people with a rooting interest in the upcoming election. They had memos from the private files of Bush's commanding officer, the late Jerry Killian, that seemed to prove the worst. In sharp contrast to his clean (some said "well-scrubbed") official record, the memos showed Bush disobeying Killian's direct order to take his flight physical. Later, they recorded pressure from higher-ups to let this infraction slide.

At best the Killian memos indicated clear special treatment for the son of a former congressman; at worst, they suggested that the president of the United States had not only dodged the draft by joining the National Guard, he had refused to fulfill even its minimal duty requirements. Narrated in Dan Rather's most somber tones, the broadcast seemed to make a clear, overwhelming case that the president had been severely derelict in his duties.

At 9:30 p.m. that evening, about half an hour after the broadcast finished, *CBS News* posted the supporting documents on their website. The effect of the show was rather electric. Colleagues at CBS sent congratulatory e-mails heaping lavish praise on producer Mary Mapes, a well-regarded investigative journalist who had recently broken the ghastly photos of Iraqi prisoners being tortured at Abu Ghraib in Iraq.

Conservative viewers reacted with predictably outraged disbelief. "If the *New York Times* would dig into terrorism as deeply as the president's service record," pouted one commenter on Free Republic, a right-wing message board, "they'd have pinpointed Osama by now."

"Documents from a dead man," snorted another. "How convenient."

Quickly, the discussion began to focus on the documents themselves, not the news media that had aired them. It was the sort of quibbling you'd expect from political partisans looking for a way to discredit explosive new information that hurt their candidate. Was the military terminology quite right? Would a commanding officer really write such a memo to his file? At comment number 47, the thread took another turn. "Buckhead" pointed out some striking anomalies:

> *Every single one of these memos to file is in a proportion-
> ally spaced font, probably Palatino or Times New Roman.*
>
> *In 1972 people used typewriters for this sort of thing,
> and typewriters used monospaced fonts.*
>
> *The use of proportionally spaced fonts did not come
> into common use for office memos until the introduction of
> laser printers, word processing software, and personal
> computers. They were not widespread until the mid to late
> 90's. Before then, you needed typesetting equipment, and
> that wasn't used for personal memos to file. Even the Wang
> systems that were dominant in the mid 80's used mono-
> spaced fonts.*
>
> *I am saying these documents are forgeries, run through
> a copier for 15 generations to make them look old.*
>
> *This **should** be pursued aggressively.*

Though a champagne glass was probably still clinking somewhere at CBS, this was the moment when Dan Rather's fortunes began to change. The *60 Minutes* story, as it turned out, wasn't going to
take down a sitting president. It was going to take out the journalists
who'd aired it.

A PROBLEM OF RECOGNITION

A fraud like this is every journalist's worst nightmare. We live in terror of making mistakes, and our greatest terror is exactly what happened here: getting a story wrong because of an obvious mistake
that *you can't even see that you're making*. It's one thing to fail because
you didn't work hard enough or do enough research; those mistakes
are bad, but they're at least fixable. It's another to botch a story because the right question never occurred to you. "To see what is in
front of your face," wrote George Orwell, "is a constant struggle."

In his 2008 book *Why We Make Mistakes*, Joseph Hallinan

dubbed this a "look but don't see" error. It isn't that journalists make more of these kinds of errors; it's that when we make them, someone usually points it out. In fact, this sort of error is nearly constant. Hallinan opens the book with a story from Burt Reynolds, who got himself into a little trouble when he told a loudmouth in a bar to stop harassing a couple at a nearby table. The loudmouth, who was rather powerfully built, swiveled his barstool to face Reynolds. And here's Reynolds describing what happened next, in an interview with *Playboy* magazine:

> I remember looking down and planting my right foot on this brass rail for leverage, and then I came around and caught him with a tremendous right to the side of the head. The punch made a ghastly sound and he just flew off the stool and landed on his back in the doorway, about 15 feet away. And it was while he was in mid-air that I saw . . . that he had no legs.

Somehow, Reynolds hadn't noticed the wheelchair folded up near the door.

You've probably had similar experiences yourself . . . okay, maybe a little less dramatic, but still. Ever spent half an hour hunting for the keys that were sitting right in the middle of your desk . . . or the glasses that were sitting on your head? How about the e-mail you accidentally sent to the whole company—how come you didn't notice all those names in the "to" field?

One of the keys to failing well is identifying the fact that you've failed, and correcting what you're doing. It sounds obvious, a bit trite, to state it that way. But it's not always so obvious when you're the one making the mistake. As we'll see, even when our failures are very obvious, we commonly resist recognizing them until it's far too late. There's a reason why the first step in any 12-step program is admitting you have a problem: it's utterly necessary, and also very hard to do.

INATTENTIONAL BLINDNESS

There is a famous psychology experiment that most undergraduate psych students are put through. You can watch it on the Web if you're interested. It consists mostly of a video containing people who are standing in a circle and passing a basketball around between them. Participants are asked to perform a simple task: to count the number of times that a basketball is passed between two people in the circle. Soon after it starts, the task gets a little more complicated, because the people start switching places as they pass. It's rather like watching the passing drills we used to run on my high school basketball team.

After the video is shown, participants are asked to submit their results, which usually roughly agree with each other. Then they're asked what else they noticed in the video.

Blank stare.

"The person in the gorilla suit?" the experimenter prods gently. "The one who came into the middle of the circle and beat on his chest before he walked out again?"

Puzzled frown.

"None of you?"

Disbelieving head shakes. And then the video is shown again, and what the *hell* is with that guy in the gorilla suit?

Psychologists call this phenomenon *inattentional blindness*: the inability to see even important and startling things when we are too focused on something else.[3] The effect is unbelievably powerful. Several years ago, I was showing this video to some friends at a party, and nope, no one had noticed the guy in the gorilla suit. But after we'd watched it a few times, one of my friends finally noticed the name of the professor who'd filmed it.

"Hey, that guy is my brother's graduate adviser!" he said. "I wonder . . . ?"

So we watched the video again. Sure enough, his brother is in the video, and he hadn't noticed. He'd been too busy looking at the basketballs, or the guy in the gorilla suit, to see that his own brother was in the video. And it's not like he's one of the Brady Bunch; he's only got one brother.[4]

It's easy to imagine how inattentional blindness can lead to big problems. But while there are obviously costs, it's also what makes Homo sapiens capable of incredible feats of concentration. After all, if it's really important to know how many basketballs were passed, then it's a very good thing not to get distracted by people in funny costumes. If a guy in a gorilla suit—or for that matter, an actual gorilla—burst onto the floor of air traffic control at JFK, I'd like to think that the guys at the radar screens wouldn't even look up. Though I'd hope someone else would call animal control.

The point is that the "problem" of inattentional blindness is not really the blindness; it's how we tell the difference between gorilla and basketball—between what's important, and what we can safely ignore. How do we keep our ability to focus, without committing so many "look but don't see" errors?

While I was preparing to write this book, I spent a lot of time reading about things going wrong, which is to say about people doing amazingly stupid things. The stories I read varied greatly—some were about individuals, some about groups and companies, and they ran from airplane crashes and lost hikers to bankrupt businesses and failed government programs. But while the particular mistakes were wildly different, in the bad stories, the tragic failures, one thing was almost always the same: the participants not only made obvious mistakes but *clung* to them.

It is a bit like watching a movie about a train going over a cliff. From a distance, you can clearly see the gaping canyon and the engine rocketing toward it, and you think that at any moment, the driver will stop the locomotive, but no matter how many times you play the video, he never does. Every time, the driver and any passengers go right over the edge without hesitation.

Most failures start with small mistakes—choosing a route that dead ends at a cliff. But most failures can be avoided if people simply recognize early on that they are on the wrong track. The tragedy is that so many of them could have ended there if the people who made the mistake had just been able to admit that, okay, that wasn't such a great idea. Instead, too often, they close their eyes to the yawning gap in front of them. Or worse, they open up the throttle and try to get up enough speed to jump the canyon.

The Killian memos offer up one of the best documented instances of a blindness we all experience from time to time. One reason that Mary Mapes and Dan Rather didn't see the obvious anachronisms is that they were looking too hard at other things.[5]

Yet the truly amazing thing about the story of Dan Rather and Mary Mapes is not that they let a hoax get on air; it's their dogged inability to recognize that they'd done so after it was pointed out to them. By the Friday after the show aired, questions about the authenticity of the documents had made the front page of the *Washington Post*.[6] Mapes called at least one writer on background to assure them that the story was 100 percent solid, with impeccable sources and experts to back up the authenticity of the documents.[7] That evening, Dan Rather issued the network's first public defense.

"My colleagues and I at *60 Minutes* made great efforts to authenticate these documents and to corroborate the story as best we could," he said. "Until someone shows me definitive proof that they are not [authentic], I don't see any reason to carry on a conversation with the professional rumor mill. I think the public is smart enough to see from whom some of this criticism is coming and draw judgments about what the motivations are." CBS echoed this point in a broadcast the next day, reiterating that they believed the documents were genuine—even though in the same broadcast they reported that one of their original sources, retired National Guard major general Bobby Hodges, now believed they were fake.[8]

As the media pursued the story, more questions emerged. One

memo mentions a commanding officer who at the time had already retired; another one had an old address that Bush had stopped using by the time the memos were supposedly written. Killian's son told ABC that he didn't believe his father had written them. "The only thing that can happen when you keep secret files like that are bad things," he said. "No officer in his right mind would write a memo like that." Killian's wife and former secretary piled on more doubts: Killian, she and the son both said, couldn't type.

One of the document examiners CBS had used to authenticate the memos told *Washington Post* reporter Howard Kurtz that he couldn't actually verify the documents because they were copies "far removed" from the originals, though he added, "I didn't see anything that would definitively tell me these are not authentic."[9] For the twelve days that they continued to defend the story, this would become the increasingly incredible CBS line: No one has proved they're fake.

The network's every utterance was joyously ripped apart by an army of conservative bloggers who apparently had any amount of time to spend researching arcane details of typewriter maintenance and 1970s-era military protocol. The CBS story was already in shreds, but the blogs and the media kept reloading the shotgun and blowing *the pieces* into smithereens. Even as conservative bloggers bitterly complained about the bias of the "mainstream media" (MSM), they became its unofficial research arm. Arguments would show up in a comment section somewhere, float upward to prominent blogs, and then appear as "further questions" in a print column the next day, backed up by consultations with old records and interviews with experts that the blogs lacked the resources to do.

The best argument for the authenticity of the documents had always been that they were aired by a major network that had vetted them with four document examiners. But as the story wore on, it became apparent that CBS hadn't vetted them quite as carefully as they'd initially implied. Some of the document examiners that CBS had consulted turned out to have raised concerns about authenticity before the show aired.

On September 16, the *Post* reported that the likely source of the documents was Bill Burkett, a retired Guardsman who was embroiled in some sort of interminable dispute with the National Guard over his benefits.[10] He also clearly had it in for George Bush; he had been pushing the story of the special treatment and scrubbed records for some time. Now, suddenly, memos proving his allegations had materialized from the private files of Lieutenant Colonel Killian—even though Killian's family had never heard of these private memos. Where had they been for thirty years?

CBS was undone by a medium that could do what the network couldn't: fail faster. Blogs have a much lower burden of proof than the mainstream media, but the back-and-forth of the medium ruthlessly pummels weak evidence, and retractions tend to be fast and common. Mistakes in the blogosphere aren't reputation killing— which makes retractions easier to issue. A theory could be floated in the far reaches of conservative or liberal cyberspace, where no one's reputation was on the line, and usually, that's where it would die. If it looked plausible, it would be picked up by bigger-name political bloggers, and if a number of them thought it looked plausible, it would gain enough attention to attract criticism from their counterparts across the ideological aisle. The collective result of all this "fast failing" was both more accurate, and much speedier, than the internal procedures of CBS, which depended on a few powerful people getting it right the first time.

For twelve excruciating days, CBS denied that it had ignored the advice of its own document examiners. It offered surprisingly weak defenses: document examination was not a hard science, and anyway, the White House hadn't denied that the documents were real! They also dug up a lone expert, a former typewriter repairman, who thought that the documents might have been produced on the IBM Selectric Composer, a typesetting machine that looked a lot like a typewriter, but with more dials and add-ons. Unmentioned was the fact that the IBM Selectric Composer cost at least as much as a good used car, and required considerable training and skill to operate.[11] It was normally used to lay out print publications, not to write memos to file in National Guard offices.

Why couldn't CBS see what everyone else saw? Why were they grasping at such tenuous straws—not merely grasping at them, but triumphantly waving them, as if they'd found a trophy? The best possible case—the one that CBS was pushing a week after the broadcast—was that in 1973, Lieutenant Colonel Killian had somehow gotten his hands on a fantastically expensive typesetting machine, and spent a great deal of time fiddling with it, all so that he could produce a document that would, coincidentally, look exactly like what you'd get if you typed up the same documents in Microsoft Word. Even if you conceded that this was a *possible* explanation, how could anyone insist that it was *likely*?

BENDING THE MAP

In *Deep Survival*, a stunning book about how people survive in extreme terrain, Laurence Gonzales writes about a phenomenon known in orienteering as "bending the map."[12] It's summed up with a pithy quote from Edward Cornell: "Whenever you start looking at your map and saying something like, 'Well, that lake could have dried up' or, 'That boulder could have moved,' a red light should go on. You're trying to make reality conform to your expectations rather than seeing what's there." Bending the map is akin to normative error—you stop paying attention to good process because you've to focused on other things.

Bending the map often turns a potentially dangerous situation—"I don't know where I am"—into a disaster: "I don't know where I am, and I don't know that I don't know where I am." Delaying the recognition that you're lost means you put more distance between yourself and the trail. It makes it harder to backtrack to a safe place. By the time the evidence that you're lost becomes overwhelming, it's a crisis—dark is coming, you have no shelter, and no idea where you are. As Gonzales points out, this makes you more likely to overreact: panic instead of anxiety, terror instead of worry. "Since most people aren't conscious of the process, there's no way to reflect on what's happening," says Gonzales. "All you know is that it feels as if you're going mad."

This is one of the reasons why many of us choose not to wander around in the woods. And yet, we can get just as dangerously lost in civilization.

After the Space Shuttle *Challenger* exploded, President Reagan appointed a special commission to investigate, including the Nobel Prize–winning physicist Richard Feynman. Feynman became suspicious of the shuttle's O-rings, which are basically what they sound like: flexible O-shaped tubes. It's difficult to engineer joints to be perfectly airtight, particularly under the stresses the Space Shuttle takes. So the shuttle used these flexible rings to ensure that connections formed a perfect seal.

But the morning of the Space Shuttle launch had been unusually cold, and Feynman believed that this had caused the O-rings to lose some of their elasticity. He famously demonstrated this thesis during a televised hearing by dropping an O-ring into ice water and showing that after it was removed, it was no longer as flexible as it was supposed to be. Congress eventually agreed that indeed, one of the O-rings had failed, allowing highly pressurized gasses to escape the joint. The heat and pressure ripped the solid rocket booster off the shuttle and ruptured the external tank. At the speeds the *Challenger* was traveling, aerodynamic forces did the rest.

It turned out that NASA had been warned of the danger before the launch. Design problems with these joints had been reported as far back as 1977, and by 1985, Morton-Thiokol, the firm that had designed the shuttle, was in the process of reengineering the connections to make them safer—but NASA had not grounded the shuttle, even though earlier flights had shown unexpected "blowby" of gases, and erosion of the O-rings. The evening before the *Challenger* launched, engineers from Morton-Thiokol expressed concerns about how the old design would hold up in the unusually cold weather (31 degrees) forecast for the next day, and suggested rescheduling.[13] George Hardy, the manager of the solid rocket booster project, told them "I am appalled. I am appalled by your recommendation."

"My God, Thiokol," said another engineer, "when do you want me to launch—next April?" The shuttle launch had already been delayed almost a week. Each delay was massively expensive, and of course, it didn't look good.

It's understandable that NASA would be upset. What is less understandable is why they chose to launch anyway. Objectively, these are crazy responses—if the O-rings wouldn't function in the cold, they wouldn't function, whether or not the launch had already been delayed. Yelling at the scientist who brings the bad news, or the engineers, wouldn't make it any safer.

In Feynman's scathing appendix to the report, he describes the extent to which NASA was bending their own "map"—the standards they should have set for determining whether a launch was safe. Looking at the history of failures in the solid rocket boosters, Feynman estimated the probability of such a failure at around one in fifty.[14] And yet NASA management insisted that the figure was much lower. "They point out that these figures are for unmanned rockets, but since the Shuttle is a manned vehicle 'the probability of mission success is necessarily very close to 1.0.'"

"It is not very clear," observed Feynman, "what this phrase means. Does it mean it is close to 1 or that it ought to be close to 1?" He went on to note that NASA's engineers put the probability of failure much higher than management did—at the same 1 in 50 number that Feynman had hit on.

So why was management so far off? What management had done was to upend the normal conventions for evaluating safety.

The blowby and O-ring erosion were unexpected. That should have been a warning that something was wrong; the design was not working as planned. Instead, incredibly, NASA's managers took it as evidence that everything was okay: the problems with the O-rings must not be serious, because nothing bad had happened yet. When the engineers at Morton-Thiokol warned that the O-rings were not designed to work under such cold conditions, NASA management refused to consider further delaying the launch unless Morton-Thiokol could prove that something bad would happen. Of course, there was no way to conclusively prove that the O-rings were dangerous except by doing what NASA did: launching the Space Shuttle.

THE CONFIRMATION BIAS

In the days before the broadcast aired on *60 Minutes*, and immediately after, the legal department repeatedly asked the producers to verify the authenticity of the documents. In e-mails, Mapes starts off fairly confident that they are real. And the e-mails keep getting more confident, though there's no new information to account for her growing certainty.

When new information did come in, it was not so positive: several of the document examiners expressed doubts or said they couldn't authenticate. During this period, Mapes became more confident still. What was happening? It's impossible to document her thought process exactly (in part because Mapes kept resolutely insisting it was a good story for years after everyone else had given up), but what's clear is that she was talking herself into believing in the documents—focusing on the reasons to believe them, and ignoring that pesky gorilla in the room.[15]

Most investigations start this way: you form a theory, and then you test your theory against the facts. It's the heart of the scientific method that you probably learned about in seventh grade, and it's also the heart of investigative journalism. Someone comes to you with a potential story. They give you a piece of information that sounds plausible. Then you check it out. Is it consistent with known facts? Do experts think it is credible? But there's a danger in forming a theory: you get invested in it, and then you start to look for reasons why it may be true, rather than evidence that it might be false.

Confirmation bias is not a sign of bad character; we do it even when we have no particular reason to care about the outcome. Of course, when we do have emotional reasons to care, this tendency is exacerbated, as anyone who has ever stayed up late arguing with a spouse, or a political opponent, can attest. But even without that emotional stimulus, people systematically err on the side of looking for confirming evidence for almost any theory they develop. Professor Nicholas Epley, who teaches behavioral science at the Booth School of Business, calls this "recruiting evidence."[16] Once you've got a theory about something, you're bound to notice stray facts that otherwise would have slipped your attention. Once you've got enough recruits, they start reinforcing each other, until you hardly notice the big hole in your left flank.

By the time conservatives kicked up a fuss about the documents, Mary Mapes had been arguing for their veracity for so long that she didn't know how to stop. Like those NASA managers, she began demanding that others prove a negative, rather than accepting her own responsibility to be certain they were real. She had bent the journalistic map so far that she was now reading it upside down.

FROM AN ERROR IN JUDGMENT TO A LAPSE IN ETHICS

Journalism's "map"—our set of commonly understood rules about how to conduct ourselves when reporting—is extremely detailed, covering everything from how to interact with sources (buying them a cup of coffee is okay; buying them a car is not) to the standards of evidence for printing explosive claims. As with any ethical code, there are always disagreements about gray areas, but these norms exert the same sort of moral force that the Hippocratic oath does for surgeons. They are strong enough that a single major normative error, such as plagiarizing or making up a quote, is generally enough to ensure that you will never work in journalism again.

When Dan Rather defended the Killian documents on the grounds that no one had conclusively proved they were fake, he violated those standards—in fact, as Mark Twain once remarked of James Fenimore Cooper, "he flung them down and danced upon them." No sane journalist thinks that it's okay to publish a probable fake as long as no one can 100 percent prove it to be false. We understand that the burden of proof is on us to authenticate documents as best we can—and to retract if we're proved wrong. I doubt that Dan Rather would disagree with any of this.

Yet even as he wandered out ever further beyond the pale, he spoke as if he stood on the high moral ground. "With respect: answer the questions," he thundered at the president on September 14,[17] six days after the initial broadcast. By refusing to admit that the documents might be fraudulent—and worse, by going on the attack—the CBS team took an error in judgment and converted it into a normative error that called into question whether they could be trusted to carry out the duties of their profession.

The longer and more stridently they delayed acknowledging their mistake, the worse Mapes and Rather made things. And yet they kept bending the map—and dragging the whole network off course with them. It was only on September 16, more than a week after the original story aired, that *CBS News* president Andrew Heyward conceded there were "unresolved issues" with the documents, and pledged to investigate.[18] Four days later Dan Rather finally faced the camera with basset-hound eyes and said "The failure of *CBS News* to . . . properly scrutinize the documents and their source led to our airing the documents when we should not have done so. It was a mistake. *CBS News* deeply regrets it. Also, I want to say personally and directly: I'm sorry." He added, "This was an error made in good faith as we tried to carry on the *CBS News* tradition of asking tough questions and investigating reports. But it was a mistake."

It was too little, too late. In November, Dan Rather announced that he was stepping down as news anchor, a position he'd occupied for twenty-three years.[19] He got off lightly compared with the others involved. After the network's internal investigation issued its report in January, Mary Mapes was fired, along with several other staffers.[20]

Conservative bloggers giddily claimed the scalps. While the bloggers were right that they had brought down a star of the "MSM," they were wrong about why. They thought they'd won because they'd exposed the bias and slipshod work of a network star. But Dan Rather and his colleagues didn't lose their jobs because they'd been taken in by a hoaxster; they lost their jobs because they waited too long to recognize what had happened. As I was writing this book, NPR's Ira Glass had to admit he'd been taken in by a series of his about Apple's operation in China. Glass is still on the air because of what he did next—not only admitted he was wrong, but did a special one-hour episode explaining exactly what mistakes he'd made.[21]

I don't think Dan Rather and Mary Mapes were engaged in a conspiracy, deliberate or otherwise, but conservatives may be right that their political biases played a big role in this story—only not in the way that they think. It's no secret that both Rather and Mapes are strong liberals who did not like George Bush. This undoubtedly made them more prone to believe documents showing that George Bush had done something wrong—just as it made conservatives more determined to show that he hadn't.

Those biases aren't entirely a bad thing. A while back, a friend in the securities industry asked me about the coverage of the financial crisis. A lot of things, he pointed out, are reported only once, and then they become the basis of other reporters' stories. How, he asked, do we prevent wrong "facts" or bias from entering into the data stream and corrupting our understanding of what happened?

I had two answers, neither of them perfectly satisfactory. The first is that journalists are competitive, and overturning, say, Andrew Ross Sorkin's account of an important meeting is a pretty major journalistic coup. The second is that this is actually what ideological journalism is good for: when facts appear that contradict people's worldviews, partisans frequently go out and exhaustively investigate those facts to see if they can be in any way mitigated or disproved.

Take an example from the UCLA political scientist Tim Groseclose, author of *Left Turn: How Liberal Media Bias Distorts the American Mind.*[22] Groseclose recounts his experience with a distorted *L.A. Times* article that made it seem as if the underrepresentation of blacks at UCLA after the passage of Proposition 209 (which banned affirmative action at state schools) was much more dramatic than it actually was. Here's how that article started out:[23]

> This fall 4,852 freshmen are expected to enroll at UCLA, but only 96, or 2 percent, are African American—the lowest figure in decades and a growing concern at the Westwood campus.
>
> For several years, students, professors and administrators at UCLA have watched with discouragement as the numbers of black students declined. But the new figures, released this week, have . . . prompted school leaders to declare the situation a crisis.
>
> UCLA—which . . . is in a county that is 9.8 percent African American—now has a lower percentage of black freshmen than either crosstown rival USC or UC Berkeley, the school often considered its top competitor within the UC system.

All this information was true—but as Groseclose noted, incomplete. UCLA was getting a lot of minority transfer students, so that overall minority enrollment had actually increased, while changes in NCAA rules, which tightened up the academic requirements for student athletes, had sent enrollment of minority athletes, who generally come in as freshmen, tumbling.

While it's undoubtedly true that some reporters consciously repress facts that threaten their prior ideological beliefs, I don't think that's really the issue in most cases. What bias does—in science, in media, in any situation where information is gathered—is affect what questions you ask. Of course, I don't *know for a fact* that the author of that article thinks affirmative action is swell, and Prop 209 was a bad idea, but one gets the strong feeling from the article that this is indeed the case.

If she had been a supporter of Prop 209, she would have looked harder for evidence that things might not be all that dire. And as Groseclose demonstrates in his book, she would have found it.

It's unlikely that she omitted those facts deliberately. Unless you know a hell of a lot about the California public college system, there is no particular reason why you should ask yourself whether almost half of UCLA undergraduates are transfers rather than incoming freshmen, or whether the NCAA had changed its rules about academic standards for athletes in a way that reduced the number of African American athletes UCLA could admit.

Confirmation bias is a personal weakness: it causes us to support theories that aren't true, because we don't ask the right questions. It manifests itself most egregiously when we are most strongly invested. But paradoxically, that same ideological fervor can be a systemic strength. It means that there is always someone who is eager and determined to ask the questions that don't occur to the rest of us.

We all have an instinctive tendency to accentuate the positive, especially when the alternative is threatening. The key to overcoming this natural tendency is to accept information from outside sources—even, maybe, outside sources who hate you. They're the only ones who can break through all the motivated reasoning, the cognitive ruts that are all too easy to get into when you're among a large group of like-minded people. One reason that Ira Glass may have responded so quickly and forthrightly is that his error was exposed by another NPR journalist. Rather and Mapes were contending with conservative bloggers, who were easily dismissed as ideologically motivated.

The secret to catching your mistakes quickly is simple: *treat outside information as if it were inside information*. When someone tells you you're off track, don't look for reasons why they may be wrong; listen for reasons why they might be right.

7 GETTING UNSTUCK

Adopting the Way of the Shark

The Buffalo Employment and Training Center (BETC) is what you do with a shirt factory when no one wants to make shirts in your city anymore. It sits on a rather dismal stretch across from another abandoned factory, the locally semifamous Trico No. 1, which housed the company that invented the windshield wiper until it decamped for Mexico in the late 1990s. The training center is New York State's attempt to provide comprehensive social services for the area's many, many job seekers. In one building you can find everything from a Mature Jobseeker's Workshop, to help accessing your veteran's benefits. It's nothing like the grim, disinfectant-sopped concrete mausoleums that people seeking government jobs must endure downstate; indeed, it's almost charming. If you're going to be unemployed, this is the place you'd like to go to look for a job, except for one small problem: there aren't any.[1]

The city's unemployment rate of a little over 8 percent actually isn't all that bad; it's close to the national average. But that statistic is deceptive. Buffalo hasn't been hit too hard by the recession only because it never participated in the prosperity that preceded it. Between 2002 and 2011, Manhattan added 80,000 net jobs—not great, but not bad considering the financial capital of America had just weathered the worst financial crisis in recent history. Over the same time period, Erie County, where Buffalo sits, added . . . 274.[2] The only reason Buffalo's unemployment rate isn't higher is that the region has been losing population for decades.[3]

I first went to the BETC in 2006, when I was doing research for an article on upstate New York's economy. At the time, the downstate

153

was booming, flush with cash from all those mortgage-backed securities that shouldn't have been sold, and I was filled with oceanic pity for the deplorable condition of western New York's economy. It turns out I was just getting a preview of what an increasing number of Americans face today. The people I met in Buffalo had a very modest set of wants that were somehow hopelessly optimistic.

Edward Bennett, a crisply pressed man in his forties, had started out as a salesman at Nabisco, the sort of job that brought generations into the middle class. "The man who had the job before me was there for thirty-two years," he told me with a shy smile. "I thought, 'I'm going to retire from this place.'" Eight and a half years later he was laid off when Kraft bought the company, an event that he clearly still found difficult to talk about. "It was the worst moment of my life," he said simply, and stopped.

Each of Bennett's subsequent jobs was like a stair-step down: worse-paid, less secure. The center helped him find a job as a manager at an Alamo rent-a-car, then he switched to part-time work so he could help take care of the kids while his wife, a nurse, became the family's main breadwinner. (Health care and the government are the only two industries in Buffalo that still offer the kind of steady, lifetime employment that used to be nearly ubiquitous.) After that, there was a stint at FedEx—"getting paid to exercise," he called it, with what looked like genuine delight—until he tore his rotator cuff and had to quit. His list of demands was pretty small at this point; mostly, he wanted something that he could stick at for a while without being catapulted back onto the job market by an injury or a corporate downsizing.

I talked to another man, a thirty-four-year-old who'd climbed to the position of manager at a fast-food place before he lost his job. He was hoping to find a similar job with a different owner, but of course, he was willing to go down to assistant manager, or even lower, to start out. "I'm very loyal to the Burger King franchise" he told me. "But I'm definitely willing to consider other opportunities." Such as? "Maybe fast casual?" he said uncertainly.

The stories were all some variation of these two. These painfully well-pressed people were straining to be upbeat in the face of an economy that had been in near-continuous decline since the opening of the St. Lawrence Seaway in 1959 scuppered the last of the barge traffic on the Erie Canal. The jobs they'd had, and hoped to have again, were not glamorous, nor spectacularly well paid. It was the everyday, tedious work that people used to bitch about—until it disappeared.

Unlike many of the crises we've been talking about, when you get fired or lose your job it isn't hard to recognize that something has gone wrong. But that still leaves the question of what to do next. How you answer this question matters a lot. The people who keep moving—sometimes literally—may find that a job loss is "the best thing that ever happened." The people who get stuck will experience some of the worst misery that a rich democracy has to offer.

So what differentiates the two? What determines who will turn the sour lemons of a job loss into the tasty lemonade of a new career opportunity?

Losing a job can shake you out of a rut. It can force you to try things that you never would have dared to do. It can be the catalyst for a new, better life. But it can also be the worst thing that ever happened to you—and sometimes, as you'll see, it can be both. Which one it becomes depends somewhat on luck, but also on what we do about unemployment. By "we" I mean people who are unemployed. But by "we" I also mean the friends, family, and fellow citizens of people who have lost jobs.

Some people get stuck and then, after a period of soul-searching, manage to unstick themselves—and discover that the process of finding an escape has equipped them to do things they lacked the skill, the knowledge, or the courage to do before. The good news is that there actually are things you can do to increase the chances that you will get unstuck. They are not foolproof (remember, there are no guarantees). But they considerably lengthen the odds in your favor.

Do the right things, and you have a good shot at turning a lost job into an opportunity. Do the wrong things, and there's a big risk of turning a failure into disaster.

To see why, let me tell you about the worst date of my life.

THE WORST THING THAT EVER HAPPENED TO ME

It was a spring evening in 2003, and the date started out well enough. He was a private equity associate who I'd been seeing for five months, and he'd planned one of those maybe-a-little-too-preciously-only-in-New-York evenings: dinner at a fancy vegetarian restaurant, and then the last performance of a successful small-theater show that was moving to Broadway. I was wearing my one really nice-looking spring dress. He held the car door for me. Dinner was excellent, the theater was petite and worn at the edges and thoroughly charming. The people sitting next to us smiled as we sat down. Then the curtain rose, and I was in hell.

He hadn't mentioned anything about the show except that it was called *Avenue Q*, and "it has puppets." This was accurate enough, as far as it went. He just hadn't told me that they were unemployed loser puppets who spent most of the show trying to find a way to make money. This was a heck of a coincidence, because at the time, I too was an unemployed loser with an empty bank account and very little in the way of job prospects—even though I had, on paper, done (almost) everything right.

I'd gotten an MBA from the University of Chicago, one of the top ten programs in the world. I tell you this not to impress you with my splendid qualifications, since my admission was a bit of luck. But a Chicago MBA was supposed to be the next best thing to a license to print money. It was a solid-gold credential that in theory should have guaranteed me a good job upon graduation.

I was a victim of the dot-com bust, but also a victim of my own stupidity—like one of those ancient Mayan ballplayers who competed to become the next human sacrifice. First, while in my first year of business school, I decided to pursue a summer internship at Merrill Lynch. And not just in any department, but in their technology investment banking group even though I had watched the legendary March 2000 NASDAQ crash from the lobby of the Merrill Lynch training center, where I was supposed to be undergoing orientation.

Joining an investment-banking firm was stupid for other reasons, most notably that I was almost nothing like any investment banker I had ever met, including the ones at Merrill Lynch. Somehow I thought that would make it an interesting adventure. What it actually felt like was interning with a rather formal, fussy baboon troop. They seemed equally puzzled by me. In earlier years, I might have passed unnoticed—at the height of the dot-com bubble, when IPOs were turning over at the rate of airport barstools, many banks hired almost anyone who could breathe and carry a briefcase. But the dot-com bubble was officially over. I spent my summer sitting in a well-upholstered office until 11 p.m. every night, not exactly to pretend that I was working—they must have known that they didn't have any work to give me—but to demonstrate that I would have been willing to work late if there was, you know, some work. Mostly I caught up on my magazine reading and debated with my officemate, a white-blond Russian national who saw nothing odd about comparing the American distaste for racist jokes with the KGB's habit of arresting people who joked about Khrushchev in public.

To no one's surprise, Merrill Lynch did not extend me an offer to join the firm full-time.

Having learned my lesson, I promptly turned around and . . . accepted a job with a technology-focused management consulting firm. Even to me, this now seems incredible, and I am unable to recall the thought process that went into that decision. I'd worked in technology before I went to school, so those jobs were easiest to get, but still, did I really believe it when they assured me that the dot-com bust wouldn't affect them because there would be, y'know, merger work, and restructurings, and that sort of thing?

I guess I must have. I certainly wanted to believe them.

I accepted the job in February, with an October start date. In April they called and explained that there had been a little hitch. Business was slow—no reason to worry, of course, just a bit less brisk than they'd anticipated, so they were pushing our start dates back a few months. I canceled a trip to Spain and asked my parents if I could move back in to their spare bedroom for a few months. I spent the summer at their co-op on the Upper West Side of Manhattan, teaching *Princeton Review* prep courses and waiting. Then on September 11, some lunatics drove planes into the twin towers. My father, who ran a trade association for the heavy construction industry, was spending sixteen-hour days at the site helping to coordinate the massive construction operations, and soon I was too.

I spent nearly a year there, doing administrative work in one of the trailers. It was not glamorous or notably important, and though I am still very glad I did it, for all the obvious reasons, it was not good for my career. A few months after 9/11, the consulting firm called to tell me that they wouldn't, after all, be able to start my associate class the following February, or for that matter, ever. I should have started looking for a new position immediately, but I was working sixteen-hour days at Ground Zero, and figured I could always look for a job later.

That turned out to be a hideous mistake. Recruiting for second-year MBA students starts in early fall, so by the time they called us to tell us we didn't have jobs, we were already in competition with the class of 2002. A year before, cuddled in the warm womb of the career department at the University of Chicago's graduate school of business, job offers had come virtually effortlessly. You went to some events, had a few interviews, and then your only problem was deciding among multiple offers. Now phone calls to those same employers went unreturned. I sent résumés the way one knocks wood in a crisis—probably won't help, but you want to feel you've done everything possible. I could have saved the fortune I spent on thirty-two-pound ecru résumé paper. They disappeared into the void.

I did all the things they told us to at the career office: arranged informational interviews, tapped my personal network, sent out those hundreds of résumés. None of it did any good. My personal contacts—aside from a bunch of freshly graduated MBAs who had their own problems—were all in my old business, installing computer networks for banks. Banking and the tech industry had both been pummeled into near-unconsciousness by the dot-com crash, so they were able to offer a great deal of sympathy, but no job leads.

Now, two years later, I was still struggling to find full-time work. Later, reporting on the Great Recession, I basically confirmed what I suspected at the time: prospective employers were tossing my résumé because they figured that if I didn't have a job, there must be something wrong with me. This is a sort of crazy belief in a recession—they had to know that lots of people, particularly people fresh out of school, were getting laid off through no fault of their own. But this was the brutal calculus of a high unemployment rate. During a recession, the few employers with jobs to offer are deluged with candidates, more than enough of whom are qualified for a given position. They are looking for reasons to get rid of candidates, not reasons to include them. You may recall the miniscandal that erupted in 2010, when CNNMoney.com reported how many employers had posted job ads stating that they wouldn't even consider someone who was out of work.[4] The public outcry that followed largely eliminated those sorts of ads. But all that did was stop employers from announcing their intentions. Employment data show that they went right on tossing out those résumés.[5]

The truth is this wasn't entirely irrational. Layoffs do tend to target the deadwood that departments have been carrying for a while. Not perfectly, of course, but somewhat. So while most unemployed people are not screwups, in a recession, a disproportionate number of screwups end up unemployed. For that reason, I'm pretty sure that when I was unemployed, hiring managers were looking at my résumé and thinking, why take the chance? The class of 2002 is full of MBAs who haven't yet been laid off.

I was getting a field demonstration of what economists call "employment scarring."[6] People who have had a bout of unemployment suffer detectable long-term effects in their career path: they are more likely to have another spell of unemployment in the future, and their incomes are lower than those of their peers who never lost a job. These effects can be large, and they seem to be permanent; one study of Stanford MBAs showed that classes that graduated into a down market still had lower average wages twenty years later.

The more troubling fact is that people actually seem to lose job skills as unemployment wears on. One study of Swedish adults found that a year of unemployment caused a 5 percent decline in basic skills.[7] And these skills were *really* basic—they were looking at scores on reading and math tests. There's good reason to think that higher-level skills decline even faster, especially in fast-changing industries: new technologies and procedures are adopted, your knowledge of the competitive landscape atrophies, and valuable personal connections fray as people switch firms, leave the industry, or retire.

But the decline in basic reading and math skills suggests something even darker: the crippling effect that depression can have on the unemployed, particularly the long-term unemployed.

Sitting in the darkened theater, as everyone else laughed at the unemployed puppets, I could feel the flush burning its way up the back of my neck. Was the choice of show deliberate? Was he trying to tell me that he was tired of buying all my meals? As Act I wore on, I couldn't help comparing myself—unfavorably—to the loser puppets. At least the puppets had their own apartments, even if they were way out on "Avenue Q"; *they* weren't still living with their parents at the age of thirty. They were fresh out of college, when you are supposed to get into this sort of scrape, and they were still doing better than I'd managed.

Your life has reached a pretty bad pass when you are wondering why the singing puppets seem to be so much more competent than you are. I was making a little money doing IT consulting for a few small businesses, including my dad's firm. But though that amount was growing, it was not enough money to live on. Indeed, it was just a little more than I needed to make $1,000 worth of payments every month on my business school loans. It was beginning to seem increasingly plausible that I had somehow inadvertently but permanently ruined my life.

WHY UNEMPLOYMENT IS THE PITS

Economic reporting tends to focus on gross domestic product. Politicians on the stump promise economic growth, and political models use it to predict who will win those elections. "Two quarters of declining GDP" is the common shorthand definition of a recession. GDP is also almost the only way we measure our economic performance against other nations; you'll often see commentators compare our national income with that of other nations as if America were but one good bonus away from really wowing the neighbors with new backyard landscaping and an in-ground pool.

But the point of economic activity is not to lead the international league tables; it is to make the citizenry prosperous and happy. And for the lived experience of the economy, GDP is nowhere near as important as employment. In fact, I'd go so far as to say that *nothing* is as important as employment. It's a double blow, psychological and economic. One that we seem remarkably unable to absorb.

One of the most surprising findings of modern psychological research is how thoroughly we habituate to even the worst events. The best and worst things that can happen to you don't make that much difference in the long run: lottery winners aren't that much happier than they were before their lives changed (in part because they frequently blow the money and end up bankrupt), and quadriplegics aren't noticeably less so. The Harvard psychology professor Daniel Gilbert says "People overestimate the negative emotional consequences of a wide variety of negative events"—they "mispredict and then misremember what they predicted."[8]

The striking exception to this rule is unemployment. A study from London's Centre for Economic Performance measured the effect on life satisfaction of six different events: layoff, unemployment, marriage, birth of a child, divorce, and the death of a spouse. All these events had immediate effects on life satisfaction, mostly in the direction you'd expect: people's satisfaction jumped in response to marriage, plummeted when their spouse died.[9] But five years later, people had mostly adapted; their happiness levels returned to about where they were before. (In fact, there are somewhat troubling charts showing that five years after they've lost a spouse, people are somewhat happier than they were when their better half was alive.)

Not so with unemployment. Life satisfaction plummeted as you'd expect—lower than everyone except widows and widowers. But while the bereaved eventually dealt with their grief and moved on, the unemployed didn't. Even five years in, they were still about as miserable as they'd been in that first year. Other research shows the same result. We may adapt to losing the use of our legs, but not the use of our time cards.

And that's in Europe, with its generous unemployment benefits, extended vacations, and fewer hours worked. What about America, where almost 80 percent of the working age population is in the labor force, and the average worker spends the majority of his waking hours either at work or commuting? If you meet someone at a party in Europe, they ask where you're from. If you meet someone at a party in America, what's the first thing they ask you? "So, what do you do?"

We have no hereditary aristocracy, no centuries-long connection to the same soil. What we have is our jobs, and to the rest of the world, in large part, our jobs are who we are. When we lose them, we're cast adrift.

It is very difficult to communicate the progressive corrosion of long-term unemployment to someone who has not endured it. If you have been through it, you never forget it, but until you have, you will have difficulty imagining the strain. People tend to think of it mostly in terms of being broke, and of course, unemployed people tend to worry about money a lot. But while it is bad to worry about how you are going to pay the bills this month, it is worse to worry about what your future will look like. Will you be forced to accept work that isn't as enjoyable as your last job? Will your pay enable you to make the mortgage? Will your job be less prestigious than the one you left, and will there be opportunities for advancement? Have you peaked at twenty-five, or thirty-five, or forty-five? Are you, in short, a failure?

Like most unemployed people, I found myself withdrawing from social relationships as time wore on.[10] It wasn't just that I didn't have the money to go out (which I didn't); the bigger problem was that I found it increasingly painful to hang out with people who had jobs. Everyone else in the theater found *Avenue Q* hilariously funny. Obviously they all had jobs and active social lives. Sitting in that darkened space, with my date's hand in mine and warm laughter welling up around me, was not the worst moment of my life. But it may have been the loneliest.

This all sounds very self-involved, and of course, it was. When you are very miserable—and being unemployed for two years is, in fact, very miserable—your universe collapses inward until it is very hard to look at anything except the black hole of despair you have created. As it turned out, I dated that man for years, and when he eventually heard my recollection of that awful, awful night, he was stunned to learn that I'd been imagining him sitting beside me, thinking of how much my life resembled the characters of *Avenue Q*.

"*Are you crazy?*" he asked incredulously. *Why, yes, yes I was.*

So I did what many unemployed people do: I stopped going out. Studies show that measures of sociability, like joining clubs and seeing friends, drop off dramatically during unemployment. Unsurprisingly, depression rises. And none of this makes you more likely to find a job.[11]

I don't remember much about the rest of that date, except that when the lights finally went up, I was desperate to get out of the theater. I rushed up the aisle and out into the spring night as if I were being physically pursued. And then I went home and played video games for about forty-eight hours straight.

THE BEST THING THAT EVER HAPPENED TO ME

I was still playing video games when my parents' phone rang. Since I was the only person in the house, I answered it, expecting one of my mother's real estate clients.

The voice on the other end of the line was British. "Hello, this is Anthony Gottlieb."

After an awkward pause, I recalled that Gottlieb was the editor of *The Economist*'s website, with whom I'd interviewed some time before. After six weeks without a callback, I'd written it off as one more lost chance.

"Hello," I said brightly. "Umm . . . how are you?"

"I'm fine," he said. "Actually, I'm calling to offer you the job."

"I'll take it!" I blurted. Gottlieb, who is a very reserved sort of man, seemed taken aback.

"Well, excellent," he said, after an amused pause. "We'll pay you $40,000."

"You'll pay me?" I said excitedly, then realized that this sounded ridiculous. ". . . . $40,000? That, um, works."

We spent a few minutes chatting about details like the start date, and then he hung up. In something of a daze, I called my boyfriend.

"Hey, Meg, what's up?" he said.

"I got a job," I said, and then, to my horror, I immediately burst into tears. Aside from my wedding, it is the only time in my life when I have cried for joy. Even today, my heart leaps when I think of it.

I used to tell that story as a sort of chin-up-there'll-be-a-happy-ending tale to soothe people who were going through their own dark period. It was only later, when memory had filed some of the raw edges off that awful, awful date that I started to realize that the ending was more than just a punch line. That job with *The Economist*—and my subsequent career in journalism—would not have been possible without the agony that preceded it.

For one thing, I got the job through my blog. I'd started it in November 2001, while I was sitting in a trailer at Ground Zero, waiting for some equipment to be delivered. For months, I'd written posts whenever there was downtime, and then I'd switched to blogging at home. At the time, the New York blog community was small and cozy; I'd met the private equity analyst there. I also met a woman named Jessica Harbour, who happened to work for Anthony Gottlieb. She was the one who had passed me the job listing.

For almost two years, I'd been pouring all the energy that wasn't going into a job into that blog. All those hours of free labor had built what was, for the early days of Web journalism, a fairly substantial audience and reputation. The readers of my blog had taught me a fair amount about how to write, and sharpened my debating skills. And all those hours had given me a large body of work that I could point to when I was asked for "clips" of my prior work. If I'd been applying for a traditional journalism job, the fact that my clips were blog posts would have been a big disadvantage, but for *The Economist's* Web team, it was a plus.

If I'd kept that job in management consulting, I would never have started that blog; I'd have been dutifully creating spreadsheets and PowerPoint presentations and accumulating frequent-flier miles like all my peers. My crushing failure to find work in a "traditional MBA" field had opened up space in my life for something completely different—and for me, much better suited.

My failure gave me something more than room, however; it gave me the freedom to pursue something that seemed, at the time, more than a little bit reckless.

When I told my parents a few months earlier that I was thinking about becoming a journalist, they reacted . . . well, about like you would expect parents to react when their child announces that they are going to take their $80,000 business degree and use it to pursue a career in a field as lucrative and stable as journalism. They freaked out.

"Are you crazy?" my mother demanded incredulously, perhaps not in exactly those words.

My father tried reasoning with me. "How would you analyze this as a problem in business school?" he asked.

"Well, I guess I'd project out the expected cash flows from my journalism earnings, and then I'd discount that for risk to calculate the expected value of the decision," I said.

"Do me a favor," he said. "Do the math."

Grumbling, I sat down and tried to calculate the expected value of becoming a journalist. I had to make some assumptions about what my future income might look like, so the computation was necessarily approximate. Nonetheless, eventually I had a number. As I recall, the expected value of becoming a journalist was roughly similar to the expected value of becoming addicted to crack. I threw the paper away, and pressed on anyway.

"I know it seems kind of crazy," I told my parents. "But what if one day I could work for *The Economist*, or *The Atlantic*?"

If this were a novel, it's the sort of ending that would make you throw down the book in disgust at its treacly improbability, but it's actually true: the two places I dreamed of eventually working were the first two journalism jobs I ever had. And this was not one of those situations where you get what you want and find out you don't really like it. I used to wake up every morning palpably happy that I was going to work at a magazine instead of a consultancy. For that matter, I still do. Not to gloat, but I have one of the greatest jobs in the world: I call smart people, and they agreeably spend hours explaining complicated topics to me. Then I write it up for people like you.

However, my first job at *The Economist* paid about a third of what I'd been expecting as a consultant, and I still had $1,000 worth of loan payments to make every single month. The $40,000 a year didn't go very far after New York City taxes, my loans, and, eventually, rent on a 435-square-foot basement apartment. My disposable income for things like food, clothing, and transportation was in the low hundreds per month. In my early years as a journalist, the menu Chez McArdle mostly featured delights such as Apples au Nothing and Ramen and Cheez Doodle Surprise—the surprise being that I was thirty-two years old and couldn't afford real food.

If I'd had a better-paying job, I doubt I would have had the courage to take the job at *The Economist*. The financial risk would have been too terrifying. Yet it was clearly the best decision I've ever made. It was only possible because I was out of other options.

I have told my story to a lot of people, some of whom were struggling with unemployment, and gotten a fair amount of skeptical feedback. "How many people could write an *Economist*-caliber blog?" one friend asked me. And it's true; no one else is going to replicate my particular career path. The lesson is not that you should simply follow your bliss and rewards will come. Most people are not going to discover an unsuspected talent for economics blogging and stumble into a career in journalism. But they may discover something else.

Do you know why we have Kentucky Fried Chicken? Because the government constructed a new highway, Interstate 75, diverting the traffic that had previously run past Harland Sanders's restaurant in Corbin, Kentucky. It was the latest in a long string of failures for Sanders, who had spent the first twenty years of his working life drifting from job to job, quitting or getting fired for insubordination. His wife eventually tired of his shiftlessness and fled to her parents with his children. He was in his forties when he finally seemed to get on his feet, running a service station and then moving across the street to start a restaurant based on the fantastic fried chicken he'd been serving weary travelers in the back room. Now he was nearly sixty-five and out of work once again.[12]

"He had a lot of hard knocks," said his daughter, Mildred Ruggles, "but he never seemed to let it get him down. He seemed to try to learn a lesson out of every experience he had, and he would try to look around the corner—'Well what can I do now?'"

So Sanders went on the road in the early 1950s, cooking his special recipe for restaurateurs and asking them to give him five cents a chicken. A Utah restaurateur named Pete Harman spotted the potential of his recipe and agreed to franchise the dish Sanders prepared, advertised on his café window as "Kentucky Fried Chicken."[13] You know the rest of the story. By the time he died, in 1980, Sanders's Kentucky Fried Chicken was one of the most successful food brands in history.

Sanders was not fulfilling his childhood dreams as a restaurant franchiser. Batter-dipped chicken was not a high destiny preordained since birth. His phenomenal success was born of a combination of bad luck and a penchant for "always looking around the corner."

THE SECRET TO FINDING A JOB

I can tell you the secret to finding a job even in a very bad market. It's breathtakingly simple: look for a job. No, really, that's the finding of all the latest, cutting-edge research. The harder you look for a job, the more likely you are to find one. It doesn't actually matter that much how you go about it: networking, informational interviews, or cruising the want ads. What matters is that you spend substantial time looking every day. The more time you spend looking, the more likely you are to land a job.

Economists talk a lot about "unemployment entry" and "unemployment exit." You can think of unemployment as a large, dark room with two unmarked doors: an entrance and an exit. People blunder through the entrance for all sorts of reasons, but it's their behavior once they're inside the room that determines how, and when, they leave. The people who sit down and wait are likely to spend a long time in the dark. The people who move around a lot looking for a way out are the ones most likely to stumble upon the exit.

You knew this, didn't you? Common sense tells you that you are unlikely to land a job while lying on your couch watching TV. Every time you leave your house, or even go on to Monster.com, you are creating openings for something to happen. The more often you do this, the more openings you have. Nor does it have to be something strictly in your field. Working at anything, be it a volunteer project or a Walmart stockroom, widens your network and creates openings you might not have thought of.

When I finally found a job at *The Economist*, I had a lot of irons in the fire. None of them was particularly promising, but all of them created openings for full-time work. The miseries of unemployment led me to create career opportunities I'd never have otherwise considered for myself. One of them, the one I actually took, was blogging and journalism. Another was small business IT consulting, which was slowly growing thanks to referrals and could, in time, have become a viable way of supporting myself. But I also had Plans C, D, and E if A and B didn't work out.

The dot-com crash gave me a chance to observe who survived and who didn't when the chips were down. Huge numbers of my friends from business school and the IT field were laid off. Some were out of work for a very long time; some never really recovered. And when it came to who flourished and who didn't, there was one defining characteristic that set them apart: either they flailed, or they failed. The people who did the best were the ones who had four irons in the fire and three backup plans and never stopped trying something to keep going. These plans weren't clever or glamorous or even particularly realistic—I'd never have guessed that my blog would ultimately save my career. But the people who weathered the storm had a lot going on. The people who went under were waiting for something to happen.

The best way to survive unemployment is to adopt what you might call the Way of the Shark: keep moving, or die.

"It can't be that simple!" you're saying, and to be sure, it's not. There are two other factors that turn out to be correlated with re-employment. The first is what economists call "lowering your reservation wage," which, stripped of the economics jargon, basically means you should take the figure you have lurking in the back of your mind, the minimum salary you'd be willing to work for, and cut it in half.

The second is even simpler: if there are no jobs where you are, move.

Yes, that's right: I'm afraid the best scientific research on employment tells us what we (ought to) already know. Beat the streets every day. Be willing to work for less. Move if you have to.

But this "common sense" can't be all that common, because we don't do it.

Shortly after the financial crisis, two economists, Alan Krueger, of Princeton, and Andreas Mueller, of the University of Stockholm, teamed up and commissioned a large-scale survey of recently unemployed people in New Jersey.[14] They found what other economists have found before them: most unemployed people quickly slack off on their job search. There's an initial burst of activity right after they lose their job, and during that period many people find a new job. But when they exhaust their contacts and the companies they know well, they tend to hunker down and wait for something to happen.

Eventually, they do get a second wind—right before their unemployment benefits run out. This may seem like common sense, but it's actually somewhat surprising. In theory, one's job search should increase over time, as it becomes more and more imperative to make money. In practice, we see the reverse—why?

That question has provoked some lively discussion in Washington policy circles. For liberals, it's evidence that workers are reacting rationally to a bad job market, withdrawing rather than wasting time looking for jobs that don't exist. For conservatives, it's evidence that unemployment benefits are encouraging people to sit at home collecting checks until their benefits run out. Pay people not to work, and that's what they'll do. It's a phenomenon that economists call moral hazard, and it plagues all forms of insurance, including unemployment insurance.

Have you ever gotten the collision damage waiver for a rental car? For $20 or so, the rental car company will allow you to crash the car, toss them the keys, and walk away without paying them anything. Consumer finance journalists, of which I am occasionally one, will tell you that you should not take the collision damage waiver; the companies make a lot of money on these policies, which tells you that you are paying them far more than the coverage is worth. But this consumer finance journalist will also admit that she's let herself be talked into it half a dozen times, usually when she was bleary and tired from a long-delayed flight. Here's the interesting thing: I have never so much as scratched a rental car when I didn't have the waiver. But three out of the six times that I've bought it, I've brought the car back with damage. And no, I was not consciously deciding not to worry about parking neatly. You do not have to be conscious of moral hazard for it to be acting on you.

Conservatives are not all wrong about the moral hazard of generous unemployment benefits. Certainly in Europe, where unemployment benefits run longer and replace more of your income, we see people taking much longer to find another job.[15] In general the more generous the unemployment benefits, the longer it takes. But even though Congress boosted them somewhat during the Great Recession, American unemployment benefits aren't a great substitute for a full-time job. Unless you make very little money, they won't replace your income, and they cut off after a couple of years. Are people really choosing a few hundred dollars a week over finding a job?

Krueger and Mueller's survey showed that after just twelve weeks, the average amount of time people spent looking for a job every day declined by 30 minutes—a huge drop, given that workers reported spending at best 70 to 100 minutes a day on their job search. Why?

Liberals tend to emphasize discouragement, and conservatives bad incentives. But Krueger and Mueller came up with a third explanation: people stop looking for a job not because they didn't want one or didn't think they'd find one but because looking was so unpleasant. They asked respondents to provide detailed information about what they'd done over the course of the previous week, and how their various activities had affected their mood. Most ranked their job search highest on stress and anxiety, and lowest on happiness.

A job search gets more unpleasant as time goes by. The longer you spend looking, the more unhappy it makes you, and the more anxious you become about being unemployed. This should make you try harder to find a job. But Krueger and Mueller found that heightened anxiety actually had the opposite effect. People tend to want to minimize the amount of time they spend feeling miserable. So they try not to think about it, which isn't a great recipe for finding a job.

THE WISDOM OF SALESMEN

Job seekers are a bit like baseball players: even the top-notch ones will spend more time striking out than making a hit. So how do they do it? How do you keep going out there, day after day, knowing that most of the time you will be rejected?

You can tell yourself it isn't personal, and mostly, that's true. Especially in a recession, employers are inundated with résumés. They have more qualified applicants than they can possibly hire. That means they're more likely to hold out for an exact match, which means you're going to be a fit at fewer places. But unless you have skin as thick as a rhinoceros hide, being turned down again and again will soon begin to feel very much like personal rejection. Luckily, there's an entire profession that has spent many hours considering the problem of getting ordinary people to willingly suffer rejection over and over and over again. I speak, of course, of sales.

"Smile and dial!" said one sales rep I interviewed. "It's the worst. But it works."[16] Salesmen face the same brutal math as job seekers: success is highly correlated to the amount of time you spend risking rejection. The single biggest predictor of success in a new territory, salesmen will tell you, is the number of calls you make.

Even experienced salespeople don't like it—that representative had been in sales for twenty years, and she still has to force herself to make the fifteen or twenty phone calls a week that she views as the minimum. I canvassed for an environmental group one long college summer, and I can testify that however long you do it, you never like having a door slammed in your face.

I was working in a long tradition: the door-to-door salesman. You don't see many of them anymore, but for decades they plied America's sidewalks, selling brushes and vacuum cleaners and other products that benefited from in-person demonstration. While successful salesmen could make good money, forcing yourself in front of weary housewives is a brutal job, and turnover tended to be high. The same is true of their modern-day descendants, the telemarketers who staff phone banks and the canvassers who sweep the suburbs every summer collecting for political causes. All of them will say that the hardest thing they do every day is walk up to that first door.[17]

Baseball players go up to bat because they have to. There's a roster, they have a place in it, and when it's their time to bat, up they go. They have a system that outsources the decision—which leaves them free to focus on making a hit. The trick for a canvassing organization or a sales team is to get new recruits through those first miserable weeks and they all do it the same way: they have a system.

"Of course they have a system!" you are thinking. "But what is it?" That's what I'm trying to tell you: the most important thing is not what the system is. *The most important thing is having a system.* Whether it's a baseball roster or a call sheet, the single most important thing you can do to get yourself to face rejection is simply to have a process.

That said, sales systems do have some elements in common. The details vary, but they tend to be based on the same four principles that are the key to getting yourself to keep up your job search day after day, week after weary week:

1. Set specific goals for input, not output.
2. Record your effort.
3. Use a script.
4. Surround yourself with other people who are going through the same thing.

Together, these four principles make the process of knocking or calling as automatic as possible. Just like a baseball roster, they take the hardest decision out of your hands. As one of my managers told me, "No one should ever be thinking about whether to knock on that door. They should be thinking about delivering the first line of their rap."

Since the days of the Fuller Brush man, managers have known how frightening a door can be. Even the monetary incentive (you don't get paid unless you sell) is not necessarily enough to overcome the fear of rejection. So instead of just giving salespeople a quota, they also gave them a process: a list of doors that they were expected to call on every day. A modern canvasser is given an area on a map and a tick sheet to ensure that they knock on every door at least twice. For a canvasser, that target is likely to be thirty or sixty houses a night. For a telemarketer, it will be much more than that, and for a salaried salesman with an expensive product, it will likely be less. The important thing is not the number. The important thing is that it is set down in advance.

And recorded afterward. Those tick sheets that canvassers carry are turned in to their managers at the end of the night. People tend to assume this is for supervision purposes—so they can be sure their employees are doing the job. But it's not actually very useful for this. After all, the canvasser spends most of the night alone, so what's to stop them from "curbstoning"—filling their tick sheet full of fake names and addresses? The answer is "nothing" and, in fact, some people do just that. However, they don't bring any money in, so they get fired pretty quickly. That's what the quota is for—to give them an incentive. But most people don't need an incentive to look for work, so we don't need to examine questions too closely.

So why collect all those tick sheets? Why not just take the names of the people who bought the product or gave money?

The answer is that while your tick sheet isn't much good to your manager, it's very useful for you. It organizes your evening, letting you know which doors you've visited and whether or not you've spoken to someone inside. Just as importantly, in a job where you get rejected at least two-thirds of the time, your tick sheet gives you a concrete achievement to focus on. Between sixty and a hundred and twenty times a night, you can check a box that says you're doing your job.

Of course, it's not enough to knock on a door if, when it opens, you start babbling. So direct-sales companies also use a script. Long before they knock on their first door, employees memorize their script, and practice it. A fair amount of time is spent developing these scripts, but they're hardly the platonic ideal of a sales pitch. By the time you're really successful, you'll almost certainly have abandoned the script for a personalized approach that plays up your own strengths—and can be customized to the person in front of you. (My most successful pitches weren't pitches at all, but the time I spent talking to people about their grandchildren or their flower gardens.) What the script does is *get nervous people to talk.*

Business schools use a variant of this, a speech my classmates and I used to call "Walk me through your résumé." It's a two-minute speech that summarizes your life and work history, a little ministory that culminates in you fulfilling your destiny as . . . an employee in whatever company you happened to be speaking to. We spent quite a bit of time refining these scripts, but that wasn't really the point. The point was that you always opened an interview strong, because you had a well-rehearsed account of why you were seeking a job at that firm.

Unfortunately, no matter how systematic you are, the process can be demoralizing. And that's why the fourth pillar of this automatic process is the part where you rebuild your morale by hanging out with other people who are in the same boat. That's why sales organizations spend a lot of time socializing together, with awards for success and a lot of commiserating over the inevitable failures. Those kids who come to your door every summer collecting for the environment are encouraged to drink together every night because it reinforces the feeling that knocking on strangers' doors is a normal thing to do, rather than a scary, awkward activity.

Nothing will ever completely dim the unpleasantness of asking someone for help finding a job. But job seekers who are stuck can help themselves get unstuck with a variant on the sales strategy. They can set daily targets for job-seeking activity, record all the calls they make or ads they respond to, write themselves a script for what they are going to say, and find groups of job-seeking friends for the support they will need to keep going.

They can also systematize the bigger decisions that are even harder to make: when to accept a lower wage, when to move. It will always be tempting to hold on for just a few more weeks to see if things work out. Setting a hard deadline will keep you from getting stuck like the people I met in Buffalo.

KNOWING WHEN TO MOVE ON

Almost every conversation I had in the Buffalo job center ended up in the south, one way or another. Florida, Tennessee, North Carolina . . . everyone had a brother or a cousin down south, it seemed, and as they approached the end of their unemployment benefits, they started to think about following. You'd imagine they'd have talked about getting away from the vicious winters, but no, western New Yorkers take a perverse pride in their ability to endure four-foot snowdrifts and inch-thick heating bills. The people flocking the job center wanted to stay in Buffalo, but they needed to go where the work was. In every Sun Belt boomtown, there are people pining for western New York while they fix up three-bedroom tract homes and crab about the air-conditioning bill. Undoubtedly, some of the people I spoke to are now among them.

But others will still be sitting at home. Some have ties to the area—parents who provide day care, spouses with good jobs. And some just can't bring themselves to say that it's over.

Since the beginning of our history, Americans have been remarkably prone to pick up and move along when the local economic
conditions faltered. That is, after all, why most of us are here: because some restless ancestor got to wondering if the pastures might
not be greener on the other side of the Atlantic. Americans seeking
better opportunities filled up the coastal lowlands, pushed west
across the Appalachians and the Rockies, and, after air-conditioning
made the summers bearable, turned the Sun Belt into the new fron-
tier.

Mobility has long been one of the secret strengths of the American economy. Our willingness to move to where the jobs are has
been one of the main factors keeping U.S. unemployment rates well
below those of our European counterparts.[18] Even when regional job
markets bog down, somewhere in America's vast labor market, there
are jobs to be had. Theoretically, the European Union should give
Europeans the same advantage, but most don't move around as
much even in their own country as Americans do. Still less do they
cross borders, changing languages and governments in search of
work.[19]

In part this is because national borders still matter. Language,
culture, the Social Security system, and even consumer goods are
different across the border. This makes it hard to move unless you
are truly desperate. And Europeans never get truly desperate, because along with laws making it difficult to fire workers, European
nations have long had extremely generous unemployment benefits
compared with the United States.[20] They replace a much higher percentage of income, and they last a very long time. Perhaps not coincidentally, so does unemployment.[21]

In recent years, American mobility has slowed down. We are not
yet at European levels, but we are headed in that direction. Two-
career couples find it hard to pick up stakes when one of them loses
a job. Then there's the two-decade push for homeownership. Advocates touted the benefits. Homeowners were building equity instead

of paying out to a landlord every month. And they were more invested in their neighborhoods. Increasing homeownership was supposed to ease the gaping wealth inequalities between poor renters and middle-class homeowners.

Unnoticed was another effect: owning a home makes it harder to move. A renter can give notice to the landlord and be out by the end of the month. A homeowner often has to wait until the house sells. And where is that likely to take the longest? In a depressed area where both the job market, and the housing market, are sluggish. After a multidecade bull market in housing, no one was worried about this possibility. But since the financial crisis, it's become clear that they should have. One study of homeowners found that people whose mortgages exceeded the value of their home were 50 percent less mobile than those who had some equity.[22]

AMERICAN LABOR-MARKET EXCEPTIONALISM

When you get knocked down by the fickle finger of fate, it's easier to bounce back if you've got somewhere soft to land—and if you've got some people around who can help you get up and dust yourself off. Being willing to move on matters, but so does living in a system that encourages it.

America used to be especially good at preventing the sort of tragedy that has afflicted the people at the Buffalo Employment and Training Center. Chart our historical unemployment rate against the rest of the members of the Organization for Economic Cooperation and Development (OECD), and we're always right there at the bottom, with Japan. Even more importantly, we experienced much less long-term unemployment than most rich countries. In a country like Greece, even before the financial crisis, almost half of the people who were out of work reported being that way for more than twelve months. The OECD average hovered around 30 percent. In the United States, it was more like 5 to 10 percent. And yet, Americans weren't less likely to lose their job; in fact, America makes it easier than almost anywhere else to fire workers. And that, as it turns out, is another reason why we have so few unemployed people.

In most of Europe, in the postwar era, governments viewed unemployment as a terrible failure, and did their best to keep it from happening. They passed laws making it very difficult to terminate an employee, at least once they're past an initial probationary period. And if a firm does go ahead and fire workers, the government usually requires very generous severance, which is then topped off with generous unemployment benefits that replace a high percentage of the former salary.

Even in a relatively business-friendly place like Denmark, letting an employee go means coming up with at least three months' worth of wages for severance pay. In France and Italy it was functionally nearly impossible to fire permanent staff—even layoffs during a downturn faced legal action, and possible reversal by a judge.[23, 24] In America, by contrast, unless you have a contract, there's no legal requirement for severance. You can be fired from one day to the next, without so much as an explanation.

Instead of preventing unemployment, the European laws ended up entrenching it. A French acquaintance recently let a nanny go rather than hire her after the trial period came to an end. He and his wife were willing to keep her on and work with her on the things that troubled them, but there was a problem: if he let her stay past the probationary period, French law would make it nearly impossible to fire her. "I felt bad," he said, "but what could I do? I can't take a chance with my child."

He and his wife eventually hired a different nanny, so the French unemployment statistics were unchanged in this particular case. But in the aggregate, what you see in countries that make it difficult to fire is that you've also made it difficult to hire. Taking on a new employee means taking on an open-ended commitment to a person you don't know very well (and who may decide to slack off once they've become unfireable). So companies go to great lengths to avoid it. Instead they rely on things like temporary contracts to round out their workforce. The people on those temporary contracts can't advance internally, and it's risky to invest in improving your skills for a job you might not have in six months. Those workers are more likely to stay on the margins of the workforce, poorly paid, with no benefits and always at risk of unemployment. It is a classic case of unintended consequences: the laws that were intended to protect people from arbitrary bosses ended up making them unhireable.

THE UNEMPLOYMENT TRAP

A version of this problem also exists with unemployment insurance. Unemployment benefits may ease the pain of unemployment, but they also seem to ensure that we have more unemployment. The generosity of European systems in the 1980s and 1990s meant that people could—and did—linger on the unemployment rolls for years, even decades. Conservatives may be right that employment insurance disincentivizes people from looking for a job, but for the wrong reason. With rent covered, you don't have to be quite so frantic about finding work. You don't have to take the first job that comes along and can hold out for a higher salary, or a more perfect fit. And that, as it turns out, can be a very dangerous thing.

It's easy to see why people would want to hold out for what they had, even when a realistic job search would probably mean accepting lower pay. Senior workers who everyone had looked up to would go back to junior workers learning the ropes in a new industry. And their pay might never recover. Facing that reality is painful. With the government paying 70 percent, even 90 percent, of your former wages, it is easier to wait for a never-never job—especially if you don't have to go to work while you wait. You could decide that you would only take a job as a steelworker doing exactly what you'd done before—even if the local steel industry has moved to another country. This is obviously an enormous fiscal drag, and it isn't great for your job prospects either. As we've seen, résumés decay, now more rapidly than ever. A seemingly generous government program thus enabled people to make a rational short-term decision with disastrous long-term consequences.

Résumé attrition is not an entirely necessary part of unemployment insurance. Denmark combines a generous system with an extremely aggressive job-retraining program: you can collect benefits for a long time, but you also have to be actively training for a new career. But it has taken the rest of Europe a long time to learn those lessons. In one of the most extreme cases, during the reunification of Germany, the government deliberately adopted policies that kept the wages of East German workers close to those of their counterparts in Western Germany, and offered them similarly generous unemployment benefits. Since East German workers and factories were considerably less productive, the result was persistent high unemployment.[25] As late as 2003, 20 percent of East Germans were still out of work.

Essentially, German policy was to keep East German workers in place, looking for jobs that didn't exist in their old towns and old industries—to keep them anchored in the past, rather than to retrain them for the future. And this also happened elsewhere. Italy, Spain, Germany, Belgium, France . . . all struggled through the same period with unemployment rates at least a third higher than that of the United States. And youth unemployment was higher still.

Over the years, Europe has gotten better about paying workers to stay in place; Germany, for example, pushed through a massive labor market deregulation known as the Hartz IV reforms, and now has an unemployment rate lower than that of the United States. Unfortunately, over the same period, America's unemployment policy became a bit more European. America may be replicating some of Europe's mistakes, not out of excess generosity, but excess fear of moral hazard.

Moral hazard does exist. I know people who have sat on unemployment until their benefits ran out without making much effort to find a job. One of them is clearly gaming the system. But another is a novelist who used the time to write a thriller, which he sold to a major publishing house in a two-book deal. The taxes he's paid on his earnings have more than repaid whatever he took out of the system. And he is not the only person to have followed this path—J. K. Rowling wrote the first Harry Potter book while living on Britain's dole.

How do we give ourselves, and everyone else, a shot at turning a job loss into the best thing that ever happened? More precisely, how do we do it without encouraging people to sit out the labor market until they're hopelessly scarred?

For starters, while we should worry about moral hazard, we should understand how it really operates. Instead of imagining that people are taking advantage of their unemployment benefits, we should understand that most of them are seeking shelter from emotional pain. So the best way to shorten unemployment is to make job seeking less emotionally painful.

Less than a month after we moved in together, the man who is now my husband lost his job. He worked for a start-up Web magazine whose financial support melted away during the 2008 crisis. Having been through this myself, I was uniquely well positioned to give him support and advice. Which I did. "I think," I told him, "you should play more video games."

This sounds crazy, but it really was true. I knew he would be anxious about his job search even when he wasn't looking. Because they're almost diabolically good at capturing our attention, video games are an excellent way to deal with anxiety. They're so good at this that researchers are conducting promising studies on the use of video games in medical settings as a way to help preoperative patients cope with pain and anxiety.[26, 27] Though he'd never been much of a gamer, he did have an Xbox, and he followed my suggestion. It turned out I was right: devoting a lot of time to playing video games kept his anxiety to a manageable level. Keeping his anxiety manageable meant that our relationship did not suffer as much strain as most relationships do when one party is unemployed. And that made both of us less anxious.

Of course, I could see that he was looking for work. We're in the same field; I knew who he was talking to, and how hard he was searching for a job. Had he escaped entirely into video games, we would have had to have another, more unpleasant, conversation. But I was confident he'd do everything he could to find another job, and I was right. Within four months, he'd landed the fellowship that eventually turned into his current job at *Reason* magazine.

Government programs have a hard time offering this kind of support, because the government can't see what you're doing. Family can offer unconditional support—and then a kick in the pants if needed. Government programs that offer the same thing risk helping people make choices that feel safer in the short term but are incredibly dangerous over longer periods.

But that doesn't mean that there is no way for governments to help; rather, it means that government help needs to stay focused on two goals: relieving short-term anxiety, and prodding people to keep moving. Denmark's training programs are one version of this. They will not let you sit on the dole indefinitely. But they will relieve you of financial worry, and give you something concrete you can do to make yourself more employable. Judging from their employment figures, this works very well.

But the United States has long had its own version. We had unemployment insurance for almost everyone—but only for a little while. Most evidence suggests that you can offer very generous unemployment checks without encouraging much moral hazard, provided that you cut the checks off fairly promptly.

However, that research was done in normal times, and these times aren't normal. During the Great Recession, the American labor market changed dramatically. You might think I mean that lots of people got laid off, but actually, that's not what happened. Layoffs only increased modestly. What really changed is job openings, which plummeted. Finding a job became like a game of musical chairs; if one person got a job, someone else had to stay unemployed.

Nonetheless, congressional Republicans fought against extended unemployment benefits as if unemployment were still under 5 percent, and a job was available for anyone who wanted one. Probably they did force some people back into the labor market. But something else happened: applications for Social Security disability skyrocketed. Work by the economist David Autor has shown that discouraged workers, particularly lower-skilled ones, are turning in greater numbers to the Social Security disability insurance system when work dries up in their area.[28] Disability benefits are hardly lavish, but they allow you to feed yourself. They also allow you to stay in place, even when there aren't any jobs. And once you're on it, there is virtually no chance that you will ever get off.

This is not necessarily because they don't want to get off, but because of the way the system is designed: in order to prevent moral hazard, Social Security disability makes it very hard for people to join the system. If you have an obvious, grievous injury, like a spinal cord injury that leaves you paraplegic, you can probably get on right away. But if you have a subtler problem, like chronic low back pain, you will need to fight through a series of appeals before you get your benefit. Then if you earn more than a nominal sum, the system will assume that you can support yourself, and kick you out again.

These rules keep people who aren't really very sick from getting insurance. But they also mean that someone on disability who finds a way to make a little money on the side, or tries going back to work to see if they can handle it, risks losing not only their benefit but their health insurance for a job that might not pan out. Unsurprisingly, almost no one takes that risk. And while it's difficult to exit long-term unemployment, America's disability insurance system is like the black hole of public policy. Once you're in its orbit, it's pretty much impossible to escape.

If we'd stayed more focused on preventing employment scarring, and helping people to move on as quickly as possible, we could have done better. If you don't like the Danish program, there are other things we could do. We could create a temporary hiring program, along the lines of the WPA, to be activated during periods of long-term unemployment, with a mandate to hire as many people as necessary to keep the unemployment rate down. These jobs would be time limited, ending when the unemployment rate dropped below its target for several months running, and they'd pay less than normal jobs—just enough to keep the lights on and prevent labor scarring. We could wave the payroll tax on new hires—one month's rebate for every month that the new hire has been unemployed. And if all else fails, we could offer people grants to move from places like Buffalo, where there are no jobs, to Bismarck or Fargo, where North Dakota's oil industry has pushed unemployment down below 3 percent.

Sadly, we were too afraid of being taken advantage of to think creatively in the face of a massive crisis. It helps no one to fixate on mythical villains—in fact, doing so is often very costly. But when catastrophe strikes, that is what we most like to do.

8 BLAME

Blamestorming and the
Moral of the Financial Crisis

A few months ago, I walked into my husband's home office and found him yelling at his video game. (It turns out that in suggesting he play video games all those years ago, I inadvertently created a monster; he now reviews video games as a professional sideline.) When I asked what was going on, he gestured excitedly at the screen. "That racist goon is talking trash to me about elves, and *I am an elf!*"

I hardly need point out that my husband is not an elf. He's a handsome, clever, and amusing but otherwise nonmagical human being. He's also six two. However, I understood exactly what he was getting at, having just spent many hours myself wiping out the Persian Empire in a game called Civilization IV. Why had I done this? For the oldest reason in history: "He hit me first!" I never attack other players, but once another player attacks me, I am implacable.

The problem is that I can't teach the Persian Empire anything. I'm playing against the computer, and the computer program is not capable of learning. It doesn't tabulate data and change strategy accordingly. It does not have Very Special Episodes where it learns that love and relationships are what really matters in life. It operates according to simple algorithms, including ones that tell it to attack me if it thinks it can get away with it. I may pursue every last Persian to the corners of the (simulated) earth, and the next time I boot up the game, they'll do the same damn thing all over again.

And yet when I am tempted to settle the war (the rational thing to do, since to continue a war, you have to divert resources away from building your economy) I can't bring myself to do it. A little voice always whispers from my inflamed id: "Are you going to let him *get away with that?*"

How can a video game trick me into thinking that it is a person? I went into a store and paid money for a disk, which I stuck into a box of bolts attached to a video screen. I should be well aware that it is not a person; people cannot be purchased for $49.95, and even if they could, you would probably not have to pay sales tax. But I can't help myself—and for a very good reason. Our brains are wired to look for agency everywhere. In fact, we look so hard that we usually find it.

HOW WE SEE THE WORLD

You sometimes hear the brain spoken of as if it were a computer, but we all know there is something wrong with that comparison; your laptop is much better at massive arithmetic problems than you are, and much worse at "simple" tasks like seeing that you typed "god" when you meant to type "dog." Peter Norvig, Google's director of research, has famously said, "What we thought was hard, things like playing chess, turned out to be easy, and what we thought was easy, things like recognizing faces or objects, which a child can do, that turned out to be much harder."[1]

The reason why the brain is so good at things computers find difficult is that it has been optimized for important tasks like walking, talking, and recognizing other people. A computer analyzes a face by systematically crunching through reams of data about it. Our brains contain shortcuts—you might call it "pattern recognition software"—that lets us tell almost instantly whether someone is a stranger or an acquaintance, friend or foe.

In fact, we're obsessive pattern makers. Have you looked for hidden pictures in the wallpaper of your childhood bedroom, or faces in the clouds? Searched the sky for the Big Dipper or Orion's belt?

That's your pattern recognition software calling order out of chaos. This software is so powerful that we literally can't help it. Take a look at the following image, composed of three triangles and three circles with wedges cut out of them.

What I described isn't exactly what you saw, is it? You probably saw a white triangle superimposed on black shapes, because that is how your brain is programmed to make sense of that kind of information.

In our natural environment, what are the odds that the missing wedges would line up exactly like that? It's much more likely that an opaque white triangle would be sitting on top of some darker shapes—and that, therefore, is what your mind is programmed to see. "The visual system," says the Yale psychologist Brian Scholl, "abhors a coincidence."[2]

"Coincidence avoidance" seems to be one of the most fundamental rules of perception. If you show people an animated movie of one ball running into another and stopping, while the other ball rolls away, they will say that the first ball made the second one move. No one will suggest that the first ball happened to hit the second ball just as the second ball was starting to move for some other reason. Nor will they name the actual reason why the second ball started to move is that the animator drew it that way.

And people will go beyond causation to motive. After World War II, a Belgian psychologist named Albert Michotte ran a series of experiments using animated films like the one I just mentioned.[3] People described balls on a screen as "hitting," "chasing," and "following" each other—very deliberate behaviors for objects that weren't real, much less alive. I've watched re-creations of some of his famous experiments myself, and even though I had already been primed by reading about them . . . well, darned if it didn't look like the little blue ball was following that big red one.

Missing triangles are not the only things our mind forces us to see. "We also seek out patterns in events," says the scientist Bruce Hood in his recent book, *SuperSense*. "Our mind design forces us to see organization where there may be none. . . . Because our minds are designed to see the world as organized, we often detect patterns that are not really present."[4]

This is especially true, Hood tells us, when we are dealing with unexpected events. We rarely seek out explanations for the things that normally happen; it is the novel and the strange that demand a cause. So when unexpected disasters do occur, our intuitions push us to see a person and a plan, rather than some complex impersonal force. We start looking, in short, for someone to blame.

THE "TRUTH" BEHIND THE CALAMITY

A few years back, I found myself embroiled in a long e-mail exchange with a 9/11 Truther. When it comes to arguing, I am a professional: a typical workday involves endeavoring to convince Republicans that tax cuts do not pay for themselves through increased economic growth, to persuade Democrats that government spending doesn't pay for itself either, and trying to induce people of all political stripes to save 20 percent of their income every year for retirement or an emergency rather than going on a much-needed vacation. As you can imagine, these efforts encounter fierce and dedicated resistance. But none of this compares to the frustrations of trying to persuade someone that the government is neither evil nor competent enough to have orchestrated the biggest terrorist attack in modern history.

The Truther was a friend of a friend. I learned of his existence when my friend forwarded a video about 7 World Trade Center to a mailing list I'm on.[5] The video starred Ed Asner, former star of *The*

Mary Tyler Moore Show, who explains that 9/11 must have been an inside job because "No steel-frame building has ever been brought down by fire."

As you'll recall from chapter 7, for a year after 9/11, I worked as a general administrative helper in a construction trailer on the Ground Zero disaster recovery site. I arrived when the twisted shards of Building One were still jutting out of the rubble, and smoke was still rising from "the pile." I spent almost twelve months in that trailer, smack in the middle of the site, talking to the workers and the engineers who were excavating the remains of the buildings. I knew these people well enough to be fairly certain that they weren't involved in one of the most colossal cover-ups in human history.

But I also knew what the buildings around Ground Zero had looked like before Al Qaeda brought them down, because in my twenties, before I went to business school, I spent several years working as a technology consultant with a firm that did a lot of business in the World Trade Center. I had been inside Building Seven—and I knew just how hard it would have been to plant something in its walls without anyone noticing. So I couldn't resist watching Ed Asner's video.

"Okay, so it's a controlled demolition," says Asner. "What's the problem with that?" As it turns out, there actually is a problem with that, which he hastens to explain: "Well, it happened on the afternoon of 9/11 . . . let's just think about this. Controlled demolitions cannot be engineered and rigged in a day. It takes months. And therefore this event must have been planned in advance."

I know better than to argue with a conspiracy theorist. Of course, I also know better than to leave the dog alone in the kitchen for "just a minute," or to order dessert on the theory that I will only take a couple of bites. That doesn't necessarily stop me. About three seconds after I finished watching the video, I started typing.[6]

Noted construction expert Ed Asner, I protested, was conveniently glossing over what is actually involved in bringing down a building. It does indeed take months, and it is not a subtle process. Demolition firms typically open up walls so that they can get to the concrete support columns, which they drill into in order to set charges. They then string detonation cord or another fuse between the columns. And since explosions take quite a bit of energy, they need an external power source to hook into.

Since the basements of all three buildings didn't explode, the charges would have had to have been set much higher up, in the offices. Needless to say, no one reported noticing a team of demolition experts doing any such thing. I attached a video interview with Mark Loizeaux, one of the world's leading experts in safely demolishing urban buildings, saying all this and noting that as explosives age, they become unstable, so you can't just build them in and detonate them sixteen years later.[7]

I hit send, and then the fun began.

My friend forwarded my e-mail to the 9/11 Truther. Loizeaux had worked for the government, the Truther said, including FEMA's operation at the World Trade Center (that's how I met him). Obviously, he was in on the conspiracy.

But was he wrong? I asked. There are loads of videos on the Web of buildings being prepped for demolition, and they all seem to show the process Loizeaux had described: walls being stripped down to the bare concrete so that crews can drill in and set the charges. Besides, there are lots of other demolition experts in the United States; why had none of them come forward to corroborate the controlled demolition theory? Truther sites offer lists of supposed experts, but they're a sorry and unconvincing bunch: a crane operator, a welder, a photographer who once worked for Mark Loizeaux's firm, a handful of people who claim to have worked with explosives in the military.

It wouldn't have been that hard for the government to pull it off, came the response. After all, the CIA, the Secret Service, and the IRS were tenants. "Clearly, this is not a tourist attraction that would invite casual attention," said my new pen pal in his next post. "Uncle Sam owns the place."

I pointed out that this was not precisely true; there were lots of financial firms located in the building, including two for whom my firm had done extensive work. I was pretty sure they would have noticed if the walls where they ran the communications cables were packed with C4 explosives.

The government undoubtedly has explosive technologies unknown to some run-of-the-mill explosives expert, came the retort. "And by the way, what exactly caused the fires to BURN FOR MONTHS?"

By now I was muttering to myself and kicking my desk as I typed. I replied that I didn't understand why *explosives* would have caused the site to burn for months. The Truthers offer countless videos of other building demolitions whose similarity to the collapse of WTC 7 is supposed to prove that explosives must have been used. But as far as I know, none of those buildings burned for months. Had the government also stuffed the building full of Duraflame logs before exploding it? There was more, much more, but I'll spare you. His views were essentially unfalsifiable; any evidence against the conspiracy simply proved that the conspiracy was even more clever and powerful than previously guessed.

"It's been a really fascinating experience—one that's really shaped my view of human nature a lot," Jim Meigs, the editor of *Popular Mechanics*, told me last year in an interview.[8] Since he took over the magazine in 2004, he has run a number of high-tech examinations of disasters like the crash of Air France Flight 447 and the wreck of the *Costa Concordia*. In 2004, he decided to cover the biggest disaster of them all.

Having spent a century reporting on how things go together and how they come apart again, *Popular Mechanics* was uniquely well equipped to provide the answers to what actually happened to the twin towers on 9/11. "I got to this magazine in 2004 and really wanted to invigorate this sleepy little brand that has a one-hundred-year history," Meigs recalls. "There was this ad taken out in the *New York Times* funded by this rich Truther, that had all of these questions, and I thought 'These are really straightforward questions. They're physical questions that have answers.' So I thought, '*Popular Mechanics* should look into it.'"

The broad outlines of the Truther doctrine are as follows: the twin towers were not brought down by two commercial airliners, as is commonly believed. Commercial airliners simply could not have generated either the force, or the heat, needed to bring those buildings down. What struck the World Trade Center and the Pentagon may not have been commercial airliners at all, but refueling tankers, or perhaps cruise missiles. Alternatively, some Truthers believe that the planes were driven into the buildings, but that this was just a bit of misdirection, the magician waving his cape to distract your eye from the rabbit he's got hidden under the table. The actual destruction of the buildings, they say, was accomplished by high explosives, possibly placed there years before. As for Flight 93, the plane that crashed into the ground near Shanksville, Pennsylvania, after its impossibly brave passengers prevented it from reaching the White House—well that was shot down or bombed, rather than crashed by frustrated terrorists when the passengers stormed the cockpit. In the most elaborate version of the conspiracy, known as the "bumble planes" theory, all the passengers from the other planes were loaded onto Flight 93 in order to conceal the fact that the twin towers and the Pentagon had been hit not by passenger liners, but by remote-controlled airplanes loaded with incendiaries.[9]

Various details from photos and news reports are offered to substantiate each of these theories. There was too little wreckage at the Pentagon and too much, dispersed too widely, from Flight 93. The size of the holes in the three buildings is not right for the planes that are supposed to have crashed into them, and the planes weren't carrying enough fuel to collapse the twin towers, much less the five other buildings in the World Trade Center complex.

Meigs assigned each of his writers to look into two or three of the most common claims. "They just started doing basic reporting," says Meigs. "What's so interesting is that the Truthers never do this: picking up the phone, talking to actual experts—they do look for documents, but they sift other Truther websites."

The *Popular Mechanics* team dove into the rabbit warren and hauled out the evidence so that they could get a good look at it. In the cold light of day, it didn't look so convincing. "Not only did the claims begin to fall apart," Meigs told me, "but we began to learn how the claims were assembled in the first place. They ranged from basic misunderstanding to seizing on early erroneous reporting."

Meigs and I shared a chuckle, the rueful camaraderie of folks who have spent a lot of time in the news factory, grinding out that sausage. Readers expect a neat story, but reporters know how rarely that happens. Eyewitnesses frequently mangle what they saw, or forget key details, and sometimes they make stuff up. Even the details that turn out to be true are often ambiguous or conflicting. Anyone who has followed a big crime story like the Boston Marathon killings, the Atlanta Olympic bombing—or the first 9/11 stories, when more than 10,000 were reported killed in the World Trade Center—will have a sense of just how often early reports prove to be unreliable.

So it wasn't at all surprising to me that early eyewitness accounts had misled some people into believing that there was some secret conspiracy being hidden from them. What was surprising was the reaction to the *Popular Mechanics* special. Instead of being happy to learn that their government probably hadn't orchestrated a massive plot to kill thousands of their fellow countrymen, the Truthers called Meigs a traitor, and flooded his mailbox with death threats.

I gave up when my correspondent started providing ever-more-obscure links to Bush family members to bolster his claim that the government was behind 9/11. It felt a bit like arguing with an ancient Greek about where lightning comes from; our worldviews were simply too far apart. I found it easy to believe that early media accounts were wrong, and impossible to believe in an effective government conspiracy on the scale that Truthers assumed. Forget the intent—governments do sometimes get up to terrible things. But the near-omniscient competence, the split-second timing, the perfect secrecy, all seemed to me flatly unbelievable. To him, they seemed more compelling than the alternative: that stories sometimes get garbled, that photos sometimes seem to show things that aren't there. The apparent tiny discrepancies were not evidence of a messy world, but the barest imperfections in a monstrous and coherent plan.

Fine, those are conspiracy theorists, you may be tempted to say. They have a screw loose and like to find evil intent lurking everywhere. But we all have a little more Truther in us than we may recognize or like to admit.

I KNOW THERE'S A VILLAIN
IN THERE SOMEWHERE

Consider the two main narratives of the financial crisis. On the right you have a story I'll call Mad Hatters and Moochers. It has a number of variants, but they all have one central theme in common: they blame government intervention for destroying the free market and causing the crisis. According to this theory, easy money from the Federal Reserve, and massive government backing for the mortgage market, caused a credit boom that drove markets to unsustainable heights. The Mad Hatters who leapt into subprime mortgages (or worse, bought subprime mortgage bonds) were driven insane by the cheap credit: because mortgage interest rates were too low, they suddenly didn't realize that you can't afford a $500,000 exurban McMansion on a $35,000 landscaper's salary.

Then there were the Moochers: people who took too much risk because they knew that if push came to shove, the government would bail them out. The theory here is that more-frequent government-organized bailouts of big financial firms have made investors and depositors too complacent and lazy to thoroughly investigate what their banks are doing with their money. Or worse, bankers knowingly gambled on highly risky investments because if their risky gamble paid off, they'd get to keep all the money, while Uncle Sam's bailouts would limit how much they could lose.

Most conservatives believe that Mad Hatters and Moochers played a big part in the financial crisis. But notice that this story isn't entirely internally consistent. Government intervention turns some bankers and investors into raving loons who stock up on dodgy mortgage bonds, and others into hyperrational geniuses who can calculate the taxpayer's losses to the last decimal. Why would they have one effect on some people, and the *exact opposite* effect on everyone else?

The Mad Hatters and Moochers story also has some factual problems. For starters, many of the banks that went bust did so in part because they had been "eating their own toxic waste": keeping the riskiest tranches of their mortgage deals on their own books, while selling off the higher-rated stuff to investors. This is hardly what we'd expect to see if they'd known the mortgages would blow up.

Besides, the financial crisis was global. Spain, for example, has no Fannie Mae or Freddie Mac to lend money into its housing market. It requires banks to keep a percentage of all mortgage securities they underwrite, precisely to guard against the temptation to defraud investors by issuing mortgage-backed securities based on dodgy loans. And their monetary policy was considerably tighter than ours, because in 2002, Spain adopted the euro, and the brand-new European Central Bank has spent the last decade demonstrating a fanatical obsession with low inflation.

And yet Spain's housing bubble was even worse than ours, and its banking crisis has also been much worse.[10] As of this writing, about 10 percent of Spanish bank loans are nonperforming. If Mad Hatters and Moochers are what makes a financial crisis, why is Spain having so much trouble?

Still, if you see a conservative on a talk show discussing the financial crisis, you will probably hear some version of the Mad Hatters and Moochers narrative.

The left-wing version is what I call Con Men and Corporate Shills. In this story, crazy free market ideologues persuaded Congress and the president to deregulate the financial sector, undoing all the wise regulations that had prevented financial crises since the New Deal. This, in turn, allowed the Con Men—rich banksters—to start systematically stealing from the poor and gullible by selling outrageously oversize mortgages to financial naïfs who couldn't possibly afford the payments, and turning those mortgages into ridiculously complex securities that they scammed still other financial naïfs into buying. Then these unscrupulous middlemen left the government holding the bag for any losses that weren't borne by the suckers on either end of the deal.

This narrative, like the conservative version, has its share of problems. For one thing, the financial naïfs weren't all that naïve. "During the great housing bubble and bust, journalists spent a fair amount of time searching for the perfect mortgage victim," writes David Leonhardt, the DC bureau chief for the *New York Times*. "This victim would be someone who played by the rules, took a conservative approach to his finances and simply wanted a decent place to live. He made his monthly payments on time, right up to the day that the bank informed him that his payments would balloon because of a fine-print technicality that no borrower could have understood. Just like that, the homeowner was facing foreclosure.

"By and large," Leonhardt reported, "these searches failed."[11]

We failed to find our perfect mortgage victim because it turns out to be pretty easy to understand that you can't afford a $500,000 house on a $35,000 salary. People thought their income would go up, or that they'd be able to refinance at a better interest rate . . . or if all else failed, to sell at a profit.

It also turns out to be hard to pin down the specific regulations that would have prevented the financial crisis. Progressives have nominated a few regulations—notably, the Gramm–Leach–Bliley Act of 1999, which repealed one of the last remnants of the 1933 Glass–Steagall Act, a ban on commercial banks owning investment banks.

If the crisis had originated in hybrid firms like JPMorgan, which had both commercial banking and investment banking arms, this might be more convincing. But it didn't. JPMorgan was fine—in fact, it had enough money to buy Bear Stearns when the government asked it to step in. It was standalone investment banks like Bear Stearns, Lehman Brothers, and Merrill Lynch—the very institutions created seventy-five years earlier when the Glass–Steagall Act mandated the separation of commercial and investment banking—that were most in trouble.

Some people point to a 2004 decision by the SEC to allow broker-dealers like Lehman Brothers to use more borrowed money to fund operations. But while that decision may have made things worse, it certainly didn't touch off the housing bubble, which was already roaring along by then.

Neither of these narratives is all wrong—there were Mad Hatters and Moochers, and Con Men and Corporate Shills aplenty. But there have always been Mad Hatters and Moochers, Con Men and Corporate Shills. None of these stories did a very convincing job of pointing to anything that had dramatically changed in the period between 1998 and 2004—at least, not anything that corresponded with the actual financial crisis.

Nonetheless, they are practically the *only* two narratives you hear about the financial crisis in the nation's news media. What's even more striking is that at bottom, they are the same story: every-thing used to be great, then some greedy fool changed the rules and ruined everything. Call it the Malefactor Model: if something went wrong, there must be a villain behind it.

A different explanation is possible. Christopher Foote, Kristo-pher Gerardi, and Paul Willen of the Fed have exhaustively ana-lyzed the various theories of what happened in 2007 and came to a compelling, but unpalatable conclusion: they're all wrong. The fi-nancial crisis happened for the stupidest reason imaginable—no one thought that housing prices would fall as much as they did.[12]

Among other evidence, Foote et al. point to a 2005 note from Lehman Brothers outlining how subprime securities would perform under various scenarios, from further dizzy escalation in housing prices to a sustained nationwide crash. Their estimates of the gains and losses were startlingly accurate. What was off was their weight-ing of the various probabilities. Lehman Brothers—and by exten-sion, all the investors who read their note—understood what would happen to the securities they held if housing prices fell all over the place, all at once. But they didn't believe it would happen. America hadn't experienced a sustained nationwide price decline since the Great Depression. And almost everyone believed that another Great Depression was impossible. After all, we had all these smart econo-mists at the Fed.

Sometimes, markets get stuck in a positive feedback loop. House prices rise, and mortgage defaults fall, because people who can't make their mortgage payment can sell before they get foreclosed on. When defaults fall, it's cheaper for banks to make loans, because they don't need to charge so much extra interest to compensate for the loans that go bad. In a competitive market, this probably means that lenders will either lower the interest rate they charge, or ex-pand credit to borrowers they might have previously considered too risky. Cheaper, more widely available credit lets people bid up the price of homes, which starts the whole cycle all over again . . . at least, until the banks run out of new buyers to lend to.

I remember having coffee in 2006 with a credit analyst who was telling me about the miraculous innovations in financial theory that had enabled us to price credit risk much more effectively than bankers of the past.

"Have we actually gotten better at pricing risk, or do we just think we have?" I asked, a little skeptically.

"Oh, no, we've really gotten better," he told me confidently. The credit analyst is, like many of his colleagues, no longer employed in finance.

Four years later, a former Bear Stearns employee would write this to me:

> I started my finance career out at Bear Stearns. I left in 2006 (lucky me) and I never ever ever would have predicted the Bear Stearns collapse let alone that I would see the entire financial system brought to it's [sic] knees.
>
> In Sept 2008 when the whole credit market froze, my trader threw out 1 mil par in (slightly sketchy) corporate bonds for a bid, and didn't get a single bid back (not even a penny).[13] I felt I had stared into the abyss. I saw firsthand a massive wholesale funding bank run.
>
> I went back to my office and had an epiphany about how fragile the system was, how uncertain history is, and life in general. I realized my previous assumptions about life, society, the markets, government, etc. took WAY too much for granted.

Bankers were hardly the only people who thought they were geniuses who could turn guesses into gold. Entire academic careers were founded on what we used to call "the great moderation": the idea that improved management of the money supply and the banking system by the Federal Reserve had essentially tamed the business cycle to the economic equivalent of a kiddie roller coaster.[14] And as for homeowners—well, who didn't have friends and family telling them to buy the biggest house they could afford because renting is just throwing your money away?

You can say that one or the other of these groups should have known better, but in a positive feedback loop, everyone is getting the same bad signal. Defaults *had* fallen. Recessions *really were* much less vicious than they used to be. Most families in America had the largest chunk of their net worth sunk into a home.

FINANCIAL GROUPIDITY

This narrative has at least as much going for it as Con Men and Corporate Shills or Mad Hatters and Moochers. Bankers will admit that they are in it for profit, not the greater social good, but they are adamant about one thing: they had no idea this was coming. At worst, they were guilty of insufficient imagination: in the occasional meeting where someone did bring up the possibility of total meltdown, says one former banker, people basically shrugged and said, "If it gets that bad, we're all so completely screwed that there's no point planning for it."[15]

There's another reason why we should consider the possibility of bad positive feedback loops: we can see them in the lab.

Vernon Smith, whom you met in chapter 2, has built asset markets in which students on computers trade with one another. The computer "securities" were built to be as realistic as possible when you're using a bunch of undergrads as securities traders: each "asset" had an expected but somewhat unpredictable payoff, and the students who accumulated the most virtual wealth could earn real money. Smith and his team were looking to see how prices emerged, but they found something unexpected: they got bubbles. Every time.[16]

According to Bart Wilson, whenever they put a group of students together to trade virtual financial securities, it didn't take long for a bubble to emerge . . . and then, inevitably, it would pop. Prices collapsed. The people who bet heavily on the inflated prices lost their shirts.

Interestingly, this happens even if you run the experiment twice in a row: the bubble emerges, and then, once again, it pops. Only when you run it a third time do people start recognizing what is happening, and stop blowing bubbles. But there's an intriguing catch: this only happens if you keep the same group. If you introduce new people, even just a few, the bubble reappears.

One can argue with this evidence, of course—experiments run in a lab using college students are not exactly like a real trading floor. But there's one thing that should keep us from arguing too forcefully: it looks a lot like what we see in real life. Remember all those banks that were eating their own toxic waste? If they knew that this stuff was all going to go bad, why did they keep so much of it around? Foote and his team think they have the answer: they underestimated the probability that the bubble would pop.

How do we know this? Because they said so. But also because they lost so much money in the crash. Dick Fuld, the head of Lehman, is reported to have lost a billion dollars, and was forced to sell off his $25 million New York City apartment along with other assets in order to pay legal bills and other expenses. He's now started his own firm, but compared with his former position, his employment prospects remain pretty dim.[17]

There's a school of thought that says he's laughed all the way to the bank—after all, Dick Fuld still has more money and real estate than I'll ever amass. But that's not how people think. Dick Fuld was forced out of the top slot at Lehman in a humiliating debacle, and has lost most of the wealth he gained over the course of his career in finance. That's not fun, even if you're still rich. You would be very sad if you lost your house and your job, even if you'd still be materially better off than the average subsistence farmer in India. And because you would be very sad, you're probably working pretty hard to avoid that fate.

As a theory, the positive feedback loop holds together at least as well as MH & M or CM & CS. Yet how often do you see it advanced in an op-ed, or pushed by a talking head on television news? You do hear it occasionally. But much more often, it's Mad Hatters or Con Men. And there is a good reason for that.

THE AGENCY DETECTION MACHINE

According to Bruce Hood, all small children share a common set of intuitions about the world that you will probably recognize in many of the adults you know:

1. There are no random events or patterns in the world.
2. Things are caused by intention.
3. Complexity cannot happen spontaneously but must be a product of someone's plan to design things for a purpose.

In other words, we have what cognitive psychologists have dubbed an "agency-detection device." We look for patterns, but not just for patterns: we look for agency, for *intention*. And we see it everywhere. Anyone who has ever been frightened by a flapping curtain during a midnight snack, or jumped away from a snake that turned out to be a stick, knows it's true.

One night not long ago, I spent five minutes trying to sneak up on my coat rack. I was alone in the house, and from the top of my stairs, the coat rack looked terrifyingly like a burglar surveying the booty. Thanks to the flickering headlights of passing cars, it even seemed to move. Obviously, I felt like an idiot when I finally got a good view of three coats and my husband's winter hat. And yet, given the environment we were designed for, my brain was engaged in basic self-preservation. It is probably not very dangerous to mistake a rock for a saber-toothed tiger, but it is very dangerous indeed to mistake a tiger for a rock.

When the question is "Tiger or rock?" it doesn't take very long to determine whether you've made a mistake. When we're dealing with more complicated problems, the quest to find an agent responsible for triggering a complex sequence of events can lead us much farther astray.

In the wake of disasters, we engage in what Cato Institute scholar Walter Olson calls "blamestorming."[18] It's just like "brainstorming" except that instead of crafting mission statements or new product names, we embark on a rapid-fire hunt for a culprit. Olson has in mind our tendency to search for a deep-pocketed corporate perpetrator whenever someone gets sick, but the general trend is ubiquitous, from politics to the PTA.

It's hard not to nod and laugh when you hear the phrase—who hasn't been to a meeting where the main object was finding a scapegoat for some spectacular screw-up? And yet it raises a sort of profound question. Why do we need to do this? And more importantly, since we all know we do it, why does it work? Why, when someone puts forth a villain, do we rush to condemn him or her, instead of asking whether a systemic explanation is more plausible?

Systemic explanations tend, in fact, to be met with outrage. I've advanced the "positive feedback loop" theory in a number of forums, and what's interesting is not the number of people who think I am wrong—I myself am much less than 100 percent confident that this is the right answer—but the number of people who think that by suggesting it, I am doing something *reprehensible*. Virtually every person who has disagreed with me has been vehemently angry that I am denying the culpability of the Moochers and the Shills. In the face of one of the most complex events in modern financial history, a whole lot of people are perfectly confident first, that there are culprits who did this semideliberately, and second, that they have accurately identified them and diagnosed what they did. In fact, they are so sure of their diagnosis that any disagreement can only mean that you yourself are one of the malefactors.

I'd argue that our hyperactive agency detection system is a big part of the reason why we tend to see culprits rather than complexity. We are driven by powerful instincts to look for intention instead of randomness, causation instead of chaos. If nature abhors a vacuum, human reason abhors a coincidence. That's why so many parents with autistic children became convinced that the vaccines their children had been given were causing it. The age at which autism is usually diagnosed is also the age at which kids in most Western countries are going through a heavy vaccination schedule. "Someone did something, and then my kid's brain went haywire" is a much more intuitively plausible story than "Sometimes this happens, for complicated reasons that we don't really understand, and possibly can't fix."

The corollary is that we also tend to favor small, concrete stories over large ones. "Vaccines cause autism" has a lot more resonance than "some unspecified combination of environmental pollutants, infectious agents, and/or genetics is causing autism." Indeed, the vaccine theory *still* seems to be more popular, even though at this point, it can be said to have been conclusively disproved: the original study that touched off the panic has been withdrawn amid revelations that the author was paid by trial lawyers looking to sue, and autism rates have increased even when vaccination rates have declined.[19]

Normal accident theory tells us that we often have to live with some background rate of disasters. But no one wants to be at the mercy of the universe. Identifying mistakes and culprits tells us that we can control those accidents, and make them not-so-normal. Perhaps it is too late for your child, but other children can be saved. One reason that we look for villains is that we want them to be there. The alternative to villains who have done something wrong is a universe where bad things sometimes happen to people who don't deserve them.

THE ILLUSION OF CONTROL

When I was growing up on Manhattan's Upper West Side, some of the streetlights had push buttons, crowned by a handsome black-and-white sign reading:

TO CROSS STREET
PUSH BUTTON
WAIT FOR WALK SIGNAL
DEPT. OF TRANSPORTATION

Longtime New Yorkers sort of suspected that they didn't do anything. And still, they pushed. Dinner parties were riven by debates worthy of the Reformation over those buttons and whether you were actually accomplishing anything by pushing them. Many people who had been pushing those buttons for decades swore that the light turned after. "I timed it," insisted a nebbishy Columbia professor at a cocktail party I attended. "At least thirty seconds faster."

Then in 2004, the *New York Times* confirmed our worst fears: the buttons had been disconnected decades before.[20] The news spread among native New Yorkers like wildfire; for weeks, every time I ran into someone I knew, the second thing out of their mouth, after "Hello," would be "Did you see the *New York Times* piece saying the crosswalk buttons don't work?"

A few years later, I found myself walking along Riverside Drive with a childhood friend who dutifully stopped at the crosswalk, and reached for the button.

"Didn't you hear?" I asked, surprised. "It was in the *Times*. The buttons don't work."

"I know," he said. His outstretched finger hesitated, and then continued toward the button as if of its own will.

"Just in case," he said apologetically.

There's a very common cognitive bias that the psychologist Ellen Langer has dubbed the illusion of control: we think we have
more influence over events than we do. Indeed, we *like* to think we
have this influence; we want a button to push, or a rabbit's foot to
carry, or a lucky rubber band to wear around our wrist.[21]

The illusion of control is generally classed as a "positive cognitive bias," because it actually makes you feel better about things.
Both humans and animals who are subjected to an unpleasant stimulus, such as a loud noise or an electric shock, exhibit less stress if
they believe they can control the negative events. In one study of
airplane noise, for example, people rarely used the switch they were
told would turn off the noise—but even so, they performed much
better on subsequent cognitive tests, like proofreading, when the
switch was there.[22]

The cumulative effect of feeling in control can be powerful. A
series called the Whitehall Studies of the British Civil Service surprised researchers by overturning the popularly held belief that
hard-charging executives drive themselves into an early grave. The
studies showed instead that low-ranking civil servants are much
more likely to die than senior civil servants, even after the researchers ruled out the influence of weight, cardiovascular fitness, and
diet.[23]

Whitehall I and Whitehall II were important because they eliminated so many of the variables that could make these results suspect. The subjects all live in the same country, work in the same
office, and get treatment from the same national health-care system.
They all enjoy the same amount of vacation, and the senior civil
servants probably work longer hours.

So why such a dramatic difference in mortality? The middle-
aged workers in the lowest tiers of the civil service were four times
more likely to die than those in the top grades. If health care, lifestyle, and environment couldn't explain this, what did?

What actually predicted how long you lived, the Whitehall researchers discovered, was how much control you had over your workday, and how much opportunity you had to develop skills. People in the study who reported low control over their work lives had three times the mortality rate of those who reported that they enjoyed high levels of control. Subsequent research has validated the idea that control reduces stress: for example, rats experiencing stress they perceived as controllable showed much lower levels of stress hormones in their brains than rats confronted with an uncontrollable stressor.[24] And as the yoga ads say, stress kills.

To be honest, I'm not so sure I wouldn't rather still be in the dark about those crosswalk buttons. It may not have made the light change any faster, but it made the wait *feel* a lot shorter—something you can readily understand if you've ever pressed the "door close" button in an elevator. I'm sad to report that most of them also don't do anything.

As with all things in this complex world, the positive illusions we seem to need in order to thrive have a downside. Finding someone to blame makes us feel like we're really doing something about the problem, even if we aren't. And of course it often has horrific implications for the people we find to blame for our misfortunes.

SCAPEGOATS AND THE RUSH TO JUDGMENT

In the early 1990s, you used to hear advocates of the death penalty argue that there was no proof we'd ever executed an innocent man. This argument doesn't get deployed much these days, because in the interim, we developed DNA testing, and discovered that there were innocent men on death row galore. Suddenly, we were given a window into all the horrifying ways that justice can go wrong. We started the new millennium with a substantial backlog of cases for which, had the crime occurred today, DNA testing would be done. In a number of these cases we discovered that we had arrested, convicted, and jailed the wrong man, sometimes for decades. It wasn't a huge fraction of cases, but a large number of individual lives had been ruined.

Often it became clear in retrospect that the police or the prosecutors had done something wrong. They coerced confessions from frightened people, often the mentally challenged, and then ignored large discrepancies between the confession and the crime scene. Evidence was mishandled. Dubious pseudoscience was pressed into the service of the case. Occasionally more blatant malfeasance has been uncovered: government forensic scientists faked evidence, or prosecutors deliberately withheld exculpatory evidence. One Mississippi medical examiner claimed to have been performing 1,200 to 1,800 autopsies a year—while also holding down a full-time job at a local medical center.[25]

What also becomes clear, however, is that none of the people who railroaded innocent defendants thought that they were condemning an innocent man to die, or spend years in jail, for a crime they hadn't committed. They were completely convinced that they had found the perpetrator. If they committed ethical lapses, it is because they were genuinely convinced that they were regrettably necessary to put a dangerous predator behind bars.

Of course, you can argue that this belief is self-interested. Often, these cases seem to be high-profile crimes that trigger a lot of outrage: stranger rapes, the assault or murder of a nice middle-class young girl.[26] These are cases where the police and prosecutors are under a lot of pressure to find the perpetrator. A lot of commentators have suggested that under those circumstances, the police deal with the pressure by finding someone—often a poor young man without the resources to mount a good defense, or the social capital to rally the public to his cause.[27]

Undoubtedly it's true that the authorities find it easier to convince themselves that a weak case is strong because their career depends on finding a suspect. But what also seems clear is that they're genuinely convinced; they're rarely simply trying to send any old person to prison.

How do they become so convinced of the guilt of someone who is not guilty? Well, how did Mary Mapes convince herself that she'd found the scoop of the century?

Unlike in the movies, it wasn't because the innocents were being framed by a devious mastermind. What usually happens is that the police settle on a defendant early on. Once they're focused, they stop "looking for suspects" and instead start "building the case." This is an important psychological shift. It means that they're no longer trying to figure out whether or not this person committed the crime. Now they're looking for evidence that they did. They become, in other words, extraordinarily prone to confirmation bias. They were recruiting evidence, not examining it critically.

In one incredible case, a man named Michael Morton was convicted of killing his wife, and jailed for decades, even though her purse was missing, her credit card was used at a convenience store in another city two days later—and her young son spontaneously told his grandmother (the victim's mother), that he had seen a scary monster in the house the day his mother was killed.[28] His account included details, like a wood cudgel and a blue suitcase thrown on the bed, that perfectly matched the crime scene.

The police not only ignored this account, they tried to convince the family that the "scary monster" described by the son was in fact his father wearing his scuba diving gear. We know that they understood that the son's testimony badly undercut their theory, because they withheld it from the defense during the discovery process. But it doesn't seem to have shaken their own confidence. Michael Morton served twenty-five years in jail for a crime he did not commit. Assured by the police that he was guilty, his wife's family believed them, even though they themselves had heard his son's exculpatory story. Morton was freed only when it became possible to do DNA testing on a bloody bandana that had been found a few hundred yards away from the crime scene.

And even then, the prosecution fought him at every step; they gave up only when DNA identified a perpetrator, and turned up a similar murder that had been committed nearby around the same time.

Why do hard-line law-and-order prosecutors fight so hard against groups like the Innocence Project? The project does DNA testing at its own expense; it costs the taxpayer nothing. And many times they end up affirming the prosecution's case. In 2006, at the behest of anti-death-penalty advocates, the State of Virginia finally agreed to allow extensive DNA testing in the case of Roger Keith Coleman, a coal miner who had been executed in 1992 for killing his nineteen-year-old sister-in-law. The lab that performed the test concluded unequivocally that Coleman was the perpetrator.[29]

Yet they do fight, even in the face of convincing evidence that something has gone wrong—when the bloody bandana came back with the DNA of Michael Morton's wife and an unidentified man, prosecutors initially argued that the blood might have been transferred to the bandana days after the murder. Once blamestorming is in its full fury, any attempt to present disconfirming evidence is siding with the forces of evil.

Of course, you could argue that there was a villain—just not the man we picked. But we convict people even when there is no human villain. Lindy Chamberlain, whose story was made into *A Cry in the Dark* with Meryl Streep, was convicted of murdering her baby because the prosecution said her story—that a dingo stole the baby—was impossible. The child's jacket was later found in the bush, where it had apparently been dragged by dingos.[30] Cameron Todd Willingham was executed for setting a fire that killed his daughters, but which actually seems to have started with a faulty heater.[31] Shaken baby syndrome, which has produced some famous trials, also appears to be overdiagnosed, raising the specter that innocent people have gone to prison for it.[32] Confronted with the worst thing we can imagine—the death of a child—it seems to be especially easy to leap from accident to intent.

"It's staggering how organized they think the world is," Jim Meigs mused shortly after he told me that his assistant had been forced to file a YouTube takedown notice of a video that had proposed him for a list of people who should be assassinated. "The conspiracy theories provide this wonderful sense of structure to the world. There's a reason for everything, everything's planned. There are these vastly powerful forces, *and they're evil.*" Just as we search for agency in randomness, we search for something like superagency in the actions of individuals and small groups. We are constantly striving to make the world more orderly and planned than it is.

The 9/11 Truthers live in a world where the U.S. government is controlled by an evil cabal that murdered thousands of its citizens in order to launch a war of revenge. That's terrible. But it's quite orderly and comprehensible, and most importantly, it's very much not random. Presumably if you could identify the cabal, and remove it, then everything would be fine.

In the world that Meigs and I live in, nineteen homicidal lunatics hatched and executed a plan that killed thousands of people, using little more than some box cutters and a couple hundred hours of flying lessons. There's no way of knowing when someone else might manage something similar. The world is an incredibly insecure place, and there's no obvious way to make it less risky.

And maybe in that world, financial bubbles sometimes happen, not because people are bad, but because we're flawed—because we get caught in positive feedback loops, and see triangles and dollar signs that aren't really there. As we'll see in the next chapter, our instinct to punish is not just costly to the people we blame; it costs us a great deal as well.

9 PUNISHMENT

Why Consistency Is the Secret to
Breaking Bad Behavior

I've spent most of this book talking about risk and redemption. I've exhorted you to eschew blame and understand failure as the natural consequence of risk and complexity. I've asked you to do your best to recognize when you're on the wrong track and to focus on fresh starts rather than retribution. But sometimes people do things that are not just risky, but wrong. Sometimes people deliberately break the rules that society has set up to protect itself. Some of those things are directly harmful to others, like theft and assault. Others, like skirting food safety regulations, create an unacceptable risk to fellow citizens. People who break the rules do not just need a fresh start. They need to be punished.

But not too much. The economists Anna Aizer and Joseph Doyle recently investigated what happens to juvenile offenders who are sent to prison, compared with those who commit the same sorts of crimes but are put under less harsh forms of supervision. The juveniles who went to a detention center were much less likely to complete high school, and much more likely to end up in jail again. Jail time not only blights young lives, it costs us more in the long run: higher crime, and the myriad of costs associated with investigating, arresting, convicting, and imprisoning them.[1]

So how do we punish people in a way that doesn't ensure they emerge from the experience ten times worse?

The prison system is where society's worst failures end up. I mean that in both senses of the word. Most of the people in prison are people who were failed by others before they failed, spectacularly, themselves. Some of them can never be rehabilitated. But others can be saved, if we go about punishing them in the right way. The problem is, we rarely do.

In the spring of 2012, I went to Honolulu to look for HOPE. In case you're wondering, you can find it on the fourth floor of the courthouse, where probationers are called on the tattered green carpet by Judge Steven Alm, a former prosecutor turned probation reformer. Under his leadership, Hawaii's Opportunity Probation with Enforcement is slowly and steadily reducing crime among probationers. It may be the best thing that's happened to crime since the invention of police.[2]

Better probation hardly sounds like a revolution. But here's the thing: almost half the people on probation in Hawaii will eventually end up in prison, having flunked the program that was supposed to keep them straight. Prison is pretty miserable, but it's a great place to meet other criminals, with whom you can commit more crime when you get out. Which is what you'll probably end up doing, because a convicted felon with a five- or ten-year gap on his résumé doesn't have a lot of lucrative employment opportunities.

Keeping probationers out of prison is good for everyone. It saves the taxpayer money. It saves the probationer the agony of years behind bars. Best of all, if it's done right, it can reduce crime, while offering someone who has failed badly the chance to build a decent future.

What HOPE teaches us about punishment also applies to the rest of us. How should we structure regulatory enforcement of environmental laws? What's the best way to keep our teenagers from going too far astray? When and how should we discipline employees who violate the rules? For those of us who want better answers to those questions, Judge Alm's courtroom offers hope.

The history of the American criminal justice system is full of programs that promise to be nicer to prisoners and to prevent crime.

The HOPE program is one of the rare ones that actually seem to work. We know this because, thanks to a minirevolution in criminal justice work, it's actually been tested. A few years ago, Angela Hawken, a public policy professor at Pepperdine, sat down at a computer with five hundred names of Hawaiian probationers. She was there to test Judge Alm's extraordinary claim: that he had taken Hawaii's worst, least compliant probationers and slashed their recidivism rate in half.

Programs that make claims like this usually turn out to have succeeded only with a highly select group of prisoners—figures from successful prison ministries, for example, tend to ignore the dropouts, or those who never sign up because they don't want to sit there and be preached at. Hawken wanted to make sure that the program's results were not due to some selection effect. So she ran five hundred names through a randomizer in the computer, and it spit out two lists: one with probationers who would be assigned to HOPE, and the other with the remainder, who would be left in the regular probation system.[3, 4]

For twelve months, she and her fellow researchers followed both sets of probationers, then they analyzed the results, which were indeed remarkable. Drug use nosedived. Twenty to 30 percent of drug tests in the regular probation system come up positive—which sounds high even before you realize that they are almost all administered at regularly scheduled monthly probation appointments. Most drugs that are tested for leave the system within a few days, so a positive test means that the probationer used drugs knowing they would be taking a drug test within seventy-two hours—and then decided to show up for an appointment even though they knew they'd test dirty.

HOPE probationers, by contrast, are all randomly drug tested at least a couple of times a month, and often more than once a week. Three months into the study, only 9 percent of the tests were coming back positive; by six months, the number had fallen even further, to 4 percent. So had missed appointments—from over 10 percent down to 1 percent. Twelve months in, only 9 percent of HOPE probationers had had their probation revoked, compared to 31 percent of the group on regular probation. People in HOPE spent about a third as many days in prison as their peers in the regular system.

Though HOPE probation costs somewhat more than regular probation, its cost is dwarfed by the money the taxpayer saves on prison. One month in prison costs five times as much as a month on HOPE probation. Then there is the material and emotional savings to taxpayers who don't have their cars stolen, purses snatched, or faces punched by a drug-addicted probationer.

The probationers like it too. The ones I spoke to, all former meth addicts, were searching for adequate superlatives. "Great" . . . "Awesome" . . . "Amazing," they told me, with the half-apologetic look of someone who feels they're not quite communicating what they're feeling.

Let's remember, they were describing being sent to jail.

Put simply, that's what HOPE does: it sends people to jail. Every single time they are caught violating a term of their probation, Judge Alm gives them at least a few days in the pokey. Oh, there are lots of other parts to it, from simplified paperwork and expedited hearings to expanded drug treatment services (which is where most of the extra cost of HOPE probation is spent). All these are necessary to make the program work—but what makes it effective is Judge Alm's true innovation: catching as many probation violations as possible, and punishing every one of them.

THE DAD TALK

Every prisoner who enters HOPE probation is brought before Judge Alm to be given what the people who run HOPE call a "warning hearing," and what I, after sitting through perhaps a dozen of them, began thinking of as "the Dad talk." Like most Dad talks, it varies slightly every time it is given, although it leans heavily on the same aphorisms, catchphrases, and hypothetical examples.[5]

Almost every day in Judge Alm's courtroom, three or four probationers come up to the defense table, some of them in shackles. There's a momentary lull as Judge Alm, a blond, hearty man in his late fifties, verifies the identity of the probationers and looks at the paperwork in front of him. Then he leans forward and looks each of them in the eye, and delivers some version of the following speech.

"Good morning," he says. "I want to start by saying that everyone in this courtroom wants to see you succeed on probation. Your attorney wants you to succeed, your family wants you to succeed, I want you to succeed. The taxpayers of Hawaii want you to succeed. It costs $50,000 a year to keep someone in Halawa prison, and $30,000 a year to ship them to Arizona. If you comply, I will never see you again. If you do violate . . . look, we're all human, we all make mistakes, including me. But how you handle that mistake makes a big difference. I'm not a mind-reader, and I can't look into your hearts. I have to look at what people do.

"Now, let's say you have an appointment with your probation officer on Monday and that morning your friend calls you and says, 'I've got a beef with my landlord, I've got to move,' and you drop everything and run over. Then at six o'clock that night"—the judge slaps his forehead—"you think, 'Oh, no! I missed my appointment!' What you do next will matter a lot. No matter what happens, you're going to do some jail time. But if you turn yourself in immediately, you'll do as little as possible.

"If you come in the next day, they're going to drug test you. If you test dirty, they'll take you into custody. But if you're clean, you're working or in school, we'll schedule a hearing later in the week, and try to have you do time on the weekend. Usually, it will only be a few days.

"On the other hand, some people on that Monday night are going to say, 'Oh, I don't want to go back to jail, so I'm going to go out and party and wait for them to find me.' If the police have to arrest you and bring you back, then I generally give you five times as much jail time as I would have if you'd turned yourself in.

"And if you get arrested on a warrant, the police have every right to check your pockets. If they find anything—drugs, or just a dirty pipe—then I have zero discretion. I have to give you the open term."

Open term is what Hawaiian courts call the five- or ten-year prison sentences generally handed out to felony offenders. He pauses briefly to let that sink in.

"During your time on HOPE," the judge continues, "you will be subject to random drug testing. You will be given a color, like Red-two. You have to call into the hotline every morning and listen to hear whether your color has been selected for drug testing that day. If your color comes up, you have until 2 p.m. to get yourself to the drug-testing facility downstairs. We have great workers, they come in at 6:30 a.m. if you need to get to an early job or school.

"The colors for the day go up at 4 a.m. Don't call until after 4. I had a guy in here the other day, he showed me his cell phone and it said "3:59 a.m." on it. That doesn't cut it.

"Over time, if you come up clean, we'll give you a new color, one that doesn't come up as often. Initially, your color will come up more than once a week. But if you keep testing clean, eventually, it's twice a month. That's random, so don't think "I got tested yesterday, they can't call my color again tomorrow. They can and do, and if you don't show up, I'm going to give you some time in jail.

"Now, if you do come in and test dirty, you have a choice. If you tell us right away, I'm going to give you a few days. But if you make us send it off to the lab to verify, and it comes back dirty, you get more jail time."

He turns to the first defendant. "Mr. Smith, where do you live?" Unless the defendant lives in one of the nearby homeless shelters, the answer is usually some distance away; downtown Honolulu is one of the most expensive real estate markets in the world. "If your battery won't start, that's not an excuse for failing to show up," he says. "You're adults; I assume you can handle these emergencies. I've been showing up to this courtroom every day I've been scheduled for thirteen years, and so have the people who work here. You can do this too."

He turns to another defendant. "Mr. Jones, who is responsible for meeting the conditions of your probation?" There is occasionally a long pause, while the probationer carefully considers his answer. In the end, however, they all come up with the right one.

"I am."

"I agree!" says the judge, in a delighted tone. "I don't see you as a victim. You've probably made a lot of good decisions in your life, along with one bad one." The third probationer catches his attention. "I'm sure you don't want to embarrass your family, do you, Mr. Brown?"

"No, your honor."

Judge Alm holds up a copy of Hawaii's *MidWeek* magazine, whose headline identifies it as the special Fugitive issue. "You don't want to show up in *MidWeek*'s Fugitive issue, do you?" He is now waving another card filled with mug shots. "Or *Hawaii's Most Wanted*, on Channel 2 at 10 PM Saturday night? Very embarrassing for your family . . ."

The probationers are all shaking their heads no.

"I guarantee that won't happen," says the judge, "unless you run. People who keep violating, or run away, I have to give them the open term. It's not that they're bad people, but they're wasting everyone's time. Don't think, 'I have to run away or I'll get the five-year term. I guarantee I won't do that if you don't run away."

With a rather severe look, he turns to the fourth probationer. "Mr. Doe, how should you handle it if you violate?"

"Turn myself in."

"Right! Everyone on the same page with that?"

Nods all around.

"You can do this, Mr. Brown, Mr. Jones, Mr. Smith, Mr. Doe. You wouldn't be here if we didn't have every expectation you can succeed on probation. So no offense, but I hope I never see any of you again."

RANDOMIZED DRACONIANISM

Out of Hawaii's 8,000 probationers, just under 2,000 have heard this speech. You might think that some version of it goes with the territory. But that is far from true, because in most places, the system simply isn't set up to deliver that kind of supervision.

According to the Reentry Policy Council, in the United States the average caseload for a probation officer is 130 offenders.[6] Just meeting with each one of your probationers for an hour a month eats up more than a standard workweek, but probation officers are creatures of the bureaucracy, and lots of other things have to get done. A mountain of paperwork has to be filled out and filed. Records must be kept. Violations must be investigated, and the court has to be kept apprised. Oh, and aren't they also supposed to be helping their probationers get the resources they need to stay straight?

The irony of traditional probation is that probation officers use the appallingly frequent no-shows to catch up on all the other tasks they're supposed to be doing. Since the least compliant people are the most likely not to show up, probation officers end up using the appointments of the people who don't show to maintain the paperwork of those who do—or, eventually, to write the lengthy reports documenting a request for revocation of parole.

Requesting a revocation of parole—asking the judge to send the probationer to serve out their prison term—is the main sanction that probation officers have. It's brutal—the local prison, Halawa, is terrifically overcrowded, and the alternative is a private prison 3,000 miles away in Arizona. Asking a judge to give someone a five-year term in prison because their car broke down seems a little extreme, and if probation officers did that for every violation, most of their caseload would be in prison.

So instead probationers rack up violations, probation officers threaten them, and eventually, when the mountain of violations gets too high, they request a revocation. But the revocation is not always granted. A request for revocation presents judges with an unpleasant choice: Do I really want to send someone to prison for five years because they have a drug habit, or a time-management problem? The answer judges often give is "No." So the cycle starts anew, until the noncompliance becomes too egregious to ignore—or, as often happens, until the violator is arrested for a new felony. At that point mandatory sentencing laws mean judges usually have little discretion; the probationer is going to prison.

When Judge Alm first came into contact with the system, he thought this was crazy. In his words, the experience of a probationer was "Nothing . . . nothing . . . nothing . . . nothing . . . nothing . . . nothing . . . bam! five-year prison term." It's what Mark Kleiman, a UCLA professor who studies crime, calls "randomized draconianism."[7]

The science-fiction writer Robert Heinlein vividly dramatized our justice system as it might be applied to housebreaking puppies: "Suppose you merely scolded your puppy, never punished him, let him go on making messes in the house . . . and occasionally locked him up in an outbuilding but soon let him back into the house with a warning not to do it again. Then one day you notice that he is now a grown dog and still not housebroken—whereupon you whip out a gun and shoot him dead."[8]

Of course, people are not puppies—but the way we learn not to do things is not all that different. If you want to teach a puppy not to do something, you need to catch him at it, and punish him immediately; if you punish him later, he will not connect the action with the punishment. (Note: rubbing his nose in it doesn't work; either catch him peeing on the rug, or don't bother.)

As anyone who has raised a kid can attest, the same is true of children: swift and consistent punishment is by far the best way to change behavior. If consequences are applied only sporadically, there is a risk you will actually reinforce the bad behavior. Consistency is probably the most important tool of parenting. As we get older, we get better at planning for the future—including avoiding punishment. But we still aren't all that good at it, and consistent consequences still go a long way toward modifying behavior.

Why is your 401(k) underfunded, your gym membership unused, and your waistline four inches bigger than you'd like? Is it because you want to have a heart attack and spend your golden years swapping Fancy Feast recipes with the other people at the senior center?

Of course not. You want to save money and get fit; the problem is that we are none of us very good at exchanging the pleasures of now for the rewards of later. We want to diet, exercise, and save—in fact, we want it so badly that we will happily commit to doing so, as long as the deprivation can be shifted later. If you ask people to sign up for a big increase in their 401(k) contribution a year from now, you'll get a lot of takers. If you ask them to do it today, not so many. It's a phenomenon known to behavioral scientists as "hyperbolic discounting," and everyone does it to some extent.

But some people do it more than others. The difference may well be at least partly hereditary, because scientists have observed big differences in the ability to delay gratification in children as young as four. In a series of famous experiments conducted at Stanford in the late 1960s, early 1970s, the psychologist Walter Mischel put four-year-old children in a room and showed them treats such as pretzels and marshmallows, then told them that if they could wait until the researcher got back, they could have a better treat (for example, two marshmallows). If they couldn't wait, they could signal, and the researcher would come back and give them their less preferred treat immediately. Then the researchers stepped out for fifteen minutes to see how long the children would wait.[9]

Some ate the treat immediately. Most held out a little while, but not for the full fifteen minutes. There was substantial variance in how long the four-year-olds could wait. Though he hadn't initially designed this as a long-term study, Mischel has done follow-ups over the years. What he found is intriguing. The kids who could delay gratification in nursery school had higher SAT scores, fewer personal problems, and better friendships than the kids who had scarfed the snack immediately.

When I went to Hawaii, I knew that the criminal justice system was mostly for people who are pretty screwed up. But it's one thing to know, intellectually, that convicted felons have troubled child-hoods and chaotic lives, and another thing to sit in court for a week and hear an endless litany of dysfunction, like the drug addict who doesn't want to go to the clean-and-sober house because where will her four kids stay? Many have so alienated their family and friends that they have no one to drive them to an assessment at a drug treat-ment center. They have the same basic problem as the kids who couldn't wait a single second to eat that delicious marshmallow.

"They're impulse ridden, they grew up impulse ridden, and they have spent their lives surrounded by people who were impulsive," says Myles Breiner, a defense attorney whose clients include HOPE probationers, told me. "They don't think rationally about problems. Their first reaction is their action."

Thomas Otake, another defense attorney, put it even more suc-cinctly: "A lot of times, someone will come to me and I think, the only difference between me and them is, I can control my urges."

So how can we train people to control their urges? It's something anyone who has eaten one too many tubs of ice cream or bought one too many pairs of shoes would like to know.

CAN CRIMINALS CONTROL THEIR IMPULSES?

Today's criminal justice system is the product of the war between two views of crime: the liberal view that criminals are victims of an unjust social and economic order who can't be expected to behave any differently, and the conservative idea that they're choosing crime out of a combination of greed and moral squalor. The justice system as it currently exists is an uneasy mixture of mandatory minimums and "three strikes laws" that hand people decadeslong prison terms for minor offenses, and revolving door systems that pump juvenile criminals back into my neighborhood in Washington nearly as fast as they can be arrested.

The British writer Theodore Dalrymple, who has long worked with patients in the prison system, points out that the people who claim that they "can't help" taking drugs, or that their boyfriends hit them because "he can't control himself," readily admit that they wouldn't do it in front of Dalrymple, or a police officer.[10] Committing a crime is a decision, not an involuntary reaction, and by moving away from punishment, the relatively gentle justice system of the 1970s made it likely that more crime would be committed.

Conservatives are right about one thing: most criminals can control their impulses if they know that they face certain punishment. But Mark Kleiman argues that conservatives largely missed a more important truth: the most important word in that sentence is not "punishment" but "certain." We spent the last three decades putting more people in prison for a much longer time, and imposing more restrictions on their lives when they got out. The problem is, the best way to fight crime is not harsher punishment; it's *inevitable* punishment. In order to prevent a thug from beating up his girlfriend, we don't need to threaten to send him away for life. All we need is to assure him that he will get caught.

Doing so required an enormous mobilization of resources—one that Judge Alm was uniquely suited to provide. Hawaii is in many ways a multicultural paradise, but it's also isolated and a bit provincial. Alm, who grew up on Oahu, was better positioned than an outsider would have been. He was a successful local prosecutor in the 1980s, and then U.S. attorney under Bill Clinton. "It took Nixon to go to China," says Breiner, "and it took a hardass former prosecutor to do HOPE. If he'd been a public defender, people would say 'no, this is just an extension of your mission as a PD.'"

When Alm started on the bench in 2002, people complained that his sentences were too tough, so the chief justice delicately suggested that he transfer to civil court. Instead, he spent a year doing misdemeanor trials for people who requested a judge rather than a plea bargain—or rather, not doing trials. After the first few times he sentenced drunk drivers to 90 or 180 days, people stopped requesting trials. "It was the most boring year I ever spent," says Alm. "We had nothing to do."

The next year, he transferred back to the circuit court, where felony trials are held. And that's when he started noticing how many violations it took for the probation officer to request a revocation hearing. "That's crazy," he told the probation officers. "I want you to bring them in front of me every time they violate. They're going to jail."

The probation officers explained that this was impossible; it took hours to write up a request for revocation. So Alm worked with them to streamline the paperwork. Now they have a one-page form on which they check off whether they're requesting punishment for a violation (most frequently a dirty drug test) or, in the case of repeat violators who refuse to follow the rules, a revocation of parole. Alm still had to persuade the probation officers to write up violations every time they occurred. He also needed to persuade sheriffs to be on hand at all times so they could take violators into custody immediately—and he needed the police to prioritize the bench warrants issued for people who missed their appointments. "Most police officers," says Judge Alm drily, "would rather be out there catching people committing crimes now, not chasing yesterday's criminals."

He quickly understood that very little improvement would be possible unless he could tackle the underlying drug problem. A clear majority of the probationers I saw standing at the defense table had used crystal meth, Hawaii's biggest problem drug, within the last few months. With a few exceptions, almost everyone else was drinking or smoking pot. I wondered if this was because there were so many arrests of nonviolent drug offenders, most of whom ended up on probation. But many of the drug users were in for other crimes— assault, robbery, theft. Several criminal justice experts set me straight: most people who are arrested for any crime have drugs or alcohol in their system at the time of their arrest.

If you don't have an impulse control problem, the best way to acquire one is by becoming addicted to drugs. Drugs essentially short-circuit the brain's reward system. When you do something good, like getting promoted or solving a hard problem, neurotransmitters are released to tell you, hey, that was awesome! Runner's high, for example, floods the brain with dopamine and other endorphins.[11] Unfortunately, so does smoking crystal meth—or rather, it floods the brain with methamphetamine, which is chemically very similar to dopamine, and can induce the same sort of euphoria.[12] Unsurprisingly, the brain often responds with strong urges to do it again. Some variant on this is the appeal of everything from nicotine to heroin—it either blocks a negative signal like anxiety, creates or enhances positive signals like euphoria, or both.

When your brain's reward system has so much artificial stimulus, it's hard to focus on less intense sources of reward, like eating or holding a job. That's why drug addicts are so skinny, and why so many of them steal or turn tricks in order to support their habit. Many drugs lower the inhibitions that help keep you from, say, taking a baseball bat to someone who groped your girlfriend. Or missing your probation appointment.

Given that a majority of probationers were using drugs, Judge Alm needed some way to help them stay clean. He found the solution in Hawaii's drug court—a special court for a hundred or so low-risk drug offenders that emphasizes treatment rather than punishment. Somewhat unusually, Hawaii's drug court had a phone-in system for randomly drug testing its clients. Alm used a similar system for probationers in the new program he set up—HOPE.

HOPE probationers would have to call in every morning to see whether their group had been randomly selected for drug testing; if their number came up, they had a few hours to get into Honolulu and take their test. Everyone who tested dirty would spend at least a few days in jail. There would be no exceptions. The punishment was consistently and predictably applied, much like tough love parenting.

"It's like with a little kid," said defense attorney Alvin Nishimura. "You have to spank them immediately."

It must mean more work for defense attorneys, I joked.

"Actually, I see my clients less often now," he said. "After a couple of times getting these little spankings, so to speak, these guys learn."

Several of the defense attorneys I spoke too suggested that HOPE was, in effect, making up for the parenting their clients never had. "Clearly, there's a cycle," Thomas Otake told me. "Many of my clients, they have parents who are on drugs or in jail." For them, he says, Judge Alm's courtroom is a "teachable moment."

Early in my visit, the judge confronted a defendant who had tested dirty, and then lied about using—only to turn himself in the next day after talking to his father.

"That's good, you listened to your father," said the judge. "Dad knows what's right, don't you, Dad?"

The defendant's father, a Hawaiian man in his fifties, waved cheerily.

"Your dad's doing great in Drug Court," Alm told the probationer. "Hopefully, you'll learn from him." He still sentenced him to fifteen days—recall that the penalty for making them send the test to the lab is at least a week in jail. But the probationer seemed content with the verdict.

Judge Alm says that he got the idea for his new program by thinking about what had worked with his own son, who just graduated from Georgetown. When his son was a kid Alm explained the rules clearly, and then followed up with immediate consequences when the rules were broken. People who were coming into his courtroom with multiple violations, he thought, weren't learning the rules; they were learning that violations had almost no risk. From the point of view of the offender, punishment was thus essentially random. You've done one thing over and over without consequence, and then suddenly one day, instead of getting another free pass, your probation officer petitions a judge to send you back to prison. Do you say to yourself, "Wow, I guess I pushed it too far"? or "I guess she was in a bad mood"?

THE IMPORTANCE OF CONSISTENCY

A lot of child rearing involves teaching kids the rules that society lives by. That means consistency. You cannot teach a child that they can pick their nose in public or kick the dog 50 percent of the time. That's why child experts will tell you that giving in to a tantrum is just asking for more tantrums. Successful parents enforce the rules every single time—when they're tired, when they're grouchy, when they really need to go home and get a couple of Excedrin. Sometimes in the moment it seems easier to give in. But you—and your kids—will generally pay for it later.

The more chaotic your own life is, the harder it is to focus on consistent discipline. Willpower is finite, and the many hassles of poverty—juggling bills, standing on your feet all day at a low-wage job, compensating for an absent partner or, worse, one who is violent or drunk or out of work or all three—quickly sap that will-power to a low ebb. Drugs drain it entirely.

Conservatives tend to assume that poor children are never disciplined. In fact, in many cases they're disciplined more harshly than middle-class Republican progeny. The problem is, they're not disciplined consistently. They spend more time unsupervised, and their beleaguered parents are frequently distracted by more pressing problems, like the fact that the electricity got shut off again. As in the probation system, parenting in dysfunctional homes often consists of multiple violations, followed by savage punishment when the parent has finally had enough. As one defense attorney told me, "Every single one of my clients in juvenile drug court has one parent, no parents, or abusive parents."

But when punishment is random, what lesson do children learn? Not that breaking rules leads to punishment, but that punishment is arbitrary, a function of luck and the mood of people more powerful than you are. This doesn't offer good incentives to change your behavior.

Since Mischel did his marshmallow experiment, a lot of researchers have performed follow-ups, trying to replicate or expand the results. A 2012 paper from researchers at the University of Rochester provided a fascinating twist.[13] Before running the marshmallow experiment, they first put the kids in a room with a jar of crayons. Kids were told that if they waited to open the jar, they could use a nicer art set when the researcher returned. In half the cases, the adults came back with the promised supplies; in the other half, they apologized for not having the promised materials and told the kids they could use the original set. They then did the same thing with a promise of stickers.

After that, the marshmallow test. The kids who had been placed in the "unreliable" environment, where promised rewards never materialized, found it much harder to control themselves than the kids in the reliable environment where the crayons and stickers showed up on schedule. In fact, children in the reliable environment waited four times longer than those who had been primed to believe that stuff didn't necessarily happen just because an adult said it would.

Most criminals are raised in extremely unreliable environments. Rewards don't show up because Mom promised; they may be derailed because Dad got laid off, or a medical bill ate the money . . . or because Mom's drug habit or Dad's temper got the best of them.

"If you interview my subjects, most of them grew up in households where there was no ability to rely on any promise," says Hawken. "I'd be very surprised if more than 10 percent of my subjects passed the marshmallow test."[14]

Successful people have what psychologists call "self-efficacy" or an "internal locus of control": they feel that outcomes mostly depend on what they do. People who believe that they can control their fate are more likely to have happy futures even if they're wrong about the extent of their control. A person who believes he can grow up to be president is probably incorrect, statistically speaking. But the person who believes he can't is never wrong.

Americans in general have more belief than people of other nations in the power of the individual to control his or her fate. Seventy-one percent of Americans—compared to just 40 percent of Europeans—say that the poor could become rich if they tried harder, and a full quarter of Europeans believe that income and success are basically all due to luck. Only 16 percent of Americans agree. As Alberto Alesina and George-Marios Angeletos noted in a 2005 paper, to some extent, either is true if you believe it is true.[15] In a society where people think that hard work is useless, few people will work hard, and everyone will be poor. In a society where people believe they can get rich just by working harder, many people will put forth enough effort to make this come true.

It's no accident that so much of "the Dad talk" Judge Alm gives to his probationers revolves around decisions and control—"Who is in charge of whether I succeed on probation? *I am*." So are the subsequent lectures that he delivers to the violators who end up back in court. Over the course of the day, the judge uses the words "decision," "choices," and "control" to almost every probationer he sees. And every verdict is concluded with the same words, delivered in that exasperated-yet-cheerful tone with which your parents send you back upstairs to finish cleaning your room: "You can do this, Mr. Smith."

The attitude, says Mark Kleiman, "is neither 'you naughty boy don't do that again' nor 'you're going to prison.'" Rather, it's "Oh, you screwed up. There's a price for that. Now try again.

"Instead of making probation violation an occasion for termination of the relationship," he says, "punishment is part of what's basically a positive relationship. The most important part of HOPE probation is the first sentence of that speech: 'Everyone in this courtroom wants you to succeed.'"

WHY TOUGH LOVE WORKS

A positive relationship in the criminal justice system? Yes. Sending someone to jail every time might strike a liberal as overly punitive. But in the case of HOPE, it not only keeps them out of prison; it hands them back some measure of control over their own fate. If they do drugs and skip appointments, they will go to jail; if they don't, they will remain free. One of the most surprising things I found about HOPE is that the probationers themselves see it as fair. What they most like about the program is the fact that violations always produce exactly the same results. But they also like the resources. Tough love is not all tough. Like good parenting, it balances punishment and reward. All the probationers I spoke to were recovering from major meth habits. They'd lost teeth, relationships, and heart tissue to the drug—and kept going.

"Had I not gone to prison, I'd be dead," said Alex, a muscular, bright-eyed woman with spiky hair and a number of tattoos. She is almost fifty, and looks a little younger, which is surprising given the toll that meth has taken on her body. Before HOPE, she was living in the kind of apartment building where there's a dealer or an addict in every other apartment, and was selling over $5,000 worth of drugs a day—in part to fuel her own habit of a daily 8-ball. "I kept two things that not many people who smoke ice do," she told me proudly, "their mind, and their teeth."

Her natural athleticism probably helped—she was a junior Olympic swimmer in 1972, and didn't start smoking ice until she was nineteen or twenty (a late bloomer, she said ruefully). Nonetheless, by the time of the arrest that led to her being placed in HOPE, she had had two heart attacks—and still she kept smoking.

"Meth made me feel invincible. Besides, I always had a job, a roof over my head. In fact," she reflected, "I was probably the worst addict because I was functioning."

She attributes going clean to three things: the randomness of the drug testing, the fact that you can't get away with a single violation, and the relationships with people like her probation officer. Interestingly, she does not attribute it to rehab, which she didn't go to.

"Most of them can stop on their own," says Judge Alm. Drug addiction is a terrible thing, and terribly hard to quit, but it is not, as some people will tell you, "impossible to control." It turns out that when they know, with 100 percent certainty, that flunking a drug test (or missing it) means several days in jail, most people are able to control their urge to do drugs. And with the drug habit under control, other aspects of their lives suddenly get a lot easier to handle.

Now, it is true that some people can't control their urges even under immediate threat. I watched a couple of probationers who were facing a choice between rehab and prison mouth off to the judge about whether they deserved to spend a month or more in jail waiting for a treatment bed. One of them snarled profanities at the prosecutor when she suggested that he didn't seem to be too amenable to probation. I was stonkered.

The sheriffs let me spend a minute inside one of the holding cells, a dark windowless room with a pedestal sink that had an undersize toilet sticking out of its side. The inmates had to ask the guards if they wanted a few sheets of toilet paper—and if there were a number of prisoners in the courthouse that day, tough luck on privacy. After a minute in that cell—without the door closed—I knew I'd have been down on my knees begging the judge to tell me what I needed to do in order to never go back there again.

For all HOPE's successes, a lot of people keep violating—a few of them extravagantly and almost joyfully, but most of them carelessly and without forethought; they use and test dirty, they skip appointments, they run. For those people, the island's residential treatment facilities are a last resort. It's an expensive last resort—HOPE probation spends about $700,000 extra a year sending people to treatment. But it's still cheaper than prison.

PUNISHMENT IS FOR TEACHING, NOT REVENGE

Like most things in life, incarceration suffers from what economists call "diminishing marginal returns," which is to say that in terms of crime reduction, the twentieth prisoner is less valuable than the second, and the deterrent effect of adding the two-millionth prisoner is probably close to zero. This is true for two reasons: 1,999,999 prisoners are already a hell of a deterrent, and by the time you're at number 2 million, the people you're adding are less dangerous and prolific criminals than when you were at, say, number 20.

In individual lives, each additional prisoner may actually serve to normalize the thought of going to prison. It's no secret that prison terms are heavily concentrated in a relatively small number of low-income communities, particularly African American neighborhoods. That's a problem because one of the things keeping people out of jail is not just the fear of jail itself, but of what your friends and family and neighbors will say. When many of them have gone to jail, they may be very sad for you, but they're not horrified at the thought that you're a felon. And if you know a lot of people who have been locked up, prison probably doesn't seem so scary. The higher the incarceration rate, the less it discourages future criminals in the communities that criminals tend to come from.

Besides, the more severe a threatened punishment, the less often it will actually be applied, as can be attested by any parent who has ever threatened to kill their kid if they touch the liquor cabinet.

And what happens to these people when they get out of jail? In many cases they find themselves locked out of student loan programs, the military, government employment, housing programs, the voting booth, and most meaningful employment. Someone who cannot get any job better than dishwasher, who cannot find a decent apartment, who finds it difficult to finance further education— is it a surprise that they turn to crime? The cost to society of turning potentially productive workers into criminals is enormous—in the direct financial costs of law enforcement, in the relationships that are broken, and in the greater fear on the streets. Rehabilitation is not only kinder than retribution; it's cheaper.

Judge Alm is not the only one to think of this. Mark Kleiman, the UCLA public policy professor who along with Hawken has studied HOPE extensively, outlined a similar proposal decades ago. In fact, he says that the Italian jurist Cesare Beccaria laid out the principles in the eighteenth century.[16] In Michigan, a similar program on a smaller scale has been getting good results for decades. And in South Dakota, a program called 24/7 Sobriety has cut both DUI fatalities and repeat offenses dramatically by the simple expedient of requiring people convicted of DUIs to come to the police station twice a day for a Breathalyzer test.[17]

What HOPE and other programs like it show us is that in a lot of cases, we can have milder punishments and fewer violations, so long as those punishments are delivered Every. Single. Time. We can make the rule-breakers better off, and everyone else, too. I've been writing about public policy programs for over a decade now, and this is one of the few I've encountered in which there are genuinely no tradeoffs. It's win-win-win all the way around.

In other words, simple, consistent sanctions and an emphasis on rehabilitation rather than retribution are curing the hardest social problem America has. Not for everyone—lots of people still go to jail. But for many, many people, we've found a better way. A sober person is better than someone who is driving under the influence. Someone with a job is better than someone who is stealing to feed their drug habit. A man at home with his family is better than a man forming new relationships in the prison yard. We can't save everyone. But shouldn't we save everyone we can?

I've spent this book arguing that we should give people room to make mistakes, and help them recover when they do. Now I'm arguing that we should, as much as we can, extend that charity even to those who do things that are not just risky or stupid, but wrong. What we've learned from doing so can change more than just the criminal justice system.

Doing this is difficult. Angela Hawken, the Pepperdine professor who helped run that first randomized controlled trial of HOPE, is now working on trials all over the country. She is incredibly optimistic about the potential of programs like this. "HOPE is changing decision making. It does seem to be affecting locus of control— recognizing that they're in charge of their own future."

But Hawken is no utopian. She thinks people who are a real public-safety risk should be incarcerated. She also warns that programs like

HOPE can't be rolled out nationally, as some overenthusiastic commentators (including me) have suggested. Each community has different rules, different problems, and a different law enforcement culture; each local implementation is different, and it takes a while to get the bugs worked out. Even when they're up and running, they tend to have an Achilles' heel—once people get complacent, the consistency starts to slip.

"You need a judge who's willing to sanction modestly but consistently. And this mostly falls on probation—they have to work so much harder. Not everyone likes that idea," she told me. After a while, when the newness has worn off, they start to slip.

That problem will be familiar to any parent who has ever said, "From now on, things are going to be run differently around here," or any manager who has attempted to implement a new performance system. In the first few weeks, things are rocky, as people adjust to the new system. Then things settle down. And then, inevitably, comes the temptation to let things slide, just this once.

Sure your kid skipped her homework, but her best friend was mean to her at lunch and she was really sad. Or maybe your boss reprimanded you and you just didn't have the emotional energy for a battle. Of course you should shut down the employees you heard trading mean gossip about a coworker, but you're on a tight deadline for a new client proposal and you don't want to disrupt the team. Or maybe one of the gossipers is your best employee, someone you like a lot. Just this once, you can pretend not to have heard.

And sometimes it's impossible to be entirely consistent. If you've promised to read your daughter a story every night, do you keep your promise even if it means violating the strict bedtime you also promised to enforce? Corporations struggle with this constantly in designing compensation systems. If you slavishly set and follow rules, you'll find that your team will invest all its energy in meeting whatever numerical targets you set—even if the sales force alienates all the customers by selling them products they don't really need, and the engineers have to cut reliability in half to meet their ship dates. On the other hand, if the rules are too loose, performance will also fall apart.

Things aren't always crystal clear, but there is a set of concrete principles we can take away. The first is that while normative errors—significant violations of the rules we live by—should have consequences, those consequences should be as immediate as possible, but also as brief as possible. Doing the wrong thing should hurt, but it should not be crippling.

The second principle is that detecting deviance is as important as being prepared to punish it. Delivering the right kind of sanctions will not do you any good if you are only witnessing one mistake out of a hundred.

The third is that occasional mercy is not merciful. Whether you are "giving them a break" because you don't want to punish a good person for a single slip, or because you just can't face the effort needed to sanction them, what you are actually doing is breaking the link between their actions and the consequences that follow. This does no one any favors.

And the fourth is that punishment should be focused on the future, not the past—on continuing the relationship, not ending it. It is for teaching, not revenge.

That last principle is the hardest one to live by. We have a deep-seated thirst for vengeance when someone has done something we think is wrong—not ill-considered, not a misjudgment, but wrong. I'm not going to argue that this thirst is wrong, either. If nothing else, the fear of vengeance deters a lot of bad behavior.

I will argue, however, that it's counterproductive more often than not. As we've seen, the line between a judgment error and a normative error isn't always as clear as we think. And if we spend too much time trying to deter, or punish, wrongdoers, we may end up imposing even greater costs on ourselves.

10 FORGIVENESS

How I Learned to Stop Worrying and Embrace
Easy Bankruptcy (Though Not Personally)

Dave Ramsey is a medium kind of guy. Medium height, medium weight, medium age. When he walks out onstage in crisp pressed khakis with his neatly trimmed goatee, you half expect to hear the quarterly production figures for the Midwest division of a widget manufacturer. Then he opens his mouth and begins to speak, and you find yourself hanging on his every word.

Ramsey has that particularly southern gift for the long yarn, and in the summer of 2009 I traveled to a minor-league hockey rink outside of Detroit to hear him work his magic.[1] His fans know he likes to take his time. But however long the story winds on, he keeps his audience entranced, reeling them in with a joke or a dramatic twist just as their focus starts to waver. The six-hour program was dotted with rigorously scheduled breaks, but I think people's bladders would have given out before their attention.

It doesn't hurt that he has a hell of a story to tell, a classic tale of catastrophic fall leading to ultimate redemption—personal, financial, religious. Thousands of people crowded into that hockey stadium to hear him describe how he'd gone to hell and back, how he'd declared bankruptcy, clawed his way out of debt and misery and ultimately ended up as a multimillionaire with hundreds of employees, a syndicated radio program, and a fabulous house next door to country music star LeAnn Rimes. For the first hour and a quarter, all he did was tell that story. With every joke, the audience roared. When he paused for emphasis, the crowd grew so quiet that you could hear the rink's ice creaking under the temporary floor.

I'm afraid I can't replicate his delivery, but I can give you the basic facts. Dave Ramsey grew up in Antioch, Tennessee, the child of two real estate agents who had him running a part-time lawn-care business at the age of twelve. After working his way through college, he married and settled down to start a family while rapidly building himself a fairly impressive real estate empire. By 1986, Ramsey had $4 million worth of property and a net worth of about a million dollars. His investments churned out $250,000 a year (about half a million in today's dollars, adjusted for inflation). It was a substantial sum, and all the more so given his age. Ramsey was only twenty-six years old.[2]

Bank deregulation in the early '80s had triggered a boom in commercial real estate lending, but then a major tax reform bill in 1986 eliminated or shrank many of the most lucrative tax deductions available for investor-owned real estate.[3] The ensuing carnage was one of the reasons we had the savings and loan crisis in the late 1980s. It also took down Dave Ramsey.

Ramsey was one of the early victims of the inevitable contraction. His biggest lender was bought up by another bank, and the new owners noticed that they had loaned $1.2 million dollars to a twenty-six-year-old who was, in Ramsey's own telling, spending a lot of money buying boats and jewelry for his young wife. The bank, as Ramsey puts it, "freaked out." His loans were callable—the bank could demand its money back at any time. Which the bank promptly did. He was given ninety days to come up with $1.2 million dollars. Then his second biggest lender, sensing something was wrong, politely requested that he also return the $800,000 they'd loaned him.

Ramsey didn't have $2 million dollars. He had millions worth of real estate, in a soft market. Over the next two-and-a-half years, everything unraveled as assets were sold off at a loss and more notes were called. "We were foreclosed on," writes Ramsey in *Priceless*, one of his early financial self-help books, "and finally—with a brand-new baby and toddler—we were bankrupt."

Over that time, he suffered all the humiliations that come with such a dramatic reversal of fortune. We think of our financial lives as private, but too much of our public face is attached to debt for that to really be true. When we can't make our payments, the neighbors see us lose our homes, our cars, even our furniture. Ramsey had asked a friend to cosign a loan for a Jaguar; he lost the Jaguar and, for a time, the friend. His marriage was shaken by the strain on two terrified people facing utter financial ruin.

When the bailiffs were getting ready to cart away his furniture, he finally declared bankruptcy. And then he made a vow. In one of the bleakest moments of his downward spiral, Ramsey, who is an evangelical Christian, came across Proverbs 22:17: "The rich rule over the poor, and the borrower is slave to the lender." This, Ramsey realized, was exactly what had happened to him. He decided he would never borrow money again.

That one simple dictum was the germ out of which a mighty personal finance industry grew. First Ramsey got his own finances together. Then he began offering financial counseling through his church. He self-published a book, *Financial Peace*, which with typical hustle, he sold out of the trunk of his car. A bankrupt local radio station asked him to host—without pay—a show called *The Money Game*. Decades later, his syndicated show is carried on hundreds of stations.

Ninety percent of Ramsey's advice to his listeners comes down to one precept: Don't borrow money. Get out of debt, he says. Cut up your credit cards and use cash, or—if you must—a debit card. Spend less than you make and save the difference. If you have to, you can get a mortgage to buy a house, but the mortgage payments should never be more than 25 percent of your take-home pay. Other than that, don't borrow. Don't be a slave to the lender.

Of course, that's not actually all he does. Ramsey offers advice on budgeting, picking mutual funds, buying insurance, negotiating with creditors, and so forth. But the message to get out of debt is so powerful that the rest is merely the icing on the cake. If you stop borrowing, plan your spending, restrict your purchases to what you can buy with cash, and plow 15 percent of your income into savings, as Ramsey advises, it hardly matters whether you're picking the optimal mutual funds. You are so far outside of mainstream behavior—so "weird," as Ramsey puts it—that prosperity is almost certain to follow. Ramsey's recipe is a near 100 percent guarantee that you will not end up, as he did, in bankruptcy courts.

BANKRUPT NATION

Why do people declare bankruptcy? There are many answers to that question, but at the most fundamental level it comes down to this: They have made promises they can't keep. They borrowed money and couldn't repay it. They had a kid, which comes with an implicit promise to support that child to adulthood. They signed up for utilities that let you pay the bill at the end of the month. They checked in to a hospital and promised they would pay the bill when they checked out. If you want to understand bankruptcy, the first thing you need to understand is debt.

You can call your promises "debt" or "obligations," but no matter what you call them, they add risk to your life. They are fixed expenses, meaning they don't go away. If you lose your job you can cut back on the grocery bill, stop going to the movies, decide to wear that shabby-looking old winter coat for another year. But you cannot decide that this month you're going to do without the car payment you agreed to last year. If you do, your lender will slap you with penalties, and if you do it again, they'll come and take the car.

Any debt you incur increases the risk that if something goes wrong, you will not be able to cut your expenses to stay afloat. One study, which looked at every bankruptcy case to go through the Delaware courts in a year, found that the single biggest predictor of bankruptcy was not illness or divorce, or job loss. It was how much debt a person had taken on. The average debtor in Delaware's bank-ruptcy court had half the income, but 10 to 20 percent more debt, than the control group. If you follow Dave Ramsey's advice you are almost certain to stay out of bankruptcy court.

Ramsey's message is not popular with everyone. Spouses of his devotees who burst through the front door proclaiming they should cut up all their credit cards are often nonplussed. People who make a living offering high-interest loans on consumer goods are not Dave Ramsey's biggest fans. And bankruptcy attorneys don't gener-ally endorse his view that you should liquidate your 401(k), sell your house, *do anything* in order to stay out of bankruptcy court. Don't file, he advises callers, unless, like me, you are forced into it by your creditors.

In 2009, in preparation for the article I was writing, my husband and I went on Dave Ramsey's plan—as Ramsey puts it, "What God and Grandma told you, only we keep our teeth in." We sat down and made out a budget, and we vowed to stick with it. Then I drove to the bank and withdrew almost $2,000 in cash. Except for a check to the landlord, that was our disposable income for the next month.

Huddled in the front seat of my car, hunched over so that no one could see what I was doing, I parceled out the money into envelopes—groceries, entertainment, gas, clothing, and so forth. As I walked around with this fantastic wad of cash on me, it felt as if everyone could see through my purse to the mugger bait. When I bought a dress using several hundred dollars from the clothing envelope, the Macy's sales associate looked at the bills as if I'd handed her an eel.

Though carrying around large amounts of cash was terrifying at first, it ended up being tremendously reassuring. I always knew exactly how much we were spending on everything; if the cash wasn't in my pocket, it was safely at home in its envelope. And by the end of the month, there were a lot of greenbacks still snuggled safe in their nests. It turns out to be a very different thing to spend cash than it is to pay for something on a card. When you swipe your credit card, you may theoretically know that your bank balance is going down, but when you pay cash, you can visibly see yourself getting poorer. You buy what you need—but not much more.

Dave Ramsey gave us something few Americans have: control over our money. There were a lot of fascinating things about eschewing credit cards and paying for everything in cash, but here's the one that surprised me most: the number of people who frankly confessed to me that they had no idea where their paycheck went every month. These weren't people I was interviewing at a credit counselor's office; they were nice Washington professionals who had idly asked me what I was working on. When I told them what I was doing, the stories came pouring out about empty bank balances, serial overdraft charges, bills left unpaid because the car broke or the kids needed something. I had no idea that so many people I knew were living from paycheck to paycheck.

In retrospect, I should have known. Three-quarters of all Americans have less than six months' worth of expenses saved. Even among people making six figures, almost one in three is living from paycheck to paycheck. America is the bankruptcy capital of the world, and no wonder: most of us spend our lives running our finances right up against the edge of disaster. On the surface it may seem paradoxical that Dave Ramsey should have become spectacularly wealthy telling people how to avoid bankruptcy—a lesson he learned by going bankrupt himself. But it's not really a paradox at all. Dave Ramsey's case perfectly captures the genius of America's bankruptcy system, which works well because it is so very forgiving.[4] Entirely by accident, America stumbled into a system that fosters innovation and risk taking, encourages entrepreneurship, and helps folks who make mistakes, even bad ones, get back on their feet. The real problem is that very few people think of it that way.

DROWNING IN DEBT

You frequently hear people described as victims of their own success. In Kennet's case, this is literally true. In 2001, after more than a decade as a commercial photographer, he had a spacious studio, a solid roster of clients, and six employees. You might call it his slice of the American Dream, except that Kennet lives in Denmark.

"Then," he says, "there was the two airplanes and 9/11 and the whole market kind of died on me." The global economy faltered. So did his business. Even as he describes his descent into financial hell, a rueful smile plays around the corners of his mouth.[5]

"We went from a turnover of 300,000 kroners [$40,000] to 50,000 kroners [$6,000] from one month to the next. The money just sort of . . . whooshed out of the company."

What happened next will be familiar to many small business owners. Kennet tried to keep things running as long as he could, tapping out his line of credit to pay salaries and the sundry expenses of running a photography studio. The commissions trickled in, but they did not recover to anything near their old levels. Eventually, when the money was close to exhausted, he did the thing he had feared most: he laid off his workers and closed his studio.

In America, that would be a sad day. In Denmark, it was sad, and very expensive. Under Danish law, every worker was entitled to at least three months' salary; some were entitled to six. The taxman, too, had to be paid, even though the business had been losing money. Kennet was forced to borrow more to pay the mandatory fees. Just as his income was cratering, he found himself saddled with a brand-new $80,000 debt, and thousands in annual interest payments.

"I was really really close to a bankruptcy," he says. "I had to sell everything I had." The $80,000 he was left with seemed "handle-able," he says.

Kennet is philosophical about his reversal of fortune. In the decade since his business failed, he has realized that he's glad he no longer has six employees to manage. Of course, he makes less money. But he's doing what he loves—taking photographs—instead of spending most of his time managing other people. He'd say it was all for the best, if it weren't for one thing: the debt. He has now paid more in interest than the original balance of his loan, and he is still paying. Nonetheless, when I spoke to him, the bank was getting ready to take his house.

Kennet is the first to admit that he has made mistakes along the way. A few years ago, he received a sizable inheritance. He ruefully muses that he could have used the money to pay down his loan, but instead he put it into fixing up the house. The idea was to increase the value enough to allow him to refinance, rolling his 12 percent loan into a mortgage with a longer term and a lower interest rate. It almost worked; Kennet estimates that he was about six months from getting clear when the financial crisis crashed the Danish housing market.

But he didn't make it. Lines of credit, unlike mortgages, are callable—the bank can demand that you repay the money if it thinks there's a high risk you'll default. And in Denmark, if they demand the money back and you can't pay, they can seize your house and sell it.

In late 2011, the loan officer he had been working with was replaced. The replacement looked over his books and decided that the loan was too risky. In the decade since Kennet's business failed, it's gotten harder to make it as a photographer. Digital cameras have dramatically lowered both the upfront cost and the skill needed to enter the profession, so he has more competition for every commission. Meanwhile, international brands, who used to do a photo shoot in every country, are now producing central campaigns that are distributed across Europe. And the portrait business has been hammered by the ubiquity of cell phone cameras and inexpensive point-and-shoot models. It is a testament to Kennet's skill and professional network that he is still making a living.

His old loan officer was willing to go along as long as he kept making his monthly payments—oh, maybe he was late a couple of times, but he always made good within a month, and he hasn't been late in several years. The new loan officer wasn't so trusting. He put Kennet on notice that the bank was getting ready to call his loan, and that they would start proceedings to take his house if he didn't pay.

"Just before Christmas I got a letter that I had ten days to pay in the full amount or they would send my case to a lawyer," he told me.

Of course, the Danish housing market is still depressed. He's tried to sell the house, but has had no takers. There's a good chance his house will not sell for enough to clear both his mortgage and his loan. If that happens, he says, he will still owe the bank the residual.

In America, Kennet would be talking about bankruptcy; in fact, he'd probably have filed, or settled with the banks, years ago. But in Denmark, this is not an option. When I ask him why he hasn't considered bankruptcy, he says simply, "Because they won't let me go." His creditors, he says, can put him into bankruptcy if they decide he's hopeless, but he cannot seek bankruptcy protection on his own. Everyone he owes money to would have to agree to a discharge, including the taxman. And in practice, the taxman almost always refuses. "You have to be mentally ill or there have to be really certain things that would make them agree on it," says Kennet. "If you're a normal, well-functioning, healthy citizen, they don't."

For ten years, his life has been driven by the need to keep making those debt payments. Now it looks as if that may be the story of the rest of his life. Asked if he sees any end in sight, he says, "Not really." At one point in our conversation, he glumly wondered if it wouldn't be better to put everything in his wife's name and work off the books. There are dangers to working in the "gray market," of course—it doesn't pay as well, and also, it's illegal. But how else can he ever hope to get clear of the mistakes of decades past?

Kennet doesn't seem to be seriously considering going underground. But it's not hard to see why someone might. And then who is better off? Not the bank, which doesn't get its money. Certainly not the person who can no longer work legally, nor the companies that might have liked to hire him above the board. Nor the fellow citizens who lose both the benefit of his work, and his tax dollars.

Dave Ramsey tells his followers to avoid bankruptcy at all costs, but there is something much worse than filing for bankruptcy, and that is being tethered to your mistakes and not being able to shed your debt. "So when you listen to Dave pound the table about avoiding bankruptcy, consider this," wrote one bankruptcy attorney. "You're listening to a man who went through bankruptcy, came out the other end and lived to tell the tale, and is now worth millions and millions of dollars. Could he have done all of that if he had all that debt hanging around his neck like a hangman's noose? Probably not."[6]

Mobsters are said to have chained concrete blocks to the legs of the corpses they didn't want to resurface, when they chucked them into a lagoon. Denmark's bankruptcy laws are the legal equivalent of this practice. It leaves unlucky businessmen drowning in debt.

WHY AMERICA'S BANKRUPTCY SYSTEM IS SO GOOD

Most Americans don't realize how uniquely generous our system is. What we call Chapter 7, the process most people think of as "bankruptcy," doesn't even exist in most of the rest of the world. If you want to declare Chapter 7 bankruptcy, you walk into a courtroom, offer up whatever meager assets you have to your creditors (often nothing), and walk out with all your debts discharged. Most countries make it difficult even to get *into* bankruptcy court, requiring debtors to attempt an out-of-court settlement, and I can't think of another country that lets you leave court without putting you on a payment plan. In Germany, the court can terminate your petition if you fail to maintain reasonable employment. In Scandinavia they can deny you a discharge if they think you spent your borrowed money frivolously. And in some places, bankruptcy isn't available at all. In Dubai, parking lots outside airports and yacht moorings have in recent years become littered with luxury cars abandoned by wealthy expats and locals who have fled the country to avoid debtor's prison.[7]

The generosity of America's bankruptcy system is basically a historical accident. America inherited an infant form of bankruptcy law from Britain, and the Constitution authorized Congress to create a new bankruptcy code (perhaps because several founding fathers, most notably Thomas Jefferson, were poor at managing their assets and were drowning in debt). But while Congress had the *right* to create a new bankruptcy code, it didn't *have* to, so it didn't get around to drafting a permanent one until the very end of the nineteenth century. By then, thanks to the Homestead Act, which gave away free land to anyone who could stay on their claim for five years, America had an unusually large number of small farmers who owed money to eastern bankers. These farmers were represented by senators, who fought hard to make it easy for them to shed their debts. And so America's first official bankruptcy code was far more lenient than its counterparts elsewhere in the world. And then, more than a century of consumer activism made it more lenient still—at least until today.[8]

When I worked for *The Economist*, I found myself covering a massive bankruptcy-reform bill as it made its way through Congress. (It eventually passed, with the unlovely moniker of the Bankruptcy Abuse Prevention and Consumer Protection Act of 2005, or the BAPCPA.) The bill's critics—mostly bankruptcy attorneys and consumer activists—were vehemently opposed to the bill, which erected all sorts of obstacles on the road to Chapter 7, from financial counseling to paperwork requirements to a means test that bounced the most affluent filers into a Chapter 13 payment plan. The word I heard most frequently when I was reporting on the new law was "draconian."

I caused immense confusion at an editorial meeting in London when I tried to describe our punitive new bankruptcy procedures. My British colleagues considered the "draconian" new process so absurdly lax and debtor-friendly that they were convinced I must have gotten it backward: surely I was describing the old law, not the crackdown that was driving consumer advocates crazy?

This is a fairly common sentiment among Europeans. During an interview for this book, one economist launched, unprompted, into a five-minute rant about our "anything goes" approach to debt relief. "It's absurd," he said incredulously. "You walk into a court and tell a judge 'I don't want to pay my debts,' and he just says 'Fine'?" He was Scandinavian.

Americans are often as shocked as Europeans to hear that our rules are so lax. We may allow easy bankruptcy, but few people really approve of it. Imagine how you'd feel if your boss told you he had declared bankruptcy. It would be a trifle awkward, wouldn't it? And wouldn't you kind of wonder if your business was in safe hands?

In my experience as a public speaker, people are even less happy when they learn that, as a result of our easy bankruptcy laws, America is far and away the bankruptcy capital of the world. Everywhere else, bankruptcy is a stigma, an enduring disgrace, a permanent stain. Here it's just as likely to be the doorway to a business empire.

People tend to feel that if we are declaring bankruptcy so often, it must be a sign that something is very wrong. But it is actually a sign that something is very right.

THE SCHOOL OF FRESH STARTS

Remember what we said back in chapter 1: most entrepreneurs fail, even if they've succeeded before. Nolan Bushnell was one of two founders of Atari, the incredibly successful video game company whose product dominated my friends' living rooms in the mid-'80s. He also founded the equally successful Chuck E. Cheese's Pizza-Time Theaters. From there he went on to found . . . a string of companies you've never heard of. His last venture, a chain of restaurants where you could order food from a computer, closed. He's now working on video games that prevent aging.

And maybe they will be a blockbuster hit! The point is that there's no way to tell from his résumé.

The entrepreneurs who do succeed, whether on their first attempt or their eighth, are responsible for the dynamism of the U.S. economy. Sometimes, like Dave Ramsey's, the failure of the previous business directly inspires the success of the next one. Bankruptcy experts have a name for this—they call it the principle of the fresh start: by wiping old debt off the books, we help the economy by speeding up the redeployment of capital—human and financial.

You're probably not convinced. Most of us are not comfortable with easy bankruptcy; we're happy enough to have it, but not to praise it. It feels too much like rewarding—nay, encouraging—bad behavior. And those who remember their coursework from Economics 101 will tell us that making default easier makes credit more expensive, for everyone.

That's the theory. But any economist will tell you that the real world is often more complicated than the simple models of Economics 101. While easier bankruptcy *should* mean more expensive credit, it's not what happens in practice. In 2005, Americans enjoyed by far the easiest bankruptcy code in the world. They also enjoyed some of the easiest access to credit.[9] (I am not the only person who received a letter addressed to her dog informing him that he'd been prequalified for a MasterCard with zero percent balance transfers.) We also had an entrepreneurial boom. By lowering the cost of failure, our bankruptcy laws made it easier for people to take risks in the first place.

We know this because the unique structure of America's bankruptcy law constitutes what economists call a "natural experiment." Bankruptcy courts are federal courts, which means that the rules are set by Congress. But exemptions—the stuff you can shield from creditors—vary from state to state. This variance gives academics a chance to study how the more or less generous provisions affect entrepreneurship.

All states allow you to protect some assets: Bank of America cannot, like the villain in a 1920's film noir, chase you down and strip the engagement ring off your finger. But which assets you can protect, and how expensive they can be, varies greatly from state to state. In Alabama and Kentucky, if you have more than $5,000 in home equity, you have to sell your house and give the proceeds to your creditors. In Texas and Florida, no matter how much your house is worth, you cannot be forced to sell it.

The amount of home equity you can shield from creditors is known as the "homestead exemption." Because it varies so widely, the economists Michelle White and Wei Fan were able to use the variance to test whether making bankruptcy more generous had any impact on people's willingness to take risks. What they found is that it matters, a lot: states with an unlimited homestead exemption have 35 percent more business owners than states with low exemptions.[10]

If you know anything about how entrepreneurship works, this is not all that surprising. In the days of Facebook billionaires, we tend to imagine entrepreneurship as a matter of having a great idea and then getting a series of venture capitalists to fund it until you can go public with a massively profitable IPO. But that's a little bit like thinking every pickup basketball player can dunk like LeBron James. Most businesses, even very successful ones, do not get their financing from Kleiner Perkins Caufield & Byers. They're much more likely to get it from Visa and MasterCard—which means that if the business fails, they're on the hook for those payments. And as we saw in chapter 3, no one can guarantee that their business will succeed.

Even after the early start-up phase, banks generally require owners to personally cosign loans until their businesses are large and well established. I've interviewed business owners who have been profitable for a decade and employ dozens of people, but still have to trot down to the bank with their credit reports and two years of personal income tax returns, along with their audited company accounts, every time they want to buy a new piece of equipment.

That means that personal bankruptcy laws have a big impact on the risk of starting a business. For small-time entrepreneurs, easier personal bankruptcy mitigates the considerable risks of starting a business. If the business goes under they may lose their capital, but they're not going to find their family out on the street. By shielding entrepreneurs from catastrophic results, we free them to take more risks—the good kinds of risks that have made America one of the most dynamic economies in the history of the world.

That's not the only way easier bankruptcy laws encourage entrepreneurship. By freeing people from the sunk costs of their failed business, we free them up to try again.

"I'm always behind, I'm always struggling to make it just for the next month," says Kennet. "It's really frustrating that you can't just draw a line in the sand and say, 'okay, now we start afresh.'" He can't expand or take risks because that crushing loan payment is always waiting at the end of the month. Taking entrepreneurial talent and strapping it to old debts is an enormous waste of a scarce resource. As we've seen, many entrepreneurs are serial entrepreneurs, and most don't get it right the first time. Rules like Denmark's run a serious risk that for those who fail the first time, there will never be a second time.

"The sad thing," Kennet told me, "the really sad thing, is that you really only get one chance."

Remember the farmers and foragers from chapter 2? Europe's bankruptcy rules are made for a farming economy, one where success is basically a function of effort and sound planning. But that's not what a modern economy looks like. Success in the modern world is more like hunting: you have to go out there and be ready to kill something and drag it home, but that doesn't mean you're going to come back with meat every day. In a complex modern economy, success and failure will always be somewhat unpredictable; even the best hunters will frequently come home empty-handed. That's why the most important thing is not being discouraged by setbacks and being willing to try over and over again.

European bankruptcy laws treat failure as if it were a simple function of effort and personal virtue. As a result, they end up punishing people whose only sin was to take a chance on starting a business. And they inadvertently punish themselves, when potential innovators decide it's not worth the risk. Compare the United States to France: we have twice the rate of new business ownership, twice the rate of early-stage entrepreneurial activity—and consequently, three times the rate of established business ownership.[11]

You might say that all this is worth it if we're punishing the profligate—keeping people from running up bills they can't pay on foolhardy ventures. And it's true: making bankruptcy more difficult probably does prevent some of that. But the price tag of easier bankruptcy is surprisingly cheap.

WHY MEMPHIS IS THE BANKRUPTCY CAPITAL OF THE WORLD

The U.S. court system publishes a handy map of bankruptcies per capita, with counties shading from palest yellow (less than 0.2 percent of the population declaring bankruptcy) to deepest red (more than eight bankruptcies per thousand people).[12] Online, you can click through the years and watch the financial crisis proceed like a terrible skin disease spreading across the face of our nation. A few red bumps appear in places like Detroit and Atlanta, quickly growing redder and darker. Then the area around them starts to look red and irritated too. The next thing you know, angry welts have metastasized all over the map, to Nevada and California and exurban Virginia, and you start wondering if the patient can survive.

If bankruptcy were a contagious disease, the CDC would be rushing epidemiologists to Shelby County, Tennessee, the darkest, reddest spot on the map. Long before other places were breaking out in bankruptcy, Memphis and its environs had a severe chronic case. Before the housing crisis, before the banks went under, more than 1 percent of the county's residents were declaring bankruptcy every year.

One percent doesn't sound like much, but when it comes to bankruptcies, that's a phenomenal number. If everyone you knew had a 1.4 percent chance of declaring bankruptcy, as residents of Memphis did in 2010, over a typical seventy-year life span more than half your friends and family would find themselves in bankruptcy court. It doesn't exactly work that way, of course—some people file more than once—but it's still more than any other place in the world. According to supporters of the 2005 bankruptcy reform, Memphis shows the danger of unchecked bankruptcy. When I was covering BAPCPA, more than one person people told me, "We don't want to end up like Memphis."

Naturally, since Memphis has a lot of bankruptcies, it has a lot of bankruptcy lawyers. The district's streamlined system makes it easy to retain one: you can roll your lawyer's fees, and your court costs, right into your payment plan. Bankruptcy is made easier because it's so common—and it's more common because it's so easy. The people behind the BAPCPA say that Memphis is a classic example of moral hazard, and it's hard to argue that they're entirely wrong.

"We have debtors who spend almost their whole life" in bankruptcy, the Memphis judge Jennie Latta told me frankly, a point that was echoed by others.[13]

"Well, you've come to the right place," said a bankruptcy attorney when I told her I was writing a book on failure. "This is where we pat failure on the ass and send it on its way."

In the spring of 2012 I went to Memphis to see for myself what moral hazard looks like when it runs amok. The Memphis bankruptcy courts are crowded with people, few of whom seem to be struggling entrepreneurs. I spent a Thursday morning observing bankruptcy trustees meeting with the debtors whose filings they oversee. The meetings take place in a long, featureless waiting room that one of the attorneys I spoke to called the Bus Stop. It was as crowded as a Greyhound station on a holiday weekend, full of the near-poor and the almost-making-it. They'd come to bankruptcy court in their uniforms, clutching folders full of unpaid bills and holding tightly to the hands of children too young to be aware of much beyond their own boredom. I watched one boy of about five or six spend fifteen minutes methodically sliding his butt up and down the wall. His mother, meanwhile, was frantic: she couldn't find her attorney in the milling crowd.

Most of these people are here because they can't seem to spend less than they make. It is a problem that even bankruptcy attorneys acknowledge. "We live in a microwave society," one lawyer told me. "We want it all immediately."

Living well below your means is hard when your means are small, especially if someone will offer to let you borrow the difference to live above them. Judge Latta ran me through the depressing seasonal math of people who come to court to explain to the bankruptcy trustee why they can't pay what they owe. "If it's September and October, it's uniforms and school supplies for the kids. If it's December, Christmas."

What about spring, I asked, does it get better then? She sighed.

"Graduations . . . proms . . ." If you're that close to the edge, it never really ends. And who wants to tell their eighteen-year-old daughter that she has to wear a $10 thrift-store dress to the prom so that MasterCard can be paid?

It's not always easy to live within your means, even when your means are more substantial. Everyone in the Memphis courts agreed that thanks to the real estate crash, they had a lot more middle-class filers than they used to. Doctors are a special problem, Judge Latta told me. They plan on working until they're sixty-five, then suddenly they get sick and can't keep working. They've got all the accoutrements of a successful professional lifestyle—high-end cars, a big house with manicured grounds and granite countertops, maybe a vacation home or a boat—all of it usually purchased with debt. It's hard to sell those big houses now, and luxury SUVs.

If we're honest, most of us aren't too different from those doctors. Ask yourself how far you'd be from bankruptcy if you and your spouse got laid off and had to take a job that only paid 60 percent of your current salary. How long until the student loans and credit card bills and the car payment and that expensive cell phone contract you're locked into ate up your savings? Could you sell the house without the bank suing you for the balance? (Contrary to popular belief, except in a minority of "nonrecourse" states, you can't just mail the bank the keys and walk away; they can come after you for the difference.)

The difference between the people at the Memphis courthouse and your average middle-class family is not so much that middle-class families are better savers.[14] It's that lower-skilled workers are more likely to be unemployed, to have their hours cut back, or to have some sort of crisis they can't absorb. If you make $100,000 a year, a $1,500 car repair bill is somewhere between annoying and painful. If you make $18,000 a year, it's a disaster.

Of course, there are struggling people in every city, but nowhere else do so many of them end up in bankruptcy court. People in

Memphis file for what seem like small reasons: their utilities are shut off, they get a small garnishment order.

One reason why so many Memphians file for bankruptcy is that—unlike the rest of the country—most file for Chapter 13. Unlike Chapter 7, where you give up whatever assets you have in order to shield your future income from creditors, Chapter 13 lets you hold on to your assets, and gives creditors a portion of your income. Chapter 13 debtors enter a payment plan, typically for five years.

That's five years for something to go wrong: a job loss, hours cut back at work, a nasty divorce. Cases regularly get dismissed because the debtor can't pay, and then reinstated when their financial situation stabilizes. None of this is ideal for the creditor, but it's better than not getting paid at all.

One of the provisions of the 2005 law was a ban on serial bankruptcy filings. It was meant to target the minority of filers who were clearly and genuinely abusive—people who would move in to an apartment, refuse to pay the rent, and file for bankruptcy to stay the inevitable eviction . . . over and over and over again. Consumer advocates complained that this provision would hurt a lot of people who made a good-faith effort to pay. I asked Judge Latta what she'd done about serial filings.

"I haven't enforced it because frankly, no one's complaining," she told me. Kicking a debtor out of Chapter 13 doesn't make it easier for the creditors to collect their money; it makes it harder. They have to go through a lot of paperwork to seize the debtor's bank account or file a garnishment order with the court to get the employer to automatically divert a chunk of their wages to the creditor. Then they squabble with other creditors over who gets the first bite of the paycheck. In Chapter 13, the bankruptcy trustee mails them a check every month. Even if a few months are missing, it costs less in the long run.

In other words, even the "out-of-control" Memphis bankruptcy culture isn't actually all that out of control. Moral hazard is real, to be sure. It just isn't that costly. It's certainly much cheaper than the alternative: driving entrepreneurs and small businessmen like Kennet out of business.

THE PARADOX OF FORGIVENESS

Every Friday, people with modest family incomes call in to Dave Ramsey's radio show and cry out, "I'm debt free!" And then they tell the story of how paying down their debts has changed their life. Ramsey is obviously right that serial debtors would be better off if they refused to borrow money, stuck to a budget, and saved 15 percent of their income as a cushion for those unexpected crises. Which is why my husband and I remained committed to paying off debt and saving even after the article ended. Some savings, and the painful discipline of cash, could keep a lot of Memphians out of the Bus Stop. But while Ramsey's powers of persuasion are formidable, they are not infinite. Plenty of people ignore his advice. Of course, people shouldn't borrow more than they can reasonably hope to pay back. But what should we do with those who do? Those who bridle at the concept of easy bankruptcy will often make a case for tough sanctions or even prison. But if easy bankruptcy for low-income people who have trouble sticking to a budget is the price of allowing more Kennerts or Dave Ramseys to get a fresh start, then America has made a very good bargain.

To see why, let us consider a problem even worse than debt: homelessness. There are a variety of issues clustered under the term "homelessness" in American policy-making, but what we normally think of are the chronic homeless, people who are not in some sort of temporary emergency but in a permanent life crisis. Most have a serious problem, like substance abuse or mental illness; many have both. They are, in the words of the professionals who work with them, the "treatment resistant" and the "hard to reach." In the past, many of these people would have been in mental hospitals. Legal and policy changes in the 1970s closed most of those hospitals and made it nearly impossible to commit someone against their will. The result is visible on the streets of every city in America.

For years, social service programs focused on getting people into treatment, often making it a condition of offering them permanent housing. Many people were helped that way. But those who refused—the ones who would rather drink or hear voices than submit to the will of doctors and social workers—stayed on the street, floating in and out of shelters as space and weather permitted.

Most people's reaction, on hearing this, is "That's a pity, but what can you do?" Or, less charitably: If you want society to give you a helping hand, you should be willing to abide by a few minimal rules—like taking your antipsychotics, or giving up the booze that is making it impossible for you to hold a job. If you can't do that, you deserve the consequences.

In the early 1980s, the clinical psychologist Sam Tsemberis found himself walking past a growing number of homeless people on the way to the hospital in New York where he worked—many of them people he'd seen in the clinic the month before. It bothered him. And eventually he hit on a novel idea: Why not solve their housing problem by . . . giving them somewhere to live? No conditions, just a clean, warm place with a bed and a bathroom and a little place to store food.

This violates every instinct we have about how to help people. After all, don't addicts have to hit rock bottom before they can recover? If we give them somewhere warm and dry where they can indulge their addiction, aren't we just enabling them?

People living on the street have already pretty much hit rock bottom, and they haven't bounced back. In many cases, if you make them give up drinking or drugs as a condition of getting housing, they'll stay on the street. And while drinking all day in your room isn't very good for you, it's even less healthy to do it on the street.

In 1992, with funding from a New York State grant, Tsemberis helped create Pathways to Housing, an agency that would offer housing to people who were still using drugs, or in the throes of acute mental illness. Their method was simple: they rented apartments from private landlords, and put homeless addicts in them. Only after the person had moved in would a team of clinical workers provide in-home services: psychiatric care, addiction and employment counseling, health checkups. By solving the most immediate and pressing problem—the one the homeless people cared most about—Pathways to Housing gained the trust, and space, they needed to tackle the deeper issues.[15]

In the first year, they housed sixty people. Since their founding, they've housed thousands.

This "Housing First" approach has spread and even won converts in the upper reaches of the Bush administration. As a result, we now have a wealth of data on it. And what the data shows is that it doesn't just get people off the streets; it also saves money. Forgiveness, it turns out, is surprisingly cheap.

That's because leaving people on the streets is stunningly expensive. All those visits to the emergency room and to prison cost a lot of money. In one famous case, a chronic alcoholic named Angelo Solis cost California hospitals $1 million in just three years living on the streets. Putting him in a motel room for $700 a month saved taxpayers hundreds of thousands of dollars in medical care and other bills.[16]

A 2009 study in the *Journal of the American Medical Association* found that Housing First participants cost taxpayers an average of $4,000 a month before they were given supportive housing. After six months in treatment, that figure had gone down to $1,400.[17] After twelve months, it fell still further, to a little under a thousand dollars a month. And that doesn't take into account the benefits to the participants, who are warm, dry, and fed and can thus turn their attention to less pressing issues, like pulling themselves together.

The success of Housing First confounds our sense of the way the world should be. It shouldn't be cheaper to give people free housing while they drink and take drugs to their heart's content, and skip their medication. It shouldn't be better to forgive people their transgressions than to insist that they stop doing clearly destructive things.

But many of America's best policies do just that: they offer people a fresh start even if they've made a lot of mistakes—even, in fact, if they keep on making those same mistakes. It's confounding, and goes against our sense of justice, but sometimes, we may have to ask ourselves: Do we want to be right, or do we want to be rich?

CULTURE VS. RULES

The magic of bankruptcy law is that frequently, we get to be both. That's because even in Memphis, not everyone who could file for bankruptcy protection does. Todd Zywicki, who teaches bankruptcy law at George Mason University, was one of the most prominent intellectuals behind the 2005 bankruptcy reform bill. He thinks bankruptcy is contagious—that knowing many people who have declared bankruptcy makes you more likely to do it yourself. Before BAPCPA, he thought there was a real danger America would end up looking a lot like Memphis. And to Zywicki's credit, he did a better job of predicting what followed the passage of BAPCPA—a dramatic decrease in bankruptcy filings—than did I, or any of his opponents.

Yet when I interviewed him, seven years after the passage of the bill, Zywicki acknowledged that however much abuse there is in the system, the surprising thing is that there isn't more.[18] Declaring bankruptcy is surprisingly painless; the worst part is probably waiting your turn in bankruptcy court. Nonetheless, most people who could benefit from bankruptcy relief soldier on, dodging creditor calls and trying to find a way to pay their debts.

Many bankruptcy experts and consumer groups consider this a crying shame. At the height of the financial crisis a number of commentators actually cheered the possibility that millions of Americans would mail in their house keys to the banks holding their mortgages, forcing bankers to suffer the losses.

In many instances they would be better off—so why don't they do it? The answer is surprisingly simple: shame. They are too embarrassed. They don't want to be thought of as deadbeats.

Bankruptcy attorneys and consumer advocates generally think that America needs two things: easy bankruptcy laws, and people who will encourage drowning debtors to take advantage of them. More conservative commentators—and bankers—tend to argue that we need tighter laws and debtors who are too proud to file. They're both right—and wrong. America benefits greatly from easy bankruptcy. And it also benefits from having Dave Ramsey to tell Americans to do everything in their power not to use them.

Dave Ramsey is right about two things: most people would be better off if they had less debt. And once they've taken it on, it's good for them to struggle as hard as possible to pay it. Not to the exclusion of everything else—if it means your kids won't have enough to eat, or you can't get the medical care you need, or you're draining your retirement account, then you should stop struggling. Turn in the keys to the car you can't afford and buy a beater, cut up the credit cards, and file for bankruptcy. But under ordinary circumstances, it is a very good thing that people struggle to pay their debts—and not just for banks.

We can have lenient bankruptcy rules precisely because we have a sound culture supporting those rules. If that culture changed so that people weren't ashamed to take advantage of the system, we'd have a situation like the one I described in Russia in chapter 2: the system would be utterly dysfunctional. The bottom 40 percent of this country has an average net worth of $12,000, much of it in exempt assets like home equity or retirement accounts.[19] In theory, every one of these people would be better off filing for bankruptcy and shedding their debts. But even in Memphis, only 1 percent actually do. If that changed—if everyone with a negative net worth decided to shed their debt—then banks would take big losses, which would be passed on to consumers in the form of higher loan rates, or a refusal to lend at all. What would follow is a push to tighten up the laws so that bankruptcy became harder to access—creating hundreds of thousands of people like Kennet, hopelessly in thrall to the bad decisions of past decades.

Bankruptcy lawyers shouldn't be criticizing Dave Ramsey; they should be thanking him. It's people like him, encouraging debtors to pay off as much as they can, who make it possible for us to maintain the easy bankruptcy laws that give relief to the clients of the consumer groups and lawyers who complain about Ramsey's message.

This is the paradox of forgiveness. In policy, just as in our personal lives, forgiveness feels dangerous. If we forgive mistakes too easily, we feel we're inviting people to transgress again. But in fact, so long as our culture makes us feel bad about our transgressions, we all end up better off.

What feels risky is often the safest course, and what feels sensible and safe is often the most dangerous thing you can do. In the spring of 2006, sensible people looking for a safe investment relied on the inherited wisdom of generations and bought the biggest house they could finance. At the same time, a handful of wild-eyed risk takers poured their effort, and money, into building a completely unnecessary Web service that let users broadcast their thoughts in 140-character chunks. Today, obviously, we'd all rather have Twitter stock than an exurban McMansion. Getting the up side of down often means letting go of your instincts, ignoring conventional wisdom, and leaping for something that no one's ever done before. Obviously, if you shoot at a target you can't see, you'll often miss. But if you can pick yourself up and try again, you may plant a flag in uncharted territory. For that to be possible, you have to be able to shed past mistakes. A resilient society lets you fail, and even lets the failure sting, but only for a moment. Then it helps you get back on track, and everyone reaps the benefit.

CODA

A year after I went to that Dave Ramsey seminar, my husband and I suddenly found that we were planning to buy a house. Thanks to the months I'd spend absorbing Ramsey's debt-free message, we'd paid off our cars and our student loans except for a few thousand dollars that for tedious reasons could not be paid off early. We were free of credit card debt and had accumulated a healthy pile of savings, which comforted me whenever I read another article on how print media was doomed to an imminent and painful death. And then before I knew it, I had agreed to plunge most of that stack of cash into several hundred thousand dollars' worth of brick and hardwood flooring.

We were not one of those couples who solemnly debates the pros and cons of ownership and then spends eighteen months dutifully trodding around open houses. We stepped into homeownership the way one steps over a doorstep. One morning, two happy renters idly decided to stop by an open house "just to look". A week later we were preparing our first offer.

Most people who are buying their first home stretch to afford as much as possible. We did exactly the opposite. Instead of asking ourselves how big a mortgage payment we could possibly stretch to pay, we asked ourselves what would happen if we both lost our jobs, and then had to take jobs making half as much. How much mortgage would we be willing (and able) to pay if that happened? We settled on a figure that was less than twice our annual income, resulting in a mortgage payment of slightly under 20 percent of our monthly take-home pay.

This was clearly a minority approach. I called my staid, boring credit union to get preapproved for a mortgage using only my income, figuring we'd add Peter if we needed to. After taking all of my information, the nice lady at the other end of the line regretfully said, "I'm afraid we can't approve you for more than . . .," naming a figure that was more than five times my annual income.

"Oh my God!" I blurted.

My husband, who had been sitting next to me while I fed her my vital stats, looked alarmed. "We're not going to be able to afford the house?" he asked anxiously.

"We can buy two!" I told him.

Obviously, our parsimonious approach required some compromise. We left the neighborhood we'd been looking in and moved about a hundred feet, across North Capitol Street, because doing so knocked $100,000 off the price. The house we finally bought, on a beautiful tree-lined street, had about two linear feet of kitchen cabinets and peeling laminate countertop, and a backyard that . . . well, if you've seen one of those gritty, depressing indie films about down-and-out heroin addicts, this is where the director would shoot a scene to let you know that the addicts had finally hit bottom. The fence sagged like old lettuce, broken blocks of concrete jutted through a sprinkling of topsoil, and everywhere you looked you saw broken glass and strange fragments of ancient metal. The only thing missing to complete the look was a car up on blocks. And nothing could be done about any of it very immediately, because we had already agreed that there would be no home equity loans. In fact, six months after we moved in, I started paying extra on our mortgage, which horrifies all the bankers I know. Lose your tax deduction paying off debt that only costs you 4.5 percent a year, when you could be getting 8 or 10 percent on that money in the market?

Their math may be correct. But life does not unfold mathematically. Our house is habitable, and slowly, it is becoming nice. It is big enough for us. And we sleep better in it than we would in a house that cost us twice as much. My husband and I are both journalists, an industry that is even less secure than it was ten years ago, when my father asked me to make that dismal projection of my expected cash flows. Taking out a little mortgage, and paying it off early, means that we can afford to take big risks where it really matters.

Don't get me wrong: we hardly live like monks. We eat at very nice restaurants at least once a year, enjoy cable television and smartphones, and even take the occasional vacation. What we've done is to minimize the fixed portion of our lifestyle, the part that could topple us into financial disaster if something goes wrong.

When I was beginning my second year of business school, and my classmates and I were nervously waiting to hear whether we'd gotten permanent offers from the firms where we'd done summer internships, a few friends and I made a bet that we wouldn't get offers. We each put a hundred dollars into a pool. Those who got offers would forfeit their hundred. Those who didn't would split the pool. The bet was what you might call "hedging your net psychic wealth." If you got a full-time offer, you'd be so glad that you wouldn't miss the hundred dollars. If you didn't . . . well, at least you'd be able to drown your sorrows in top-shelf liquor.

I hit the jackpot. Everyone got an offer but me. I got to go to dinner at one of Chicago's best restaurants. Considering the summer I had at Merrill Lynch, I was probably better off with the dinner.

Five years later, after I'd been dumped by my long-term boyfriend and was beginning to think I'd never get married, a grad school friend made me another bet: she bet me two bottles of very expensive champagne that I'd be married within three years. As you know if you read this book, I happily lost that bet in 2010.

I think of our mortgage in the same way I think of those bets: they're future insurance. They allow you to face the unknown with a certain amount of equanimity.

As I have now argued for hundreds of pages, it matters enormously what happens after you have failed. But it is much easier to do the right thing if you have prepared yourself for failure beforehand. And the best way to prepare yourself can be summed up in four words: don't count on it.

If you want to be able to take big risks, and then recover and move on, you cannot have everything riding on any one outcome. Diversify your emotional and financial investments. Hedge against the future. Minimize your fixed obligations. Maximize your net psychic wealth.

Of course I don't mean that you should avoid all commitments. But you should maximize your commitment to the things that matter. Marriage. Kids. Parents and siblings. Friends. Your passions. You can make more of the commitments that count when you have fewer commitments to granite countertops, sunroofs, and cell phone contracts.

If you absolutely have to have one thing happen or your life will be over and you can never be happy again, you are giving hostages to fate. Fate, you will have noticed, is not a very nice negotiator.

So we sent in a SWAT team to get them back. We assumed the worst, and made sure that we could live with it. That meant living with a little bit of the worst now, in the form of neighbors who I am sure talk among themselves about our backyard.

But it also meant that when I got the chance to do a personal project that meant not having a paycheck for six months, I could take it. We didn't need to worry about the mortgage, or our car payments. We could easily cut our spending in half without feeling much pain, because we were cutting the things that were nice but not necessary: dining out, trips, new clothes. The stuff we needed was still easily taken care of. If we'd had a mortgage and debt payments stretched up to the limits of our take-home pay, as most Americans do, that would have been terrifying. As it was, I could accept without even thinking about it.

The result is the book you hold in your hand.

ACKNOWLEDGMENTS

If it takes a village to raise a child, it takes at least a small neighborhood to birth a book. Innumerable people and institutions have supported me during the years that this book was happening, starting with the folks who paid my check. I owe a huge debt of gratitude to Anthony Gottlieb and innumerable other editors at *The Economist*, which hired me, taught me to write, and gave me the ideas that eventually turned into this book. Also to Tina Brown and *Newsweek*, where editors Damon Linker, Justine Rosenthal, and Sarah Blustain patiently lived through much of its writing. And I owe especial gratitude to *The Atlantic*, where much of the material in this book first appeared in one form or another—David Bradley and James Bennet for hiring me and giving me a series of extraordinary opportunities, James Gibney and Don Peck who edited many of the pieces, and Bob Cohn, the Web editor, who didn't even blink when I told him I needed to shut down the blog for a while while I went off and started to write this book thing.

The New America Foundation gave me a fellowship to develop the ideas in this book, which not only gave me valuable resources to do research but also gave me a moral obligation to actually produce a book at the end. Without their support, and the interaction with many brilliant fellow fellows, both this book and I would have missed a lot. Thanks also to the Legatum Institute's Summer School, where I got to try out an early draft of these ideas on an audience of incredibly accomplished people.

Gail Ross, my agent, also deserves credit for crossing her arms and demanding that I produce a book proposal, stat—and then working and reworking it until it actually made sense. Without her and colleague Howard Yoon, this book probably wouldn't exist. And it certainly wouldn't be coherent without the heroic and tireless efforts of my editor, Joy de Menil, who somehow managed to produce hundreds of pages of edits at the same time she was producing a beautiful baby. Writing a book for the first time is a nerve-wracking experience, particularly if you are a fixed mind-set sort of person. Joy took what were essentially ten 8,000-word magazine features and coached me through making them into the book you are now holding.

I need to give special thanks to the people who helped set up reporting trips and generously gave of their time: Memphis bankruptcy judges Jennie Latta and Paulette Delk, along with many, many others in the Memphis bankruptcy courts; Bart Wilson, Vernon Smith, and the rest of the experimental economics program at Chapman University; Judge Steven Alm and the amazing staff of the HOPE program. Thank you for helping me understand what was really going on.

A number of very patient people read early drafts of this manuscript and helpfully pointed out all the weak bits. Thanks to Mark Kleiman, Tyler Cowen, Gabriel Rossman, Kevin Drum, Jonathan Rauch, Jeremy Senderowicz, and Tim Carney for wading through rough drafts and being honest enough to tell me what wasn't working.

And of course, there is my family, who supported me for years before I even thought about writing a book, and went ahead and kept supporting me when I insisted on doing this crazy thing. My father, who talked through many of the concepts (and put up with a lot of distracted moments on the phone when I realized I needed to go edit something again). My mother, who graciously allowed me to write about her illness, and didn't even insist on final approval of the manuscript. My sister, who ran errands so that I could stay chained to the keyboard. And most of all, my husband, who endured dirty dishes, unchecked weeds, seven outlines, dozens of chapter drafts, and at least four separate readings of the same book, and never even mentioned divorce. Without his judicious editing, remarkable patience, and indefatigable moral support, this book could literally never have been written.

NOTES

CHAPTER 1

1. You can watch Peter Skillman's talk at http://vimeo.com/3991068.
2. Jim Manzi, interview with the author, August 7, 2012.
3. I spoke with Jeff Stibel several times about leading startups and corporate turnarounds. Quotations in this chapter are taken from a phone interview in March 2012 and a visit to Dun & Bradstreet Credibility Corp's Malibu offices in July 2012.
4. For a concise discussion of the dopamine reward system and how it motivates learning, see Roy A. Wise, "Dopamine, Learning, and Motivation," *Nature Reviews: Neuroscience* Volume 5 (June 2004), p. 1.
5. Carol Dweck, interview with the author, September 2, 2012.
6. For a comprehensive overview, see Carol Dweck, *Mindset: The New Psychology of Success* (New York: Ballantine Books, 2006).
7. S. Berglas and E. E. Jones, "Drug Choice as a Self-Handicapping Strategy in Response to Noncontingent Success," *Journal of Personality and Social Psychology* 36(4) (1978), pp. 405–417.
8. Hirt, McRea, and Boris, " 'I Know You Self-Handicapped Last Exam': Gender Differences in Reactions to Self-Handicapping," *Journal of Personality and Social Psychology* Volume 84, number 1 (2003), pp. 177–193.
9. The experiment is described in Claudia M. Mueller and Carol S. Dweck's "Praise for Intelligence Can Undermine Children's Motivation and Performance," *Journal of Personality and Social Psychology* 75 (1998) pp. 33–52. I have also drawn from my interview with Dweck and her article, "Brainology," *Independent Schools* magazine, Winter 2008.
10. Benedict Carey, "Some Protect the Ego by Working on Their Excuses Early," *New York Times,* January 5, 2009.
11. A description of Mark Twain's sad decade can be found in many places; for reference, I used Ron Powers's *Mark Twain: A Life* (New York: Free Press, 2005).
12. Ron Alsop, *The Trophy Kids Grow Up: How the Millennial Generation Is Shaking Up the Workplace* (San Francisco: Jossey-Bass, 2008).
13. "High School Grades Hit By Inflation," *CBS News*, February 11, 2009.
14. Justin Pope, "Admissions Boards Face Grade Inflation," Associated Press, November 18, 2006.
15. Tulgan, Bruce, *Not Everyone Gets a Trophy: How to Manage Generation Y* (San Francisco: Jossey-Bass, 2009), Kindle edition, location 129.
16. Jenny Anderson and Rachel Ohm, "Bracing for $40,000 at New York City Private Schools," *New York Times,* January 27, 2012.
17. Erik Larson, "Why Colleges Cost Too Much," *Time* magazine, June 24, 2001.
18. Lois Lee, "Admit Rate Holds Steady at 12.3 Percent," *The Daily Pennsylvanian,* March 28, 2012.

19. Peter Jacobs, "Breaking Down the Numbers for the Class of 2016," Ivygate.com, accessed September 24, 2012.
20. "2,032 Admitted to Class of '16," *Harvard Gazette,* March 29, 2012.
21. Andrew Carnevale and Stephen Rose, "Socioeconomic Status, Race/Ethnicity, and Selective College Admissions," *America's Untapped Resource: Low-Income Students in Higher Education* (Manassas: Century Press, 2004).
22. Richard Perez-Pena, "Harvard Students in Cheating Scandal Say Collaboration Was Accepted," *New York Times,* August 31, 2012.
23. Ron Haskins, Harry Holzer, and Robert Lerman, "Promoting Economic Mobility by Increasing Post-Secondary Education," *Report of the Pew Economic Mobility Project,* May 2009.
24. John Scalzi, "Being Poor," Whatever Blog, September 3, 2005.
25. Larry Frum, "Nearly Half of All Video Gamers Are Women," CNN.com, August 11, 2013.
26. "A Literature Review of Gaming in Education," research report from Pearson Assessments, http://www.pearsonassessments.com/hai/Images/tmrs/Lit_Review_of_Gaming_in_Education.pdf.

CHAPTER 2

1. Spencer Abraham, "Remarks by U.S. Secretary of Energy Spencer Abraham," U.S. Chamber of Commerce, National Energy Summit, March 19, 2001.
2. For an overview of the California energy crisis, see the Congressional Budget Office, "Causes and Lessons of the California Electricity Crisis," September 2001, and the Federal Energy Regulatory Commission's report on its response to the California crisis: "The Western Energy Crisis, the Enron Bankruptcy, and FERC's Response," pp. 1–6.
3. "Joint Hearings before the Subcommittee on Energy Policy, Natural Resources and Regulatory Affairs and the Committee on Government Reform," April 10–12, 2001.
4. Ed Mendel, "Energy Crisis Cited as Turning Point for Davis," *San Diego Union-Tribune,* September 2, 2003.
5. Paul Krugman, "Reckonings; California Screaming," *New York Times,* December 10, 2000.
6. For more on California's reliance on the spot market and the trading strategies that Enron exploited, see Christopher Weare, "The California Electricity Crisis: Causes and Policy Options" (San Francisco: Public Policy Institute of California, 2003), p. 26.
7. Agis Salpukas, "Power Deregulated. Consumers Yawn; California's Effort to Promote Plan for Electricity Is Off to a Slow Start," *New York Times,* February 26, 1998.
8. Bart Wilson, interview with author via instant messenger, February 3, 2013.
9. Joseph A. Schumpeter, *Capitalism, Socialism and Democracy* (London: Taylor & Francis, 2009), Kindle edition, location 1941.
10. Personal biographical information was taken from the autobiographical ac-

count provided to the Nobel Prize committee by Vernon Smith, "Vernon Smith—Biographical," Nobelprize.org.

11. Bart Wilson, interview with author, June 2012.

12. Russ Roberts tells this story in his April 2010 podcast with economist Paul Romer at Econtalk.org, http://www.econtalk.org/archives/2010/04/romer_on_charte.html. I have heard this story from other economists, who may have gotten it from Russ.

13. Noam Chomsky, *The Chomsky Reader* (New York: Pantheon, 1987) p. 153.

14. "A Lurch Toward Love," *Newsweek,* February 18, 1996.

15. Bart Wilson, interview with the author, February 2013.

16. "No Negligence in Chimp Attack," *Praetoria News,* June 4, 2012

17. Interview with Brian Hare, assistant professor at the Duke Institute for Brain Sciences. Claudia Dreifus, "Why Bonobos Don't Kill Each Other," *New York Times,* July 5, 2010.

18. Anke F. Bullinger, Alicia P. Melis, and Michael Tomasello, "Chimpanzees, *Pan Troglodytes,* Prefer Individual over Collaborative Strategies Towards Goals," *Animal Behavior* 82 (5) November 2011.

19. Michael Tomasello, "Origins of Human Cooperation," lecture delivered at Stanford University in October 2008.

20. For an extensive and accessible discussion of reciprocal altruism and the gift economy, I recommend David Graeber's *Debt: The First 5,000 Years* (Brooklyn: Melville House, 2011).

21. "Noble or Savage?" *The Economist,* December 19, 2007.

22. Jonathan Haidt, *The Righteous Mind: Why Good People Are Divided by Politics and Religion* (New York: Random House, 2012) Kindle edition, location 3023.

23. Hilly Kaplan, interview with the author, May 9, 2012.

24. Kaplan has published a number of papers on the Aché, including: K. Hill, H. Kaplan, K. Hawkes, and A. Hurtado, "Foraging Decisions Among the Aché: New Data and Analysis," *Ethology and Sociobiology* 8 (1987) pp. 1–36; H. Kaplan and K. Hill. "Food Sharing Among Aché Foragers: Tests of Explanatory Hypotheses," *Current Anthropology* 26 (2) (1985) pp. 223–246; H. Kaplan, K. Hill, K. Hawkes, and A. Hurtado. "Food Sharing Among Aché Hunter-gatherers of Eastern Paraguay," *Current Anthropology* 25 (1984) pp. 113–116.

25. Gurven, Hill, and Kaplan, "From Forest to Reservation: Transitions in Food Sharing Behavior Among the Aché of Paraguay," *Journal of Anthropological Research* Volume 58, number 1, Spring 2002.

26. Hillard S. Kaplan, Eric Schniter, Vernon L. Smith, and Bart J. Wilson, "Risk and the Evolution of Human Exchange," *Proceedings of the Royal Society of Biological Sciences,* published online April 18, 2012, doi: 10.1098/rspb.2011.2614.

27. Jonathan Haidt, "What Makes People Vote Republican," Edge.org.

28. Paul A. Gompers, Anna Kovner, Josh Lerner, and David S. Scharfstein, "Performance Persistence in Entrepreneurship," HBS Working Papers, July 2008.

29. Niels Bosma, Sander Wennekers, and José Ernesto Amorós, "GEM Consortium 2011 Global Report," *Global Entrepreneurship Monitor,* January 2012.

30. Dane Stangler, "High-Growth Firms and the Future of the American Economy,"

Kauffman Foundation Research Series: Firm Formation and Economic Growth, March 2010.

CHAPTER 3

1. Paula Parisi, *Titanic and the Making of James Cameron: The Inside Story of the Three Year Adventure that Rewrote Motion Picture History* (New York: Newmarket Press, 1998) p. 180.
2. Claudia Puig, "Epic-Size Troubles on 'Titanic,' " *Los Angeles Times*, April 19, 1997.
3. Nathan Ditum, "Why Titanic Is Still King of the World," Virgin Media, April 6, 2012.
4. DiCaprio's previous roles in big-budget pictures included heroin addict Jim Carroll in *The Basketball Diaries,* Meryl Streep's mentally ill son in *Marvin's Room,* and Johnny Depp's mentally retarded younger brother in *What's Eating Gilbert Grape?*
5. William Goldman, *Adventures in the Screen Trade* (New York: Grand Central Publishing, 2012), Kindle Edition, location 800.
6. Ben Taylor, *Apocalypse on the Set: Nine Disastrous Film Productions* (New York: Overlook Duckworth, 2012), Kindle edition. Chapter 8 covers the disastrous troubles of *The Abyss*, while Chapter 9 contains the account of *Waterworld's* convulsions.
7. William Goldman, *The Big Picture: Who Killed Hollywood? And Other Essays* (New York: Applause, 2001), Kindle edition, locations 152 to 157.
8. Georgette Jasen, "Journal's Dartboard Retires After 14 Years of Stock Picks," *Wall Street Journal*, April 18, 2002.
9. Philip E. Tetlock, *Expert Political Judgment: How Good Is It? How Can We Know?* (Princeton, NJ: Princeton University Press, 2006), Kindle edition, locations 957–958.
10. P. S. Wang, R. L. Bohn, E. Knight, R. J. Glynn, H. Mogun, and J. Avorn, "Non-compliance with Anti-Hypertensive Medications: The Impact of Depressive Symptoms and Psychosocial Factors," *Journal of General Internal Medicine* July 2002; 17(7), pp. 504–511. doi: 10.1046/j.1525-1497.2002.00406.x.
11. Malcolm Gladwell, *The Tipping Point* (New York: Little Brown, 2000).
12. Duncan Watts, interview with the author, April 2012.
13. Duncan J. Watts, *Everything Is Obvious: Once You Know the Answer* (New York: Crown Business, 2011), Kindle edition.
14. For more about the Mona Lisa's theft, see "The Theft that Made the Mona Lisa a Masterpiece," *National Public Radio*, July 30, 2011, p. 60.
15. Matthew Sagalnik and Duncan Watts, "Web-Based Experiments for the Study of Collective Social Dynamics in Cultural Markets," *Topics in Cognitive Science* 1 (2009), pp. 439–468.
16. Jim Manzi, interview with author, September 2010.
17. Data on *Titanic's* performance comes from Box Office Mojo.
18. For a discussion of movie audience demographics and how Hollywood targets them, I recommend Lynda Obst's *Sleepless in Hollywood: Tales from the*

NEW ABNORMAL in the Movie Business (New York: Simon and Schuster, 2013). Obst, a longtime producer, is scathing and funny about the results of the overreliance on the young male audience, particularly the global young male audience, on movies.

19. Bernard Weinraub, "Who's Lining Up at Box Office? Lots and Lots Of Girls; Studios Aim at Teen-Agers, a Vast, Growing Audience," *New York Times*, February 23, 1998.

20. Jason Deparle, *American Dream: Three Women, Ten Kids, and a Nation's Drive to End Welfare* (New York: Penguin Group, 2004), Kindle edition, location 1414.

21. Carol B. Stack, *All Our Kin: Strategies for Survival in a Black Community* (New York: Basic Books, 1997), Kindle edition.

22. William Julius Wilson, *When Work Disappears: The World of the New Urban Poor* (New York: Vintage, 1997).

23. Gordon Berlin, "Experimentation and Social Welfare Policymaking in the United States," speech delivered in November 2007 to Lancement du Grenelle de l'Insertion: Les Rencontres de l'Experimentation Sociale, a conference sponsored by the French government in Grenoble, France, to discuss the role of experimental studies in reducing poverty and helping the unemployed reenter the labor market.

24. I took my account of the "new consensus" and welfare experimentation from Jason Deparle, *American Dream*, and from Jim Manzi's book on experimentation, *Uncontrolled: The Surprising Payoff of Trial-and-Error for Business, Politics, and Society* (New York: Basic Books, 2012) pp. 182–186.

25. "Taxation and the Family: What Is the Earned Income Tax Credit?" *The Tax Policy Briefing Book: A Citizens' Guide for the 2012 Election and Beyond* (Washington: Tax Policy Center, 2012) II-1-7.

26. Poverty figures come from the Census Bureau www.census.gov/hhes/www/censpov.htm.

27. "Most people who entered the system did leave within two years. But a substantial minority stayed, and over time they came to dominate; the average woman on the rolls at any given moment would draw aid for ten years," from Jason DeParle, *American Dream,* Kindle edition, locations 1638–1639. He is referring to the report commissioned by the Department of Health and Human Services, M. J. Bane and D. T. Ellwood, *The Dynamics of Dependence: Paths to Self-Sufficiency* (Cambridge: Urban Systems and Engineering, June 1983).

28. Jason DeParle's *American Dream* and LaDonna Pavetti's "Time on Welfare and Welfare Dependency: Testimony Before the House Ways and Means Committee, Subcommittee on Human Resources," May 1996.

29. Barbara Vobejda and Judith Havemann, "2 HHS Officials Quit Over Welfare Changes," *Washington Post*, September 12, 1996.

30. Peter Edelman, "The Worst Thing Bill Clinton Has Done," *The Atlantic*, March 1997.

31. For data and a fuller picture of welfare caseloads post-reform, see "How Has the TANF Caseload Changed Over Time," Urban Institute, March 2012, and

H. Luke Schaefer and Kathryn Edin, "Extreme Poverty in the United States, 1996 to 2011," *National Poverty Center Policy Brief #28,* February 2012.

32. Census Bureau, "Income, Poverty, and Health Insurance Coverage in the United States: 2010."

33. Glenn Begley and Lee Ellis, "Drug Development: Raise Standards for Preclinical Cancer Research," *Nature* 483 (March 2009), pp. 531–533.

34. The history of the LA Unified School District's culinary adventures were mainly drawn from two news accounts: "LAUSD Students Roundly Reject Healthier School Lunch Menu," *CBS Los Angeles,* January 19, 2012, and Teresa Watanabe, "L.A. Schools' Healthful Lunch Menu Panned by Students," *Los Angeles Times,* December 17, 2011.

35. A rather wistful history of the New Coke decision can be found at the Coca-Cola Company's website, http://www.coca-colacompany.com/stories/coke-lore-new-coke. But for the full story, you need to read Mark Pendergrast's *For God, Country, and Coca-Cola Definitive History of the Great American Soft Drink* (New York: Basic Books, 2000).

36. Quotations on New Coke all come from Mark Pendergrast, *For God, Country, and Coca-Cola,* Kindle edition, location 8681.

37. Some have questioned whether researchers actually saw the Hawthorne Effect at the Hawthorne Electric Plant in Cicero, Illinois. But it is a well-documented phenomenon in other areas. You may be familiar with one of the most common examples: the "white coat effect," which causes peoples' blood pressure to rise when a doctor or nurse takes it, even though it is steady when measured by machine. (See A. Botomino, B. Martina , D. Ruf, R. Bruppacher, and K. E. Hersberger, "White Coat Effect and White Coat Hypertension in Community Pharmacy Practice," *Blood Pressure Monitoring* 2005 Feb, 10[1], pp. 13–8.) If you are interested in the research that gave us the Hawthorne Effect, see "Harvard Business School and the Hawthorne Experiments (1924–1933)," *Baker Library Historical Collections.*

38. Grover Whitehurst, "Can We Be Hard-Headed About Preschool? A Look at Head Start," Brookings Institution The Brown Center Chalkboard, last accessed October 2013, http://www.brookings.edu/blogs/brown-center-chalkboard/posts/2013/01/16-preschool-whitehurst. He discusses data from the Head Start Impact Study, one of the most comprehensive and rigorous studies ever undertaken of large-scale early-childhood interventions. (Available from HHS here: http://www.acf.hhs.gov/sites/default/files/opre/head_start_report.pdf.) A related recent study from Brookings Papers on Economic Activity showed some impact for low-income students from universal preschool, but fairly disappointing in relation to the money spent. Elizabeth Cascio and Diane Schanzenbach, "The Impacts of Expanding Access to High-Quality Preschool Education," paper delivered at the Brookings Papers on Economic Activity, September 19–20, 2013.

39. The story of *Heaven's Gate* has been told many times, but I took my account from Ben Turner, *Apocalypse on the Set,* Chapter 2. I learned about *Fatal Attrac-*

tion's reshoot from Daniel Cerone, "Why Director Adrian Lyne Went for the Jugular," *Los Angeles Times*, February 18, 1992.

40. Harvey Mackay, "Embrace Mistakes as Opportunities to Grow," February 11, 2013. The story also appears in Edgar Schein's *Organizational Culture and Leadership* (San Francisco: John Wiley, 2010) and is a staple of the motivational speaker circuit.

CHAPTER 4

1. The most widely cited figures on preventable deaths—and they are shrouded in considerable uncertainty—come from Institute of Medicine, *To Err Is Human: Building a Safer Health System*, (Washington: National Academies Press, 1999). It is available for free at http://www.iom.edu/Reports/1999/to-err-is-human-building-a-safer-health-system.aspx.

2. My belief in checklists came, of course, from Atul Gawande's *The Checklist Manifesto: How to Get Things Right* (New York: Metropolitan Books, 2009) p. 82.

3. D. Mike Hardin Jr, "Acute Appendicitis: Review and Update," *American Family Physician* 60(7) (November 1999) pp. 2027–2034. As Dr. Hardin notes, "The mortality rate in nonperforated appendicitis is less than 1 percent, but it may be as high as 5 percent or more in young and elderly patients, in whom diagnosis may often be delayed, thus making perforation more likely."

4. Most of this chapter was written while my mother was in the hospital and immediately after, while she was upstairs in my office, recuperating on the adjustable bed we'd been sold the day before she came home by a Sleepy's salesman who didn't hesitate to take advantage of my emotional state. The story is therefore composed of live observations and very fresh memories—mine, my sister's, my husband's, and my mother's.

5. Statistics on texting and cell phone usage while driving were taken from the CDC "Distracted Driving," http://www.cdc.gov/motorvehiclesafety/distracted_driving/, but a recent study from AT&T suggests that the problem may be even worse than these figures suggest; their survey found that half of all commuters now text while driving. "Nearly Half of Commuters Admit to Texting While Driving," att.com March 28, 2013, http://www.att.com/gen/press-room?pid=23969&cdvn=news&newsarticleid=36217.

6. D. L. Strayer, F. A. Andrews, and D. J. Crouch, "A Comparison of the Cell Phone Driver and the Drunk Driver," *Human Factors* 48(2) (Summer 2006), pp. 381–391.

7. Foundation for Traffic Safety, "2012 Traffic Safety Culture Index: Motorists Admit to Driving Drowsy," December 2012.

8. US Department of Transportation National Highway Safety Administration, "2010 Motor Vehicle Crashes: Overview," *Traffic Safety Facts Research Note*, February 2012 revision.

9. James Reason, "Human Error: Models and Management," *British Medical Journal* 320 (March 2000), pp. 768–770.

10. Charles Perrow, *Normal Accidents: Living with High Risk Technologies* (Princeton: Princeton University Press, 1999), Kindle edition.

11. Tadataka Yamada, ed., *Principles of Clinical Gastroenterology* (Hoboken: Wiley-Blackwell, 2008), p. 277.

12. R. M. Klevens, J. R. Edwards, C. L. Richards Jr, T. C. Horan, R. P. Gaynes, D. A. Pollock, and D. M. Cardo, "Estimating Health Care-Associated Infections and Deaths in U.S. Hospitals, 2002," *Public Health Reports* 122 (March 2007).

13. Atul Gawande, "The Checklist," *The New Yorker*, December 10, 2007, last accessed September 2013. This is the article that spawned his excellent book and much of its content is replicated there.

14. Charles Bosk, *Forgive and Remember: Managing Medical Failure, 2nd Edition* (Chicago: University of Chicago Press, 2013). This book, originally his PhD dissertation, is a landmark in the study of how doctors handle learning and error. I had a very nice interview with Charles Bosk in March 2012, shortly after my mother's illness. Never walk onto a hospital floor where a relative is a patient empty-handed, he told me. Always bring donuts or pizza, because once you've given people a gift they feel obligated to you. Aside from giving me this invaluable advice, the interview and his book greatly informed my thinking on medical error.

15. David Lee Roth, *Crazy from the Heat* (New York: Hyperion, 1997).

16. To get a sense of just how important antibiotics have been to human health, I recommend Brad Spellberg's *Rising Plague: The Global Threat from Deadly Bacteria and Our Dwindling Arsenal to Fight Them* (Amherst: Prometheus Books, 2009).

17. David Hyman, "Medical Malpractice and the Tort System: What Do We Know and What (If Anything) Should We Do About It?" *Texas Law Review* 80:7 (June 2002), pp. 163–169.

18. We remember the Enron scandal, and you probably know the name of Worldcom, but who remembers the major restatements at Rite Aid and Dollar General? No one—even though Rite Aid's auditor actually resigned over the poor quality of their accounting. Mark Maremont and James P. Miller, "Rite Aid Says KPMG Quit as Auditor; Doubts on Management Statements," *Wall Street Journal*, November 19, 1999.

CHAPTER 5

1. "The Best Thing That Ever Happened to Me," Survey Monkey, June 2012. You can take the survey yourself at https://www.surveymonkey.com/s/6B95JC2.

2. Kay Hymowitz, Jason S. Carroll, W. Bradford Wilcox, and Kelleen Kaye, "Knot Yet: The Benefits and Costs of Delayed Marriage in America," The National Marriage Project.

3. Data on GM's profits and employment in 1955 taken from the 1955 Fortune 500 List, which is archived at CNN Money.

4. For more on Henry Ford and financing, see Steven Watts, *The People's Tycoon: Henry Ford and the American Dream* (New York: Vintage Books, 2005), p. 343,

and Lendol Calder, *Financing the American Dream: A Cultural History of Consumer Credit* (Princeton: Princeton University Press, 1999).

5. "Advertising the Ford Model T," Exhibit of the Henry Ford Museum, p. 111.

6. Wage data taken from GM's 1955 Annual Report and the Social Security Administration's National Average Wage Index.

7. Ad in the *Sarasota Herald Tribune*, April 27, 1947, p. 12.

8. James Schrager, interview with author, November 2011.

9. Turnaround expert Thomas Kim, interview with author, November 2011.

10. "For years, aviation safety experts could not understand why passengers did so little to save themselves in plane crashes. They would sit in their seats instead of going to an exit. Those who did get up had an infuriating tendency to reach for their carry-on baggage before leaving." Amanda Ripley's *The Unthinkable: Who Survives When Disaster Strikes—and Why* (New York: Crown Publishing Group, 2008), Kindle edition, locations 2409–2410.

11. Tom Jepson, "How to Survive a Plane Crash," *The Telegraph*, November 5, 2010.

12. David McRaney, *You Are Not So Smart: Why You Have Too Many Friends on Facebook, Why Your Memory Is Mostly Fiction, and 46 Other Ways You're Deluding Yourself* (New York: Gotham 2011).

13. "If a flight attendant stood at the exit and screamed at people to jump, the pause all but disappeared, the researchers found. In fact, if flight attendants did not aggressively direct the evacuation, they might as well have not been there at all," from Amanda Ripley's *The Unthinkable*.

14. The phenomenon of depressed people having more accurate self judgments is called "depressive realism." A good summary of the research can be found in Lorraine G. Allan, Shepard Siegel, and Samuel Hannah's, "The sad truth about depressive realism," *The Quarterly Journal of Experimental Psychology* 60:3 (2007), pp. 482–495.

15. "Solyndra: Illustrating a Recovery Act Supply Chain," White House Blog, May 26, 2010. http://www.whitehouse.gov/blog/2010/05/26/recovery-supply-chain.

16. One of the best pieces of reporting on Solyndra is Juliet Eilperin's "Why the Clean Tech Boom Went Bust," *Wire*, February 2012. Much of my understanding of what happened came from this article, as well as my contemporaneous research about the financial side.

17. Alison Vekshin and Mark Chediak, "Solyndra Plant Had Whistling Robots, Spa Showers," *Bloomberg News*, September 28, 2011.

18. Jim Snyder and Christopher Martin, "Obama Team Backed $535 Million Solyndra Aid as Auditor Warned on Finances," *Bloomberg News*, September 12, 2011.

19. Joe Stephens and Carol D. Leonnig, "Solyndra Loan: White House Pressed on Review of Solar Company Now Under Investigation," *Washington Post*, September 13, 2011.

20. Saqib Rahim, "Republicans Probe Whether DOE's Effort to Save Solyndra Violated 2005 Energy Act." *New York Times*, October 11, 2011.

21. "20 Questions," Gamblers Anonymous.

22. Amos Tversky and Daniel Kahneman, "The Framing of Decisions and the Psychology of Choice," *Science*, New Series, Volume 211, number 4481 (January 30, 1981), pp. 453–458.

23. I interviewed Paul Ingrassia in early 2012 and he helped frame my understanding of GM's trajectory. The quotations are taken from his book *Crash Course*, Kindle edition, locations 823–846, 996–998.

24. You can read more about GM's "cost wedge," as experts refer to it, in the article I wrote on the subject, "Can GM Get Its Groove Back," *The Atlantic*, November 2010. Information on GM's cost wedge comes from an interview with David Cole of the Center for Automotive Research in August 2010.

25. "The stories of aggrieved dealers were hitting Wagoner emotionally, because of Oldsmobile's long heritage at GM. The result: the pain of closing Oldsmobile doused discussion of eliminating more GM brands, just as the 1998 Flint strike had made talk of confronting the UAW strictly off-limits. Wagoner's 'Go Fast' was becoming, in effect, 'Don't Rock the Boat,' " from Paul Ingrassia's *Crash Course*.

26. John Stoll, "GM Director Says Board Stands Behind CEO Wagoner," *Wall Street Journal,* May 28, 2008.

27. GM's U.S. market share in September 2013 stood at just a shade above 16 percent, according to *Wall Street Journal* auto sales data (http://wap.wsj.com/mdc/public/page/2_3022-autosales.html). A far cry from the days when it had 50 percent of the cars on the American road.

28. As of May 2013, the *New York Times* reported that GM was still using massive incentives—$3,793, compared with $592 for the Honda Accord and $1,946 for the Ford Fusion—to move the Chevy Malibu, one of its stalwarts. There were plans to revamp the sedan yet again to reduce the need for incentives, but such promises have been made before and as this book went to press, it was too early to tell whether this time they were working. Bill Vlasic, "To Compete, G.M. Alters a Sedan," *New York Times*, May 31, 2013.

CHAPTER 6

1. "Free Republic Comment Thread," September 8, 2004, last accessed October 2013, http://www.freerepublic.com/focus/f-news/1210662/posts?page=47#47.

2. Joseph Hallinan, *Why We Make Mistakes: How We Look Without Seeing, Forget Things in Seconds, and Are All Pretty Sure We Are Way Above Average* (New York: Broadway Books, 2009), Kindle edition, locations 201–202.

3. Daniel J. Simons and Christopher Chabris, "Gorillas in Our Midst: Sustained Inattentional Blindness for Dynamic Events," *Perception* 28 (1999), pp. 1059–1074.

4. You can watch the famous gorilla video yourself at http://www.youtube.com/watch?v=vJG698U2Mvo.

5. The inside narrative of Dan Rather's final, fatal scoop is taken from Dick Thornburgh and Louis Boccardi's "Report of the Independent Review Panel on the September 8, 2004, 60 Minutes Wednesday segment 'For the Record'

Concerning President Bush's Air National Guard Service," January 5, 2005, available at cbsnews.com http://www.cbsnews.com/htdocs/pdf/complete_report/CBS_Report.pdf.

6. Michael Dobbs and Mike Allen, "Some Question Authenticity of Papers on Bush," *Washington Post*, September 10, 2004.

7. One writer who Mapes contacted told me about it in a private email after reading an early draft of this chapter.

8. Howard Kurtz, "Rather Defends CBS Over Memos on Bush," *Washington Post*, September 11, 2004.

9. Howard Kurtz, "Document Experts Say CBS Ignored Memo 'Red Flags,'" *Washington Post*, September 15, 2004.

10. Michael Dobbs, "CBS Guard Documents Traced to Tex. Kinko's," *Washington Post*, September 16, 2004.

11. Teresa Nielsen-Hayden, "Back When IBM had Balls," *Making Light*, August 20, 2006, last accessed September 2013, http://nielsenhayden.com/makinglight/archives/007893.html.

12. Laurence Gonzales, *Deep Survival: Who Lives, Who Dies, and Why* (New York: W. W. Norton, 2003), Kindle edition, locations 2386–2387.

13. The engineer, we now know, was Roger Boisjoly. Howard Berkes, "Remembering Roger Boisjoly: He Tried to Stop Shuttle Challenger Launch," National Public Radio, February 6, 2012. http://www.npr.org/blogs/thetwo-way/2012/02/06/146490064/remembering-roger-boisjoly-he-tried-to-stop-shuttle-challenger-launch.

14. Richard Feynman, "Personal Observations on the Reliability of the Shuttle," appendix to official report of the Space Shuttle commission.

15. For example, document examiners expressed some reservations about the presence of a superscript "th" in one of the documents, which most typewriters couldn't have made in the 1970s. Early Tuesday evening, Mapes was reportedly "spooked" by this, but by midnight, she was apparently "over" it, even though no positive information seems to have come in during that time. (Thornburgh and Boccardi, "Report of the Independent Review Panel," p. 110.) Even after the network came under fire, she was absolutely certain the documents were genuine—so much so that she surprised others at the network. (Thornburgh and Boccardi, "Report of the Independent Review Panel," pp. 178–180.) As late as 2005, Mapes was still proclaiming that the documents were genuine.

16. Nicholas Epley, interview with the author, 2008.

17. Joe Hagan, "Dan Rather to Bush: Answer the Questions," *New York Observer*, September 20, 2004.

18. Howard Kurtz, "Rather Concedes Papers Are Suspect," *Washington Post*, September 16, 2004.

19. Howard Kurtz, "Dan Rather to Step Down at CBS," *Washington Post*, November 24, 2004.

20. "CBS Ousts 4 Over Bush Guard Story," Associated Press, January 10, 2005.

21. Ira Glass, "Retraction," *This American Life*, Episode 460, March 16, 2012.

22. Tim Goseclose, *Left Turn: How Liberal Media Bias Distorts the American Mind* (New York: St. Martin's Press, 2011), Kindle edition.
23. Rebecca Trounson, "A Startling Statistic at UCLA," *Los Angeles Times,* June 3, 2006.

CHAPTER 7

1. I went to the Buffalo Employment and Training Center in 2006 for a story that never ran in *New York Magazine.* I stopped by again around the time of the financial crisis, for a story that never ran in *The Atlantic.* At last, I am telling the story.
2. Employment figure calculated from data available at Census.gov and Bls.gov.
3. Ramon Garcia, "Population Trends in Buffalo Niagara," Partnership for the Public Good, Buffalo Brief, October 2, 2012, last accessed October 2013, http://www.ppgbuffalo.org/wp-content/uploads/2011/01/population-2012-garcia2.pdf.
4. Chris Isidore, "Looking for Work? Unemployed Need Not Apply," CNN Money, June 16, 2010.
5. As of September 2013, data from the Bureau of Labor Statistics showed that short-term unemployment was actually lower than 2007. But the number of those who have been unemployed for more than twenty-seven weeks remains cruelly elevated to several times 2007 levels. There are more people in this group than in any of the short- and medium-term categories of unemployed.
6. Wiji Arulampalam, Paul Gregg, and Mary Gregory, "Introduction: Unemployment Scarring," *The Economic Journal,* Volume 111 (November 2001).
7. Per-Anders Edin and Magnus Gustavsson, "Time Out of Work and Skill Depreciation," *Institute for Labor Market Policy Evaluation Working Paper,* September 2005.
8. Daniel Gilbert, interview with the author, 2012.
9. Andrew E. Clark, Ed Diener, Yannis Georgellis, and Richard E. Lucas, "Lags and Leads in Life Satisfaction: A Test of the Baseline Hypothesis," Centre for Economic Performance Discussion Paper (November 2007).
10. Helen Russell, "Friends in Low Places: Gender, Unemployment, and Sociability," *Work, Employment and Society,* 13 (June 1999), pp. 205–224.
11. Frances McKee-Ryan, Zhaoli Song, Connie Wanberg, and Angelo Kinicki, "Psychological and Physical Well-Being During Unemployment: A Meta-Analytic Study," *Journal of Applied Psychology* Volume 90(1) (January 2005) pp. 53–76. doi: 10.1037/0021-9010.90.1.53.
12. Josh Ozersky, *Colonel Sanders and the American Dream* (Austin: University of Texas Press, 2012), Kindle edition.
13. Lee Benson, "About Utah: Story of first KFC shows anything can happen," *Deseret News,* January 20, 2012.
14. Alan Krueger and Andreas Mueller, "Job Search and Job Finding in a Period of Mass Unemployment: Evidence from High-Frequency Longitudinal Data," CEPS Working Paper No. 215, January 2011.
15. Data on long-term unemployment in the United States and Europe from the Organization for Economic Cooperation and Development statistics site, last

accessed October 2013. http://www.oecd-ilibrary.org/employment/long-term-unemployment-12-months-and-over_20752342-table3.

16. Manufacturer's representative interviewed at International Home and Housewares Show, March 2012.

17. For a great history of the modern sales organization, see Walter A. Friedman's *Birth of a Salesman: The Transformation of Selling in America* (Cambridge: Harvard University Press, 2004), Kindle edition. I have added to that great history with my own experience as a canvasser, and later at a firm that employed telemarketers—and my years of interviewing various entrepreneurs and sales people and asking them how they manage to do one of the hardest jobs in the world.

18. "Labour Mobility in a Transatlantic Perspective," Conference Report, European Foundation for the Improvement of Living and Working Conditions, Dublin, October 30–31, 2007.

19. Barry Eichengreen, "Is Europe an Optimum Currency Area?" National Bureau of Economic Research Working Paper No. 3579 (January 1991).

20. Data on unemployment benefit replacement rates in the United States and Europe from Organization for Economic Cooperation and Development statistics site, last accessed October 2013. http://www.oecd.org/els/benefitsand wagesstatistics.htm.

21. See, for example, Lawrence Katz and Bruce Meyer, "The Impact of the Potential Duration of Unemployment Benefits on the Duration of Unemployment," NBER Working Paper No. 2741 (July 1990), and Henry Farber and Robert Valletta, "Do Extended Unemployment Benefits Lengthen Unemployment Spells? Evidence from Recent Cycles in the U.S. Labor Market," Federal Reserve Bank of San Francisco Working Papers Series, Working Paper 2013-9 (April 2013).

22. Fernando Ferreira, Joseph Gyourko, Joseph Tracy, "Housing Busts and Household Mobility," *Journal of Urban Economics*, Volume 68 (2008), pp. 34–35.

23. Martin Schindler, "The Italian Labor Market: Recent Trends, Institutions and Reform Options," IMF Working Paper WP/09/47 (March 2009).

24. "Euro Area Labor Markets and the Crisis," European Central Bank Structural Issues Report, October 2012.

25. Christian Merkl and Dennis Snower, "East German Unemployment: The Myth of the Irrelevant Labor Market," Kiel Institute for the World Economy Working Paper No. 1435 (July 2008).

26. J. I. Gold, S. H. Kim, A. J. Kant, M. H. Joseph, and A. S. Rizzo, "Effectiveness of Virtual Reality for Pediatric Pain Distraction During i.v. Placement," *Cyberpsychology, Behavior, and Social Networking* 9(2) (April 2006), pp. 207–12.

27. A. Patel, T. Schieble, M. Davidson, M. C. Tran, C. Schoenberg, E. Delphin, and H. Bennett, "Distraction with a hand-held video game reduces pediatric preoperative anxiety." *Paediatric Anaesthesthia.* 2006 October;16(10), pp. 1019–27.

28. David Autor, "The Unsustainable Rise of the Disability Rolls in the United States: Causes, Consequences, and Policy Options," NBER Working Paper No. 17697 (December 2011). Autor discusses what his paper means with Russ

Roberts for the Econtalk podcast in April 2012. http://www.econtalk.org/archives/2012/04/autor_on_disabi.html.

CHAPTER 8

1. Nick Heath, "What Happened to Turing's Thinking Machines?" *Between the Lines*, June 22, 2012.
2. Brian J Scholl, "Innateness and (Bayesian) Visual Perception," *The Innate Mind: Structure and Contents*, Peter Carruthers, Stephen Laurence, and Stephen Stich, eds. (Oxford: Oxford University Press, 2005).
3. Johan Wagemans, Rob van Lier, and Brian J. Scholl, "Introduction to Michotte's Heritage in Perception and Cognition Research," *Acta Psychologica* 123 (2006), pp. 1–19. You can view some of Michotte's demonstrations online at http://cogweb.ucla.edu/Discourse/Narrative/michotte-demo.swf.
4. Bruce Hood, *SuperSense: Why We Believe in the Unbelievable* (New York: Harper Collins, 2009), Kindle edition.
5. Email exchange, January 2012.
6. "Architects and Engineers—Solving the Mystery of WTC 7," Youtube. https://www.youtube.com/watch?feature=player_embedded&v=hZEvA8BCoBw.
7. "Mark Loizeaux – President of Cont. Demolition Inc.," Youtube. http://www.youtube.com/watch?v=Nj6ZtXt6W90.
8. James Meigs, interview with author, March 2012.
9. The Editors of *Popular Mechanics, Debunking 9/11 Myths: Why Conspiracy Theories Can't Stand Up to Facts* (New York: Hearst Books, 2011).
10. Simone Foxman "Spain's Housing Bubble Is Forcing Its Banks to Sell Homes at Half of What Was Paid for Them," *Quartz*, December 12, 2012.
11. David Leonhardt, "Buyer, Be Aware," *New York Times Magazine*, August 10, 2010.
12. Christopher L. Foote, Kristopher S. Gerardi, and Paul S. Willen, "Why Did So Many People Make So Many Ex Post Bad Decisions? The Causes of the Foreclosure Crisis," NBER Working Paper No. 18082, April 2012.
13. By "1 mil par" he meant that he had offered bonds with a face value, or redemption value, of $1 million—which is to say that when the bonds mature, whoever holds them will get $1 million cash. He couldn't get anyone to bid even a penny for them.
14. He was not the first to use the term, but a speech by Ben Bernanke is probably the best and most accessible explanation of it. Ben Bernanke "The Great Moderation" remarks to meetings of the Eastern Economic Association, Washington, DC, February 20, 2004.
15. Interview with author, November 2011.
16. Vernon Smith, Gerry Suchanek, and Arlington Williams,"Bubbles, Crashes, and Endogenous Expectations in Experimental Spot Asset Markets," *Econometrica* Volume 56, number 5 (September 1988), pp. 1119–1151. This is the paper that started the twenty-year experimental literature on asset bubbles.
17. Joshua Green, "Where Is Dick Fuld Now? Finding Lehman Brothers' Last CEO," *Businessweek*, September 12, 2013.

18. Walter Olsen, interview with author, March 2012.

19. Jeffrey Gerber and Paul Offit, "Vaccines and Autism: A Tale of Shifting Hypotheses," *Clinical Infectious Diseases* Volume 48 (2009) pp. 456–461.

20. Michael Luo, "For Exercise in New York Futility, Push Button," *New York Times*, February 27, 2004.

21. Ellen Langer, "The Illusion of Control," *Journal of Personality and Social Psychology* Volume 32, number 2 (1975) pp. 311–328.

22. Sheldon Cohen, "Aftereffects of Stress on Human Performance and Social Behavior: A Review of Research and Theory," *Psychological Bulletin* Volume 88, number 1 (1980) pp. 82–108.

23. M. G. Marmot, G. D. Smith, S. Stansfeld, C. Patel, F. North, J. Head, I. White, E. Brunner, and A. Feeney, "Health Inequalities Among British Civil Servants: The Whitehall II Study," *The Lancet* 337 (1991) pp. 1387–1393.

24. Y. Friedman, R. Bacchus, R. Raymond, R. T. Joffe, and J. N. Nobrega, "Acute Stress Increases Thyroid Hormone Levels in Rat Brain," *Biological Psychiatry*, Volume 45, Issue 2 (January 1999) pp. 234–237.

25. Radley Balko, "Despite Evidence from Discredited Medical Examiner, Mississippi's Jeffrey Havard Nears Execution," *The Huffington Post*, November 29, 2012.

26. Bill James, *Popular Crime: Reflections on the Celebration of Violence* (New York: Scribner, 2011).

27. Brandon Garrett, *Convicting the Innocent: Where Criminal Prosecutions Go Wrong* (Cambridge: Harvard University Press, 2011).

28. The details of Michael Morton's case are taken from an incredible two-part series commissioned by the *Texas Monthly*. Pamela Colloff, "The Innocent Man," *Texas Monthly*, November/December 2012. 29. Maria Glod and Michael D. Shear, "DNA Tests Confirm Guilt of Executed Man," *Washington Post*, January 13, 2006.

30. Malcolm Brown, "Dingo Baby Ruling Ends 32 Years of Torment for Lindy Chamberlain," *The Guardian*, June 12, 2012.

31. David Grann, "Trial by Fire: Did Texas Execute an Innocent Man?" *The New Yorker*, September 7, 2009.

32. Joseph Shapiro, "Rethinking Shaken Baby Syndrome," National Public Radio, June 29, 2011.

CHAPTER 9

1. Anna Aizer and Joseph Doyle, "Juvenile Incarceration, Human Capital and Future Crime: Evidence from Randomly-Assigned Judges," NBER Working Paper No. 19102 (June 2013).

2. I spent the week of March 20, 2012, in Honolulu's state courthouse, interviewing Judge Alm, probation officers, probationers, and defense attorneys, as well as the staff who support them. With the exception of Mark Kleiman and Angela Hawken, all quotations and observations in this chapter are from that week. Where possible, I have identified the people I spoke to; where they asked me not to give their name, I did not.

3. Angela Hawken and Mark Kleiman, "Managing Drug-Involved Probationers with Swift and Certain Sanctions: Evaluating Hawaii's HOPE," submitted to the National Institute of Justice, December 2009.
4. Phillip Bulman, "In Brief: Hawaii HOPE," *National Institute of Justice Journal* 266 (June 2010).
5. Alas, I was unable to write quite as fast as Judge Alm talked, and recording was not possible in the courtroom. While the Dad Talk hit all the same elements each time, it varied in delivery. This is a reconstruction from my notes of multiple talks. As should be obvious, the names are fictionalized.
6. Council of State Governments, Reentry Policy Council. *Report of the Re-Entry Policy Council: Charting the Safe and Successful Return of Prisoners to the Community* (New York: Council of State Governments, January 2005).
7. Mark Kleiman, interview with author, March 2012.
8. Robert Heinlein, *Starship Troopers* (New York: Ace, 2010), Kindle edition, location 1788.
9. W. Mischel, O. Ayduk, M. Berman, B. J. Casey, I. Gotlib, J. Ionides, E. Kross, T. Teslovich, N. Wilson, V. Zayas, and Y. Shoda, " 'Willpower' Over the Life Span: Decomposing Self-Regulation," *Social Cognitive and Affective Neuroscience* 6(2) (April 2011) pp. 252–256.
10. Theodore Dalrymple, *Life at the Bottom* (Cheltenham: Monday Books, 2010), Kindle edition.
11. David Linden, "Exercise, Pleasure and the Brain," *Psychology Today,* April 21, 2011.
12. National Institute on Drug Abuse, "Drug Facts: Methamphetamine," revised March 2010.
13. Celeste Kidda, Holly Palmeria, and Richard N. Aslin, "Rational Snacking: Young children's Decision-Making on the Marshmallow Task Is Moderated by Beliefs About Environmental Reliability," *Cognition* Volume 126, Issue 1, (January 2013) pp. 109–114.
14. Angela Hawken, interview with author, May 31, 2013.
15. Alberto Alesina and George-Marios Angeletos, "Fairness and Redistribution," *American Economic Review,* 95(4) (2005), pp. 960–980.
16. Mark Kleiman, "The Outpatient Prison," *The American Interest,* March/April 2010.
17. Beau Kilmer, Nancy Nicosia, Paul Heaton, and Greg Midgette, "Efficacy of Frequent Monitoring with Swift, Certain, and Modest Sanctions for Violations: Insights from South Dakota's 24/7 Sobriety Project," *American Journal of Public Health* Volume 103, number 1 (January 2013) pp. e37–e43. doi: 10.2105/AJPH.2012.300989.

CHAPTER 10

1. Megan McArdle, "Lead Us Not into Debt," *The Atlantic,* December 2009. I traveled to Detroit to see Ramsey's live event, and mingle with his followers, in August 2009.

2. Dave Ramsey, *Priceless: Straight-Shooting, No Frills Financial Wisdom* (New York: Thomas Nelson, 2002), Kindle edition. This chronicles Ramsey's rise and fall, and rise again. Much of the biographical detail can be gleaned from listening to his podcasts regularly, which I still do, four years after I first wrote about him.

3. *Commercial Real Estate and the Banking Crises of the 1980s and Early 1990s* (Washington: Federal Deposit Insurance Corporation, 1997). Chapter 3 explains the origin and development of the banking crisis that took down Dave Ramsey's highly indebted real estate empire.

4. I first gathered data on America's marvelously lax bankruptcy laws for an article for *The Economist*. "Morally Bankrupt?" *The Economist,* April 15, 2005. I spoke to multiple bankruptcy experts in the course of writing this book, and no one believed that this had changed.

5. Kennet, last name withheld, interview with author via Skype, April 2012.

6. Jay Fleischman, "Why Dave Ramsey Hates Bankruptcy," *Bankruptcy Law Network*, September 2007.

7. Anthony Bond, "Dumped in Dubai: The Luxury High Performance Cars Left Abandoned by British Expats Who Fear Being Jailed Because of Debts," *Daily Mail,* August 28, 2012.

8. David Skeel, *Debt's Dominion: A History of Bankruptcy Law in America* (Princeton: Princeton University Press, 2001).

9. On consumer credit in the United States, see, for example, Gunnar Trumball's "Regulating for Legitimacy: Consumer Credit Access in France and America," HBS Working Paper (November 2010).

10. Wei Fan and Michelle White, "Personal Bankruptcy and the Level of Entrepreneurial Activity," *Journal of Law and Economics* Volume 156 (October 2003).

11. S. R. Xavier, D. Kelley, J. Kew, M. Herrington, and A. Vorderwülbecke, "Gem Consortium 2012 Global Report," Global Entrepreneurship Monitor, January 2013, last accessed October 2013.

12. "Bankruptcy Filings per Capita, by U.S. County," United States Courts. http://www.uscourts.gov/Statistics/BankruptcyStatistics/BankruptcyFilingsPerCapita.aspx.

13. I spent the week of May 18th in Memphis, talking to judges, trustees, and advocates at the courts. All quotations and observations in this section come from that week, unless otherwise noted.

14. According to the Consumer Federation of America, the median middle-class family has less than $4,000 in their checking account. "The Financial Status and Decision-Making of the American Middle Class," The Consumer Federation of America, September 2012.

15. Sam Tsemberis, Leyla Gulcur, and Maria Nakae, "Housing First, Consumer Choice, and Harm Reduction for Homeless Individuals with a Dual Diagnosis," *American Journal of Public Health* 94–4 (April 2004) pp. 651–656.

16. Sarah Arnquist, "Million Dollar Patient," *Daily Republic*, June 13, 2006.

17. M. E. Larimer, D. K. Malone, M. D. Garner, D. C. Atkins, B. Burlingham, H. S. Lonczak, K. Tanzer, J. Ginzler, S. L. Clifasefi, W. G. Hobson, and G. A. Marlatt,

"Health Care and Public Service Use and Costs Before and After Provision of Housing for Chronically Homeless Persons with Severe Alcohol Problems," *Journal of the American Medical Association* 301–13 (2009), pp. 1349–1357.

18. Todd Zywicki, interview with author, January 2012.
19. Edward Wolff, "The Asset Price Meltdown and the Wealth of the Middle Class," NBER Working Paper No. 18559 (November 2012) Table 4.

INDEX